Queer Pop

QUEER FUTURES

———

Edited by
Kathrin Dreckmann, Bettina Papenburg and Jami Weinstein

Volume 1

Queer Pop

Aesthetic Interventions in Contemporary Culture

Edited by
Bettina Papenburg and Kathrin Dreckmann

DE GRUYTER

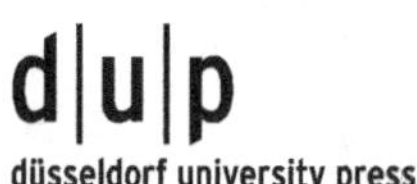

düsseldorf university press

We acknowledge support by the Open Access Publication Fund of the University of Freiburg.

ISBN [Paperback] 978-3-11-144730-8
ISBN [Hardcover] 978-3-11-079586-8
e-ISBN [PDF] 978-3-11-101343-5
e-ISBN [EPUB] 978-3-11-101415-9
ISSN 2940-2344
DOI https://doi.org/10.1515/9783111013435

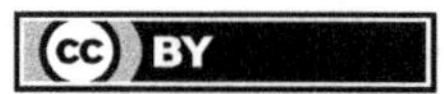

Library of Congress Control Number: 2023942768

Bibliographic information published by the Deutsche Nationalbibliothek
The Deutsche Nationalbibliothek lists this publication in the Deutsche Nationalbibliografie; detailed bibliographic data are available on the Internet at http://dnb.dnb.de.

Cover image: wacomka – stock.adobe.com [2]. Composing & Artwork: Silvia Sunderer
Typesetting: Integra Software Services Pvt. Ltd.

www.degruyter.com
dup.degruyter.com

Acknowledgements

The editors of the present volume would like to thank their cooperation partners and a number of institutions and individuals who facilitated the international and interdisciplinary symposium on Queer Pop held at Freiburg University in January 2020, and who enabled the publication of the present volume, which grew out of the symposium. The Center for Popular Culture and Music at Freiburg University hosted and partially funded the event. The Cultural Office of the City of Freiburg, the Ministry of Science, Research and the Arts of the State of Baden-Württemberg, and the Dean's Office of the Faculty of Philosophy at the Heinrich Heine University Düsseldorf all provided financial support for the symposium.

The Publication Fund of Freiburg University generously supported the open access publication of the present volume. A big thank you goes to Antonia Lauterborn, Maxi Kisters, Susanna Kothen, Sandra van Opbergen, and Max Höfer for their meticulous work in preparing the manuscript for publication. We are especially grateful to Sarah Rüß and Emma Rüter for tirelessly copy-editing all contributions and liaising with the contributing authors. We thank Don MacDonald for his accurate proofreading work. Last but not least, Anne Sokoll of De Gruyter / dup deserves special thanks for supporting the idea for the Queer Futures series already in its initial stages, for her continued support, and for seeing this volume through to completion. Without her, the series and the volume would not exist.

Berlin and Dusseldorf, February 2024
Bettina Papenburg and Kathrin Dreckmann

Contents

Part III: **Queer Affect**

Part IV: **Queer Futures**

Bettina Papenburg and Kathrin Dreckmann
Introducing Queer Pop

1 Queer Aesthetics and the Question of Politics

Taking as its point of departure the debate between those who argue that queer has no future[1] and those who envision the future as the purview of queer,[2] this volume considers the potentials and futurities of the concept of "queer" in the field of popular culture. How do musicians, performance artists, film directors, television producers, show masters, and photographers who claim the notion of "queer" contribute to reimagining possible futures? To offer a variety of answers to this question, the assembled contributions discuss selected case studies from popular music, film, television, magazine culture, curating, and performance art. They engage with forms of expression that employ stylistic means such as citation, parody, and remixing, among others.

It is our contention that aesthetic considerations play an important role in thinking about queer futures – be they utopian, dystopian, or otherwise. In the context of media and cultural studies, we understand the aesthetic as the capacity of media environments and representations to profoundly change and re-orientate our perception. To this end, *Queer Pop* assembles theoretically advanced research on a range of creative expressions by queer and trans* artists that materialize futures and forms of community. Contributions address the aesthetics of sexual and gender identities and engage critically and creatively with persisting hegemonic ways that cultural artifacts are produced and exhibited. They explore how individual artists and artistic and popular cultures translate, appropriate, critique, and redefine the concept of "queer" and the visions of the future it generates.

Media studies engage with phenomena from popular culture and scrutinize them critically and affirmatively. In doing so, the field takes up the tradition of critical theory and takes inspiration from British cultural studies. The present volume combines stances from British cultural studies with US-American queer theory. It aims at facilitating a broader diffusion of these perspectives in German-speaking scholarship by connecting Anglo-Saxon theory with discussions in German-speaking academia and cross-linking the latter internationally.

Cultural studies direct attention to the representation of subordinate and socially marginalized groups and focuses on the culture of everyday life and popular culture. Scholars working in this field considered and continue to consider how visual repre-

---

1 See, for instance, Lee Edelman: *No Future: Queer Theory and the Death Drive*. Durham, NC / London 2004.

2 See, for instance, José Esteban Muñoz: *Cruising Utopia. The Then and There of Queer Futurity*. New York, NY 2009; Kara Keeling: *Queer Times, Black Futures*. New York, NY 2019.

sentations shape ideas about members of social groups.[3] They thus speak to the social sciences, which negotiate the question of "representation" through concepts such as marginalization, cultural participation, equality, and social justice. The present volume follows in this vein and studies how aesthetic and political dimensions relate to one another in queer popular culture, namely to counterbalance those positions in media studies today that deal with "representation" primarily as an aesthetic concept and ignore its political dimension.

The contributions assembled here gain decisive theoretical impulses from queer theory, a field of study established in literary studies and philosophy in the USA in the 1990s that has been constantly developed ever since. The interdisciplinary orientation of queer studies is evidenced, among other things, by the fact that in its early years, it took literary analyses, statistical studies, and sociological and ethnological observations in everyday and subcultural contexts as starting points for developing theoretical concepts.[4]

Researching the history of those human beings who suffered exclusion remains a desideratum in the German-speaking world.[5] The research approach offered by queer theory, which has undergone rapid development in English-speaking academia over the past thirty years, has hardly been addressed in German discourse until 2010; this approach has been gaining some currency over the past ten years.[6] Historians work-

---

3 See, for instance, E. Ann Kaplan (ed.): *Women in Film Noir* [1978]. London 1998; Richard Dyer: *Now You See it: Studies on Lesbian and Gay Film.* London / New York, NY 1990; bell hooks: *Black Looks. Race and Representation.* Boston, MA 1992; Kobena Mercer: *Welcome to the Jungle. New Positions in Black Cultural Studies.* New York, NY 1995; Stuart Hall (ed.): *Representation: Cultural Representations and Signifying Practices.* London 1997; Richard Dyer: *White.* London / New York, NY 1997; Kobena Mercer: Skin Head Sex Thing: Racial Difference and the Homoerotic Imaginary. In: *The Masculinity Studies Reader*, ed. by Rachel Adams / David Savran. Malden 2002, 188–200.

4 See, for example, Eve Kosofsky Sedgwick: Queer and Now. In: *Tendencies.* ed. by Michèle Aina Barale / Jonathan Goldberg / Michael Moon. London 1994, 1–8.

5 See, for instance, Richard Kühl: *Der Große Krieg der Triebe. Die deutsche Sexualwissenschaft und der Erste Weltkrieg.* Bielefeld 2022. See also Nicholas Maniu: *Queere Männlichkeiten. Bilderwelten männlich-männlichen Begehrens und queere Geschlechtlichkeit.* Bielefeld 2023, 62–78.

6 For a historically-rooted and forward-thinking perspective located at the intersection between queer theory and expanded cinema, see Astrid Deuber-Mankowsky: *Queeres Post-Cinema. Yael Bartana, Su Friedrich, Todd Haynes, Sharon Hayes.* Berlin 2017; for a framing of queer cinema as an art form that articulates the precarious, see Astrid Deuber-Mankowsky / Philipp Hanke (eds.): *Queeres Kino / Queere Ästhetiken als Dokumentationen des Prekären.* Vienna 2021; for critical reflections in activism and artistic practices on the affective politics implied by social inequality and power relations, see Käthe von Bose / Ulrike Klöppel / Katrin Köppert / Karin Michalski / Pat Treusch (eds.): *I is for Impasse. Affektive Queerverbindungen in Theorie_Aktivismus_Kunst.* Berlin 2015; for a reconsideration of queer maculinity and sexuality in German fanzine culture, see Peter Rehberg: *Hipster Porn. Queere Männlichkeiten und affektive Sexualitäten im Fanzine Butt.* Berlin 2018; for a consideration of queer motives in rock and pop music, see Doris Leibetseder: *Queere Tracks: Subversive Strategien in der Rock und Popmusik.* Bielefeld 2010; for an examination of a variety of examples from different media, see Sebastian Zilles (ed.): Queer(ing) Popular Culture. Special Issue, *Navigationen: Zeitschrift für Medien- und Kulturwissenschaft* 18/1 (2018). http://dx.doi.org/10.25969/mediarep/1920; for a collection of Ger-ing on queer German history even go so far as to identify a "queer moment"[7] in recent years, referring to a watershed in gender and sexuality studies in German-speaking academia and, more specifically, of academic work at the intersection of a German cultural canon and queer topics.[8]

In contrast to some current German-language publications in the field of queer studies whose merit lies primarily in the translation of English-language key texts into German, *Queer Pop* distinguishes itself by demonstrating what the transfer of predominantly Anglo-American theory into cultural studies discourse in German-speaking academia can contribute to a more comprehensive understanding of contemporary forms of aesthetic expression. Furthermore, the volume explores how studying the various present-day forms of artistic self-staging enables one to gauge the current state of queer theorizing. Unlike existing publications on queer cultures in English,[9] the assembled contributions do not consider queer pop culture in isolation as an aesthetic issue but discuss the staging of the body as socially significant representations that address, hinder, and promote social inclusion and cultural diversity.

To position this book on *Queer Pop* as the first in the *Queer Futures* series means to make an initial attempt at bringing into conversation queer theory and the aesthetic expressions by queer artists. We are currently witnessing the successful marketing of queer, Black, and trans* artistic personas, especially in the field of pop music. This development demands including in the discussion liminality and hybridity – not only as concepts that media cultural theory utilizes but also as practices in art and pop culture. In the context of Black art, liminality refers to an aesthetic strategy that underscores the cross-linking of the experience of a traumatic past and the imagining of a possibly liberating future. Temporal hybridity is seen as specific to a *jazz aesthetic*[10] that spans music and literature and includes many more art forms. Pointing to the interweaving of liminality with Black posthumanism and Afrofutur-

---

man translations of canonical readings in the field of queer theory and some exemplary applications of the perspectives offered, see Mike Laufenberg / Ben Trott (eds.): *Queer Studies. Schlüsseltexte.* Frankfurt 2023.

7 Sébastien Tremblay: Review of *The Queer Art of History: Queer Kinship After Fascism.* By Jennifer V. Evans. Durham, NC: Duke University Press. *German History* 41, No. 4 (2023), 632. See also Sébastian Tremblay: *A Badge of Injury: The Pink Triangle as Global Symbol of Memory.* Berlin 2024.

8 The scholarship of Adrian Daub and Ervin Malakaj, among others, provide evidence for this observation. See, for instance, Ervin Malakaj: *Anders als die Andern.* Montréal / Berlin 2023. We thank the anonymous reviewer of the manuscript for this insightful hint and the invaluable comments on the individual contributions and the book as a whole.

9 See, for instance, Thomas Peele (ed.): *Queer Popular Culture: Literature, Media, Film, and Television.* Basingstoke 2011; Stan Hawkins: *Queerness in Pop Music: Aesthetics, Gender Norms, and Temporality.* New York, NY / London 2016.

10 In his description of a "jazz aesthetic," Swiss-US-American scholar of African American literature Jürgen E. Grandt emphasizes temporal hybridity. He writes: "the 'blackness' of black culture, of both the music and the literature, in fact thrives on hybridity, harnessing the energies inherent in the tension-filled process of cultural product as well as simultaneously affirming the African American (literary)

ism, US-American scholar of literature Kristen Lillvis stresses that "contemporary black artists, writers, filmmakers, musicians, and theorists record and reconfigure the black subject's experiences of liminality by blending references to the past and present with predictions for the future."[11]

These ideas and practices resonate, on a positive note, with reflections on temporality in queer theory. In his future-oriented imagination of queerness, Cuban-US-American performance studies scholar José Esteban Muñoz asserts:

> Queerness is not yet here. Queerness is an ideality. Put another way, we are not yet queer. We may never touch queerness, but we can feel it as the warm illumination of a horizon imbued with potentiality. We have never been queer, yet queerness exists for us as an ideality that can be distilled from the past und used to imagine a future. The future is queerness's domain.[12]

And US-American critical theorist and film studies scholar Kara Keeling starts her reflection on the intersection of queer theory and critical race studies from "the generative proposition *another world is possible*, the insistence that such a world already is here now."[13]

2 Queering the Concept of "Pop"

The English term "queer" exists as a noun, adjective, and verb. Since the late nineteenth century, the noun "queer" has been used as a derogatory term for a male homosexual. In the early 1990s, as queer theory was gaining currency in the United States, the term underwent a critical re-evaluation:[14] the research approach celebrated difference in regard to the sexual norm and broadened the concept of "queer" to include the intentional subversion of social conventions and the conscious and strategic destabilization

---

tradition." Jürgen E. Grandt: Prelude: So What? In: *Kinds of Blue. The Jazz Aesthetic in African American Narrative*. Columbus, OH 2005, xviii.

11 Kristen Lillvis: Introduction. In: *Posthuman Blackness and the Black Female Imagination*. Athens, GA 2017, 13.

12 Muñoz: *Cruising Utopia*, 1.

13 Keeling: *Queer Times*, ix [italics in original].

14 This usage of the term "queer" can be traced back to Teresa de Lauretis' introduction to a special issue of *Differences* on "Queer Theory: Lesbian and Gay Sexualities" and the conference of the same name held at the University of California at Santa Cruz in February 1990. See Teresa de Lauretis: Queer Theory: Lesbian and Gay Sexualities An Introduction. In: *Differences: A Journal of Feminist Cultural Studies* 3/2 (Summer 1991), ed. by Teresa de Lauretis, iii–xviii. Many scholars recognize this text as the founding publication of queer theory, in conjunction with Judith Butler: Critically Queer. *GLQ: A Journal of Lesbian and Gay Studies* 1 (1993), 17–32.

of classificatory systems,[15] thus opening up new spaces for thinking and ways of living "otherwise." The term queer, however, carries a problematic legacy, since it is mainly associated with white gay male history and thus only partly operative for lesbians, People of Color, or trans*, intersex, and non-binary people.[16] This begs the question whether "queer" is still a useful concept.

In the academic context, there is some debate on the question whether "queer" primarily signifies sexual orientation and homosexual practices or whether it goes beyond sexual orientation. Some scholars argue that sex matters and insist that "queer" should not be untied from homosexual identity, same-sex desire, and homosexual practices, and primarily focus on the potentialities for social transformation that identity politics instigate.[17] Other scholars working in queer studies use the interdisciplinary space that this field opens up to include perspectives from postcolonial studies and critical race theory,[18] transgender theory,[19] transnational feminism,[20] disability

---

15 French historian Michel Foucault who, in his *History of Sexuality*, pinpointed how sexology invented the homosexual in the late nineteenth century, also pointed to the historical formation of specific "epistemes" and highlighted the possibility to change them. See Michel Foucault: *History of Sexuality*, vol. 1, *An Introduction* [French original 1976], trans. by Robert Hurley. New York, NY 1978, 42–44 and Michel Foucault: *The Order of Things: An Archaeology of the Human Sciences* [French original 1966], London / New York, NY 2005, especially "Preface," xvi–xxvi, and the chapter "Mathesis and 'Taxinomia,'" 79–85.

16 For a lesbian critique of the term queer see, for instance, Julia Parnaby: Queer Straits. *Trouble and Strife* 26 (1993), 14; see also Susan J. Wolfe / Julia Penelope: Sexual Identity / Textual Politics: Lesbian {De/Com}positions. In: *Sexual Practice, Textual Theory: Lesbian Cultural Criticism*, ed. by Susan J. Wolfe / Julia Penelope. Cambridge, MA 1993, 5; for a Queer of Color critique see, for instance, José Esteban Muñoz: *Disidentification: Queers of Color and the Performance of Politics*. Minneapolis, MN 1999; Roderick A. Ferguson: *Aberrations in Black: Toward a Queer of Color Critique*. Minneapolis, MN 2004; for an emphasis on intersectionality in queer studies see, for instance, David L. Eng / Jack Halberstam / José Esteban Muñoz: What's Queer About Queer Studies Now? *Social Text* 23/3–4, (Fall–Winter 2005), 1, 3, 4; for a trans* critique of "queer" and queer studies see, for instance, Susan Stryker: Transgender Studies: Queer Theory's Evil Twin. *GLQ: A Journal of Lesbian and Gay Studies* 10/2 (2004), 212–215, here: 214. Stryker also alludes to the kinship between transgender studies and "disability studies and intersex studies, two other critical enterprises that investigate atypical forms of embodiment and subjectivity that do not readily reduce to heteronormativity, yet that largely fall outside the analytic framework of sexual identity that so dominates queer theory."

17 See, for instance, Leo Bersani: *Homos*. Cambridge, MA 1996; Lauren Berlant / Michael Warner: Sex in Public. In: *Publics and Counterpublics*, ed. by Lauren Berlant / Michael Warner. New York, NY 2002, 187–208; see also Rehberg: *Hipster Porn*, 8–11.

18 See, for instance, Phillip Brian Harper / Anne McClintock / José Esteban Muñoz / Trish Rosen: Queer Transexions of Race, Nation, and Gender. An Introduction. *Social Text* 52/53 (Fall/Winter 1997), 1.

19 For instance, Jack Halberstam: *In a Queer Time and Place: Transgender Bodies, Subcultural Lives*. New York, NY / London 2005, 1.

20 For instance, Jasbir K. Puar: *Terrorist Assemblages: Homonationalism in Queer Times*. Durham, NC / London 2007.

studies, and critical animal studies.[21] Taking the concept of "queer" as their point of departure, yet another group of scholars examines all the diverse meanings of further critical terms and puts experimental writing forms to the test.[22] Some scholars reach ethical conclusions that are socio-critical in their outlook; others unfold decidedly utopian visions.

If we are to speak of queer pop, then we also have to problematize the term "pop." While in the English language "pop" is just shorthand for "the popular," in German-language discourse the term has certainly led to controversies regarding the different methodological approaches in attempts of defining it. Because most contributions to this volume grow out of German-speaking academia, it is especially productive to gain insight into German methodological approaches to the term "pop" and pop culture. This might also facilitate a better understanding of the academic background of the contributors and further elucidate the perspectives this volume and its contributions are written from. For example, German pop theorist Diedrich Diederichsen distinguishes "pop music" from "the popular" and considers "pop" as a system that emerged only after 1955. He writes:

> I therefore distinguish between pop music, whose history begins in 1955 give or take five years, and the popular and popular culture that existed before pop music and continues to exist. Finally, one can also speak of a more recent pop culture, which is the result of the influence of pop music as a cultural, artistic, and culture-industrial model on other arts and culture-industrial formats.[23]

Another attempt at a definition which distinguishes between the "mass culture" of old and "popular culture" highlights the development of the first youth subcultures that stimulated a specific pop cultural experience after 1945.[24] Above all, the demarcation of

---

21 For instance, Mel Y. Chen: *Animacies: Biopolitics, Racial Mattering, and Queer Affect*. Durham, NC / London 2012.

22 For an example in experimental collective writing that queers the ideology promoted by the Silicon Valley, see Caroline Bassett / Sara Kember / Kate O'Riordan: Feminist Futures: A Conditional Paeon for the Anything-Digital. In: id.: *Furious: Technological Feminism and Digital Futures*. London 2020, 1–22.

23 Diedrich Diedrichsen: *Über Pop-Musik*. Cologne 2014, xii [Own translation, B.P.].

24 In regard to the emergence of popular culture, English cultural and media historian Jon Savage points to the invention of the teenager through the invention of an independent consumption-oriented life stage between childhood and adulthood. This took place precisely after the Second World War, and it was only from that point on that this idea, starting in the USA, spread throughout the countries of the Western hemisphere. The socially relevant notion of the teenager as the bearer of a specific concept of culture applicable to this life stage only – namely youth culture – emerged. Although certain reform movements since the twentieth century accentuated and even glorified youth (one might think for example of the Wandervogel, of certain instrumentalizations in the National Socialist terror system and in the USSR), the societal width and consumerist entrenchment of youth culture is a laborious "invention" of the 1940s and 1950s.

youth as a sociologically addressable group and its attachment to musical concepts gave rise to the first subcultures starting in the late 1950s up to punk in 1977 in England.[25]

Punk opened up new possibilities for self-definition by following a postmodern vein, the dismemberment of the world and recomposition of its individual parts. Although punk caused a rivalry between the fragmentation of the status quo and a new aesthetic that interconnected media to create new gendered codes, it was nevertheless shaped by a history of white, mostly heterosexual youth. Artists such as David Bowie and Brian Ferry can be credited with questioning and subverting gender relations and role clichés. Both these artists as well as others played an instrumental role in shaping the iconography of the punk movement.[26] In this context, the performances of Grace Jones between 1978 and 1986 deserve special attention. She expanded the understanding of performance art, for example, and hinted at a connection between postcolonialism and postmodernism.

German scholar of literature Thomas Hecken traces the various concepts of pop historically. In Hecken's view, especially the concept of the "culture industry," coined by the German philosophers Theodor W. Adorno and Max Horkheimer, developed a great impact. The two representatives of the first generation of the Frankfurt School elaborated upon the concept in their *Dialectic of Enlightenment*, which they wrote in 1944 while in exile. The book became one of the most widely-quoted texts of critical theory and played a decisive role in developing the concept of "pop."

In the canonical formulation of their position in the chapter on culture industry, Horkheimer and Adorno discuss the impact of an industrial form of cultural production. It is not an exaggeration to declare this chapter to be one of the most influential works of mass media analysis and cultural theory, at least in Europe. The very concept of the culture industry makes it clear at which point Horkheimer and Adorno

---

And it is only in this constellation that a traditional mass culture, to which categories such as generation and age were largely extraneous, and which even tended to target older consumers, became pop culture in the modern sense. The catalyst of this process was the invention of another cultural strategy, namely pop music as a specific system in the 1950s. It is precisely at this point in the 1950s that the contours finally form which became the starting point for all further pop cultural differentiations. Pop culture refers to the mass-media reception of entertaining contents and their complex concatenation and transfer into a form of life. Pop as a form of life means offering a set of possibilities for cultural reflection and related patterns for action. Since the 1950s, having an affinity to pop culture means not only having certain musical preferences but also wearing certain clothes, advocating certain attitudes and world views, driving certain vehicles, and practicing certain ways of life. See Jon Savage: *Teenage. The Creation of Youth Culture*. New York, NY / London 2007.

In his reflections on the concept of "queer time," Jack Halberstam proposes that the "queer temporalities" which subcultural lifestyles open up challenge such a division into lifespans. Taking queer time as the starting point, he suggests "that we rethink the adult/youth binary in relation to an 'epistemology of youth' that disrupts conventional accounts of youth culture, adulthood, and maturity." Halberstam: *In a Queer Time and Place*, 2.

25 Dick Hebdige: *Hiding in the Light. On Images and Things*. London 1988.

26 See Simon Reynolds / Joy Press: *The Sex Revolts. Gender, Rebellion and Rock'n'Roll*. Cambridge 1995.

start. From their perspective, the universe of late capitalist popular culture essentially consists of the mass media of film, television, radio, and the press and appears as a single large industrially and profit-oriented context of use. The products of the culture industry, according to Horkheimer and Adorno, cheat people out of their happiness by presenting them with false ideals and opportunities for distraction in order to keep them from realizing their true situation. The perfidy of the culture industry – according to the authors – lies in the fact that it transfers the already problematic modes of production of capitalist society to cultural products of all kinds, including products of high culture, thus creating a conformist cosmos, or, as the authors put it, "the reproduction of sameness,"[27] which does not allow for intellectual and aesthetic variety. Starting from a traditional Marxist theory of manipulation of the masses by the entertainment industry, Horkheimer and Adorno go even further, and Adorno then also pointedly elaborates on this in his later work, for example, on television. According to Adorno, the diabolical thing about the forms of the modern entertainment industry is precisely that they make an implicit pact with the unconscious of the recipient. To put it simply, the lowest instincts of the viewer are tapped into in order to create an intellectual training for an anesthetized existence in late capitalism.

> Entertainment is the prolongation of work under late capitalism. [. . .] The culture industry endlessly cheats its consumers out of what it endlessly promises. [. . .] Fun is a medical bath which the entertainment industry never ceases to prescribe. It makes laughter the instrument for cheating happiness.[28]

The point of Horkheimer and Adorno's argument is that the tendency for cultural decay characteristic of the culture industry is infectious and also corrodes parts of high culture. This implies that the culture industry promoted stereotypical images of characters in regard to race, class, and gender. A continuity of the same bound the gatekeepers of yore to decisions that conveyed a commercial and thus simplistic and self-perpetuating image in regard to race, class, and gender.

Thus, the culture industry in particular also significantly contributed to the fact that the history of female, as some scholars have argued,[29] and queer pop artists has hardly been addressed. Already in the early 1980s, British cultural theorist Angela McRobbie pointed out the lack of visibility of female bands and fans. She was able to identify very early and very clearly gaps in the historiography of pop.[30] McRobbie,

---

27 Max Horkheimer / Theodor W. Adorno: The Culture Industry: Enlightenment as Mass Deception. In: id.: *Dialectic of Enlightenment*, ed. by Gunzelin Schmid Noerr, trans. by Edmund Jephcott. Stanford, CA 2002, 106.
28 Horkheimer / Adorno: *The Culture Industry*, 109–112.
29 See Christa Brüstle: *Popfrauen der Gegenwart. Körper – Stimme – Image. Vermarktungsstrategien zwischen Selbstinszenierung und Fremdbestimmung.* Bielefeld 2015.
30 See Angela McRobbie / Jenny Garber: Girls and Subcultures. In: *Resistance through Rituals. Youth Subcultures in Post-War Britain*, ed. by Stuart Hall / Tony Jefferson. London 1976, 209–222.

English media theorists and sociologist Dick Hebdige,[31] British journalist Vivien Goldman,[32] Diedrich Diedrichsen,[33] as well as English music journalist Simon Reynolds and US-American music journalist Joy Press[34] all highlighted that pop is a genuinely heterosexual cis-male cultural field. An alternative history of pop, the authors argue, could be written as a history of female bands and musicians. In doing so, they perpetuate the binary understanding of male versus female. Hence, lesbian, bisexual, and trans* musicians have been left out of the evolved structures of the culture industry, women's historiography, and also the "Fringe of the Fringe."[35] This begs a number of questions: How can pop historiography counter a perpetuation of the clear-cut distinction between male and female? How does the concept of queer promote a critical and creative rewriting of the history of pop culture? Should genres be rethought?[36]

3 A Queer Historiography

As such cursory consideration of pop historiography shows, the various academic and journalistic discussions on the notion of "pop" employ a binary and non-inclusive approach. In other words, the discussion surrounding the concept of pop perpetuates the politics of exclusion prevalent in mainstream culture. To intervene in this discussion from a decidedly queer and intersectional perspective, we propose the compound term of "queer pop." In doing so, our aim is twofold: Firstly, we seek to critically interrogate the problematic academic legacy of pop cultural historiography by pointing to its omissions that become apparent through an intersectional lens.[37]

---

31 Dick Hebdige: *Subculture: The Meaning of Style.* London 1979.

32 See Vivien Goldman: *Revenge of the She-Punks: A Feminist Music History from Poly Styrene to Pussy Riot.* Austin 2019.

33 See Diedrich Diederichsen: And then they move, and then they move – 20 Jahre später [preface to the new edition]. In: id.: *Sexbeat.* 2nd edition. Cologne 2002, i–xxxiv.

34 See Reynolds / Press: *The Sex Revolts.*

35 See Kathrin Dreckmann / Elfi Vomberg / Linnea Semmerlin (eds.): *Fringe of the Fringe. Queering Punk History.* Berlin 2023.

36 See Jack Halberstam: Trans* Feminism and Punk Performance. In: *Fringe of the Fringe. Queering Punk Media History*, ed. by Kathrin Dreckmann / Elfi Vomberg / Linnea Semmerling. Berlin 2023, 35–45.

37 Here, we take inspiration from US-American film historian Laura Horak's archival study on cross-dressing women in US-American films from 1908 until 1934. Horak's study intervenes in film historiography by showing that the well-known examples of Marlene Dietrich, Greta Garbo, and Katherine Hepburn had a host of predecessors pertinent to establishing imaginations about lesbian identity. Considering representations of gender and sexuality in regard to class and race, Horak makes it clear that gender-bending performances abound in American cinema before the Hays Code was established. See Laura Horak: *Girls will be Boys: Cross-Dressed Women, Lesbians, and American Cinema, 1908–1934.* New Brunswick, NJ / London 2016.

Secondly, we want to draw attention to the contributions of LGBTQI* artists to popular culture and appraise such contributions by bringing them into conversation with approaches from the academic fields of queer studies, transnational feminism, and critical race studies.

To this end, we distinguish between queered pop and genuine queer pop. The category of "queer" as a positive term of self-identification has only become established in academia and everyday language during the past 20 to 30 years. Thus, if one wants to look historically at practices of queering in pop music, one must be aware that the term "queer" may seem anachronistic in regards to contexts that predate the 1990s. While gay and lesbian artists have in parts shaped pop discourse phenomenologically since its beginnings, their influence has largely gone unnoticed and the queer undertones and subtexts of their contributions have received little critical acclaim.[38] Public discussion and academic discourse tended to reduce artists who would go by the term "queer" today to their subcultural status, while the artists themselves cultivated a distinct coding culture. Today, music videos like Queen's *I Want to Break Free* from 1984 can certainly be read as queer statements. However, the codes the band utilized in the video were not so clearly noticeable in the 1980s. Consider also the cover to the album *The Man Who Sold the World*, released by David Bowie in 1970. The cover, designed for the UK market, features Bowie wearing a dress by fashion designer Michael Fish. The album was not available in the US. Examples abound that prove the heteronormative view of the time.

In her 1964 essay *Notes on 'Camp,'* which queer theorists often quote,[39] Susan Sontag refers to the specific culture of homosexuals as a forerunner of the camp aesthetic. Sontag describes the concept of "camp" in 58 theses[40] and underscores how exaggeration works especially with regard to the unsettling of gender roles. Highlighting the intertextuality between high and low and emphasizing the pop cultural, Sontag points out how eclectic concepts circulating between lowbrow and highbrow culture often follow a logic of citation.[41] The process of reinterpretation and denaturalization of texts coming from a heterosexual culture perceived as dominant was of interest to queer theorists and artists alike. Sontag's essay even gained some currency in pop culture. David Bowie, for instance, heavily annotated his personal copy of the essay, as exemplified by the respective exhibit in the traveling exhibition *David Bowie Is.*[42]

---

38 See, for instance, the artists' talk in the present volume.

39 See, for instance, Jack Babuscio (ed.): *Queer Aesthetics and the Performing Subject: A Reader*. Edinburgh 1999.

40 Susan Sontag: Notes on "Camp." *The Partisan Review* (Fall 1964), 515–530. See also: Dolores McElroy: Camp. In: *Gender: Laughter*, ed. by Bettina Papenburg. Farmington Hills, MI 2017, 293–310.

41 Sontag: *Camp*, 515–530.

42 "David Bowie Is," touring exhibition curated by Victoria Broackes and Geoffrey Marsh of the Victoria and Albert Museum, London. See also: Victoria Broackes / Geoffrey Marsh: *David Bowie Is.* London 2013.

The culture industry has only been classifying music by queer artists as such for the last few years. In the previous decades, one-dimensional, patriarchally organized mainstream culture provided clear role models and propagated clear-cut categories. Only a few connoisseurs knew provocative albums like those by bands such as The Slits. Singer-songwriters such as Maxine Feldman had little audience. In the 1990s, at long last, K.D. Lang and Melissa Etheridge committed openly to a mainstream lesbian culture. However, a small number of performances by artists whom the cultural industry promoted present an exception. Those artists employed distinct codes intelligible to only a small portion of the audience. Bowie, for instance, invented the androgynous concept of "outer-space" – which refers to space travel and to a space outside of the normative social order – and the related narratives revolving around figures such as Ziggy Stardust, Major Tom, and Aladdin Sane. Bands such as Queen and artists such as Prince and Grace Jones likewise provided codes that were intelligible for a homosexual subculture. The phenomenon of "queering" artists to enhance their promotional value, however, occurs only recently. Consider, for instance, the biopic of Freddy Mercury in 2018.[43] Artists such as Lil Nas X, Janelle Monáe, Arca, and Mykki Bianco who openly identify as queer have only hit the stage and achieved public success in the last five years.

4 Mainstreaming "Queer"

The performance of marginalized identities, which in the 1980s still came to pass in cultural niches, increasingly spread into the cultural mainstream over the past thirty years, as demonstrated by the commercial success of artists such as Lady Gaga and Janelle Monáe. Until the 1990s, gay musicians (such as Freddy Mercury, David Bowie, and Prince) who became commercially successful and received public recognition did not, for the better part of their careers, openly identify as gay. They used specific codes that the gay community would understand. Their public acceptance and commercial success, however, depended on not labelling their work and themselves as gay.

The situation today is a quite different one. Openly identifying as queer, bisexual, trans*, or pansexual has become a selling point. Such self-identification allows artists to not only present themselves as "cool" and "with it" but also to reach a broader audience and extend their community of fans. In regard to some artists, one could devalue such self-fashioning as inauthentic – the public response online and in various social media channels points in this direction – and argue that it simply serves the purpose of commercialization. On the other hand, however, the public performance of highly visible artists who embody an LGBTQI* persona enhances visibility of the

---

43 Bohemian Rhapsody. Directed by Bryan Singer. 20th Century Fox / Regency Enterprises / GK Films / Queen Films, USA/UK 2018. The film presented Freddy Mercury's homosexuality as problematic.

community and facilitates acceptance of individuals who have experienced discrimination or would experience it under different cultural circumstances.

The censorship occurring in social media notwithstanding, a new culture of debate via social media opens up new possibilities for exploring sexual identity, which not only curtails the influence of gatekeepers such as labels and television channels – who, for a very long time decided whom to include and whom to leave out – but sometimes also pushes theory to its limits.

Pop culture today includes and references an extensive history, quoting from a varied repertoire of works by sexually ambiguous musicians, film-makers, authors, photographers and performers, including – but not limited to – members of different LGBTQI* communities. This applies to the creative expressions by artists who worked or are still working at the margins of their respective fields as well as to those whose work was critically acclaimed or received public recognition. Artists who identify as queer draw inspiration from filmmakers Rainer Werner Fassbinder, Rosa von Praunheim, Todd Haynes, and Jennie Livingston, for instance, as well as writers such as Pat Califia and Octavia E. Butler, photographers such as Claude Cahun, Robert Mapplethorpe, and Catherine Opie, and performers such as Ron Athey, to name but a few. Bowie's work remains a continued reference for queer performances,[44] as does the work of Prince, Freddy Mercury, and Grace Jones.[45]

Many musicians, particularly very successful ones, have been engaging with LGBTQI* issues in recent years and positioning themselves in a queer pop culture discourse. For example, Black US musician, singer, and performance artist Janelle Monáe construed a pop cultural persona that explicitly plays with gender roles. In the short film *Many Moons* which promoted her album *Metropolis: Suite 1 (The Chase)* in 2007, for instance, the artist wears a bow tie and appears as both dandy and diva. Monáe exemplifies a queer pop concept. In her stage shows and music videos, she cites, enacts, and shines a critical light on the gender-specific policies of the various music genres.[46] Monáe also addresses issues of race. In *Metropolis*, she develops a narrative – which unfolds across a number of studio albums – in which Black subjects, who have been attributed the status of objects for centuries, live as androids in an imaginary future. In this form of embodiment, they continue to experience oppression and continue to struggle for liberation.

In *Dirty Computer*, a 50-minute narrative film – or "emotion picture," as she herself terms it – from 2018 that showcases her album of the same name, borrows from and breaks down aesthetics from previous eras, focusing above all on the media aesthetics of David Bowie. The shape and design of the "vulva pants" that Monáe wears

---

44 See Kathrin Dreckmann: Notes on Pop. Campy Popästhetiken in Musikvideos. In: *Musikvideo reloaded: Über historische und aktuelle Bewegtbildästhetiken zwischen Pop, Kommerz und Kunst*, ed. by Kathrin Dreckmann. Berlin / Boston 2021, 141–157.

45 See Diederichsen: *Sexbeat*, xix.

46 See Halberstam: *Trans* Feminism and Punk Performance*, 35–45.

in her music video *Pynk* recall the Kansai Yamamoto jumpsuit worn by David Bowie back in 1973. At the same time, she expresses femininity and self-empowerment: *Pynk* can be seen as surmounting a male-dominated world.[47] Monáe communicates her message as a highly successful Black and openly pansexual musician who identifies as a feminist.

Playing with gender roles and gender identity, however, does not count as a brand-new phenomenon in mainstream pop culture. At the MTV Video Music Awards in Los Angeles in September 2011, performance artist, singer, and actress Lady Gaga appeared in men's clothing as the macho Jo Calderone, the boyfriend of prize winner Lady Gaga. In her drag performance, Lady Gaga remained true to her signature outlandishness.[48] The gender and sexual orientation of the artist have been hotly debated ever since she shot to fame in 2008. This debate sparks questions about artists who talk, sing, and perform in public within the framework of gender, race, class, and erotic desire: How does their self-positioning affect their utterances? What drives the public discussion that aims to pin down the biological and social gender of a person, a labeling that the term "queer" decidedly rejects? How can changing perceptions through empowering representations of members of marginalized groups, as art can do, provide impulses for interventions in the field of the social?

5 Structure of this Volume and Contributions

This volume brings together contributions from emerging and renowned scholars from mostly German-speaking academia who employ concepts from queer theory such as homonormativity, homonationalism, erotohistoriography, and queer temporality in fields including media aesthetics, critical theory, cultural studies, and literary studies. They analyze a variety of case studies that we gather under the rubric of what we call "queer pop." With this volume, we launch the English-language series on *Queer Futures*. The contributions assembled here take up the social and political responsibility of cultural studies and examine the aesthetic strategies that artists who occupy marginalized subject positions and whose history has not yet been comprehensively documented and researched have employed in their self-fashioning over the last forty years. The essays collected in this volume examine how queer artists intervene in a mainstream cultural discourse and explore how they use aesthetic means to promote social justice and inclusion. The contributions are loosely organized around four thematic foci: firstly, "Queer Aesthetics in Pop Music"; secondly,

---

47 Kathrin Dreckmann: "PYNK" beyond forests and thighs: Manifestations of Social Utopia in Current Music Video. In: *Music Video and Transculturality: Manifestations of Social Utopia?*, ed. by Kathrin Dreckmann / Christofer Jost. Münster 2024.
48 Jack Halberstam: *Gaga Feminism: Sex, Gender, and the End of Normal.* Boston, MA 2012, 4.

"Homonationalism and Homonormativity in Television"; thirdly, "Queer Affect"; and fourthly, "Queer Futures." The "Creative Interlude," situated between the third and fourth parts, includes reflections of practicing feminist and queer artists on their positioning in the male-dominated arena of pop culture and on the question of how the public discussion of queer topics has changed during the past 30 years.

Part I – Queer Aesthetics in Pop Music

As we have shown above, academic and public discourse on pop culture as well as pop historiography reproduce the normalizing distinction between men's history and women's history. A queer history of pop is still to be written. The contributions assembled in this part attempt at such a critical rewriting. They do so, for instance, by assessing and reevaluating selected works by commercially successful pop artists in regard to the queer motives they allude to or openly present. Kathrin Dreckmann promotes such a queer historiography by tracing the history of the visual motives and tropes evoked in the music video *Montero (Call Me By Your Name)* from 2021 by US-American rapper and queer Black icon Lil Nas X back to the discussion on same-sex desire going on in ancient Greek philosophy. Highlighting the politics of citation at work in current pop music, Dreckmann not only shows how Lil Nas X references homoerotic desire and non-binary ideas of gender that had already circulated in Plato's *Symposium*. She also tracks postcolonial practices of empowerment in *Montero* by pointing to how the artist appropriates feudal accoutrement used at European courts in the eighteenth century, such as the wig, in an ironic pose of self-fashioning. In regard to colonial and neocolonial practices of cultural appropriation, Dreckmann argues, this seizure comes into view as an empowering gesture of asserting hybrid identity at the intersection of race and sexuality.

Franziska Haug's contribution dwells on the topic of the music video and lingers with the subject of the commercially successful non-white pop artist. Haug analyzes how selected music videos by artists such as Beyoncé, Rihanna, and Madonna, but also Britney Spears, collude in the mainstream manufacturing of gender identity and erotic desire. She assesses how such artists in their lyrics and performances reflexively address such production of gender and desire. Reconsidering the question of the relation between aesthetics and politics, Haug unravels the aesthetic strategies that the music video employs to shape – and possibly change – normative ideas about gender. To this end, Haug combines materialist and social constructivist approaches and includes perspectives from monist philosophy and psychoanalysis.

While artists such as Lil Nas X, Beyoncé, Madonna, and Rihanna address issues of gender identity and erotic desire head-on, these topics play a more subdued role in the oeuvre of the British pop duo Pet Shop Boys. In his close reading of selected songs, albums, cover artwork, and music videos by the Pet Shop Boys, dating from 1984 to 1990, Daniel Baranowski discerns queer topics and unfolds queer moments that function, as he argues, borrowing a term from French philosopher Jacques Derrida, as an "eccentric center" that is an unobtrusive yet significant starting point allowing for a slow unwrapping of the key motif of the oeuvre by directing attention to its margins.

Part II – Homonationalism and Homonormativity in Television

The contributions assembled in the second part shift the subject focus from pop music to television. Both contributors of this part firmly anchor their analyses in queer theory, taking up some of the problems and concepts that scholars in this field are currently debating and reconsider them in light of selected case studies. Katharina M. Wiedlack investigates how the embodiment of the white Russian drag persona Katya by Irish-American comedian Brian McCook in the US-American reality television show *RuPaul's Drag Race* (2009–present) supports a homonationalist program. The term "homonationalism,"[49] coined by queer theorist and postcolonial critic Jasbir Puar, refers to a collusion of nationalist and sexual rights discourses that strategically enlists lesbian and gay politics into an orientalist and racist agenda. Taking the persona of Katya as her example, Wiedlack stresses how a show such as *RuPaul's Drag Race*, which deliberately promotes liberal pro-gay discourse, concomitantly asserts Western hegemony by exploiting the stereotype of the racialized Other.

Sarah Rüß considers how the US-American television series *The L Word* (2004–2009) and *The Fosters* (2013–2018) endorse ideas and practices of homonormativity. The term "homonormativity,"[50] propagated, among others, by US-American historian Lisa Duggan, refers to a politics of enrolling lesbians and gay men into a heteronormative, consumption-oriented, capitalist lifestyle that conforms to a nationalist agenda. Rüß considers how television series such as *The L Word* and *The Fosters*, while enhancing the visibility of lesbians by presenting a variety of lesbian characters to a wider audience, advance a repressive and exclusionary politics of shame. Such politics devalues lifestyles that deviate from the homonormative ideal. To this end, Rüß reads selected scenes from both series through the lens of affect theory.

Part III – Queer Affect

Since the formation of queer theory in the early 1990s, "affect" has emerged as a crucial concept. Shame, stigma, embarrassment, and pain as consequences of the experience of social exclusion, devaluation, and misrecognition, as well as the trauma

---

49 Puar: *Terrorist Assemblages*, 336–339.

50 Lisa Duggan: The New Homonormativity: The Sexual Politics of Neoliberalism. In: *Materializing Democracy: Toward a Revitalized Cultural Politics,* ed. by Russ Castronovo / Dana D. Nelson / Donald E. Pease. New York, NY 2002, 175–177.

ensuing from this experience have all been focal points for queer theorizing.[51] In the noughties, politically progressive queer theorists disengaged from the affect trajectory promoting a move from shame to pride, in response to conservative activists pushing the renaming of Christopher Street Liberation Day to Gay Pride. Instead, scholars insisted on dwelling on affects such as shame and anger and suggested investigating the capability of negative affect for instigating social change.[52] By foregrounding the transformative capacities of negative affect, scholarship in queer studies resonates with a feminist tradition of taking negative individual affective experience as a starting point for political activism that denounces social ills and formulates political demands.[53]

Many studies that combine queer theory and affect theory take up Eve Kosofsky Sedgwick and Adam Frank's work on shame as a heuristic pedagogical tool.[54] In regard to Sedgwick and Frank, London-based feminist philosopher Clare Hemmings, for instance, emphasizes the fact that "[s]hame itself [. . .] has a resonance well beyond its homophobic generation, enabling queer subjects both to identify the bodily resonances

---

51 See, for instance, Heather Love: *Feeling Backward: Loss and the Politics of Queer History*. Cambridge, MA 2007, 3.

52 See David M. Halperin / Valerie Traub: Beyond Gay Pride. In: *Gay Shame*, ed. by David M. Halperin / Valerie Traub Chicago, IL / London 2009, 3–4; see also Clare Hemmings: Invoking Affect. Cultural theory and the ontological turn. *Cultural Studies* 19/5 (2005), 549. The Gay Shame conference, held at the University of Michigan in Ann Arbor in 2003, gave a decisive impulse. US historian of sexuality David M. Halperin and US literary and women's studies scholar Valerie Traub state in the introduction to the edited volume that followed from the conference: "Gay pride has never been able to separate itself entirely from shame, or to transcend shame. Gay pride does not even make sense without some reference to the shame of being gay, and its very successes (to say nothing of its failures) testify to the intensity of its ongoing struggle with shame." They conclude: "Perhaps, then, the time has come to consider some alternate strategies for the promotion of queer sociality." Halperin / Traub: *Beyond Gay Pride*, 3–4. Gay pride labeled the gathering of bodies of people who have been shamed. It enabled an identity politics that were and still are the politics of gay pride. The questions the Michigan conferences sought to address were: Can there be a politics after gay pride? What gets lost through the affirmation of pride instead of shame? Negative affect – for instance, disgust – that the bodies of gays, and perhaps, to a lesser extent, lesbians, elicit in those who shame them can become a starting point for reflection about affective responses circulating in the culture of the majority, and, by extension, can prompt participants in this culture to reflect about stereotypes and prejudices.

53 See for instance, Audre Lorde: Eye to Eye: Black Women, Hatred, and Anger. In: *Sister Outsider: Essays and Speeches by Audre Lorde*. Freedom, CA 1984; Ann Cvetkovich: *An Archive of Feelings: Trauma, Sexuality, and Lesbian Public Cultures*. Durham, NC / London 2003; Sara Ahmed: *The Cultural Politics of Emotion*. New York, NY 2004; Sara Ahmed: *The Promise of Happiness*. Durham, NC 2010; Barbara Tomlinson: *Feminism and Affect at the Scene of Argument: Beyond the Trope of the Angry Feminist*. Philadelphia, PN 2010; Ann Cvetkovich: *Depression: A Public Feeling*. Durham, NC 2012.

54 See Eve Kosofsky Sedgwick / Adam Frank: Shame in the Cybernetic Fold: Reading Silvan Tomkins. In: *Shame and Its Sisters: A Silvan Tomkins Reader*. Durham, NC 1995, 1–28; see also Eve Kosofsky Sedgwick: *Touching Feeling*. Durham, NC 2003.

of a heterosexual status quo and to create community through empathy and shared experience."[55] However, as Hemmings aptly points out, questions of intersectional positioning need to be addressed here. For whom does bodily knowledge open up new possibility for connecting? Hemmings rightfully foregrounds "that only for certain subjects can affect be thought of as attaching in an open way; others are so over-associated with affect that they themselves are the object of affective transfer"[56] – for instance, the prostitute or the Black person.

Joanna Staśkiewicz's contribution investigates how queer forms of neo-burlesque stage performance in Warsaw and New Orleans employ humor and laughter as strategies for transforming individual and collective pain ensuing from the experience of social exclusion into an experience of community and belonging. Considering 2018 neo-burlesque performances by New Orleans-based artists Dick Jones Burly and Lefty Lucy as well as Warsaw-based artists Lola Noir and Gąsiu, Staśkiewicz argues that queer performance art offers a space outside of the normative temporal order. It temporarily frees the performers and the audience from the pressure that a capitalist and heteronormative lifestyle exerts. Staśkiewicz employs the concept of "erotohistoriography,"[57] as coined by US-American scholar of literature Elizabeth Freeman and which refers to a corporeal rewriting of history, to argue that queer performance art allows for a glimpse of a utopian world in which trauma may be processed and from which a collective politics may ensue.

Peter Rehberg proposes what he calls "affective sexuality" as a form for gay men to relate to one another sexually that significantly differs from performance-oriented gay male sexuality as it is represented, circulated, and perpetuated in mainstream visual gay pornography. Rehberg discerns this specific form of gay male sexuality in the photographic staging of the male nude in the English-language Dutch gay and queer fanzine *Butt* (2001–present). Situating *Butt* in the discourse on post-pornography and taking his cue from Michel Foucault and Lauren Berlant, Rehberg critically reevaluates the evasion of the topic of sexuality in current queer affect theory and insists on tethering the debate in this field to sexuality.

Part IV – Queer Futures

The subjects considered in Staśkiewicz's and Rehberg's contributions – queer performance art and post-pornographic queer magazine culture – already provide a glimpse at what queer futures may look and feel like and what pleasurable and enriching forms of community they may enable. The contributions collected in the final part of

---

55 Hemmings: *Invoking Affect*, 549–550.
56 Hemmings: *Invoking Affect*, 561.
57 Elizabeth Freeman: Time Binds, or, Erotohistoriography. *Social Text* 23/3–4 (2005), 59.

this volume further elaborate on forward-looking aesthetic strategies that explore how they can rework and transform the experience of discrimination and social exclusion so that new forms of relating to one another and to a variety of different subject positions may materialize.

Vera Mader's contribution traces a Black feminist chronopolitics in three music videos of 2013, 2014, and 2022 by British pop artist FKA twigs. Combining stances from Black feminism with concepts from Afrofuturism and ideas from a strand of German media theory inspired by cybernetics, Mader argues that the aesthetic staging of a time out of joint in FKA twigs' music videos challenges a linear conception of time that was and still is at the bedrock of ideas on Western supremacy. To complicate such a linear understanding of time by emphasizing gaps, intervals, and including retrograde and sideways moves implies, as Mader suggests, an interrogation of historical and present power relations responsible for oppression and marginalization. In such practice, which deliberately addresses the ambivalence of media technology, a more just and inclusive future shimmers through.

Josephine Hetterich, in the final contribution to this volume, dwells on the concept of queer temporality and connects it to the practice of queer reproduction. Hetterich asks how a focus on queer reproductive labor brings into view different conceptions of the future. To answer this question, the author examines how the Netflix series *Pose* (2018–2021), which pays homage to the Black and Latinx queer and trans* ballroom culture in Harlem of the 1980s and 1990s, revisits audiovisual materials relevant to queer and trans* historiography. In doing so, Hetterich identifies three forms of queer reproduction in *Pose*: a narrative focus on the topic of care, the writing of a queer and trans* history, and a publicizing of such history. The engagement with the past that *Pose* offers, the author concludes, can be read as a future-oriented strategy of resistance.

The past that queer media practices address has been and still is subject to orders of knowledge that largely remain unconscious. We can only rework and overcome such epistemes if we render them conscious. And it is here that the present volume aspires to contribute to the ongoing discussion, namely by assembling contributions that bring into view past and present forms of articulation of queer identity and queer desire, thus offering a foretaste of a queer future.

Bibliography

Ahmed, Sara: *The Cultural Politics of Emotion*. New York, NY 2004.
Ahmed, Sara: *The Promise of Happiness*. Durham, NC 2010.
Bassett, Caroline / Kember, Sara / O'Riordan, Kate: Feminist Futures: A Conditional Paeon for the Anything-Digital. In: *Furious. Technological Feminism and Digital Futures*, ed. by Bassett, Caroline / Kember, Sara / O'Riordan, Kate. London 2020, 1–22.
Babuscio, Jack (ed.): *Queer Aesthetics and the Performing Subject: A Reader*. Edinburgh 1999.

Berlant, Lauren / Warner, Michael: Sex in Public. In: *Publics and Counterpublics*, ed. by Berlant, Lauren / Warner, Michael. New York, NY 2002, 187–208.

Bersani, Leo: *Homos*. Cambridge, MA 1996.

Broackes, Victoria / Marsh Geoffrey: *David Bowie Is*. London 2013.

Brüstle, Christina: *Popfrauen der Gegenwart. Körper – Stimme – Image. Vermarktungsstrategien zwischen Selbstinszenierung und Fremdbestimmung*. Bielefeld 2015.

Butler, Judith: Critically Queer. *GLQ: A Journal of Lesbian and Gay Studies* 1 (1993), 17–32.

Chen, Mel Y.: *Animacies: Biopolitics, Racial Mattering, and Queer Affect*. Durham, NC / London 2012.

Cvetkovich, Ann: *An Archive of Feelings: Trauma, Sexuality, and Lesbian Public Cultures*. Durham, NC / London 2003.

Cvetkovich, Ann: *Depression: A Public Feeling*. Durham 2012.

de Lauretis, Teresa: Queer Theory: Lesbian and Gay Sexualities. *An Introduction*. In: *Differences: A Journal of Feminist Cultural Studies* 3/2 (Summer 1991), ed. by de Lauretis, Teresa, iii–xviii.

Diedrichsen, Diedrich: *Sexbeat*. Cologne 2002.

Diedrichsen, Diedrich: *Über Pop-Musik*. Cologne 2014.

Dreckmann, Kathrin: Notes on Pop. Campy Popästhetiken in Musikvideos. In: *Musikvideo reloaded: Über historische und aktuelle Bewegtbildästhetiken zwischen Pop, Kommerz und Kunst*, ed. by Dreckmann, Kathrin. Berlin / Boston 2021, 109–124.

Dreckmann, Kathrin / Semmerling, Linea / Vomberg, Elfi (eds.): *Fringe of the Fringe. Queering Punk Media History*. Berlin 2023.

Dreckmann, Kathrin: "PYNK" beyond forests and thighs: Manifestations of Social Utopia in Current Music Video. In: *Music Video and Transculturality: Manifestations of Social Utopia?*, ed. by Dreckmann, Kathrin / Jost, Christofer. Münster 2024.

Deuber-Mankowsky, Astrid: *Queeres Post-Cinema. Yael Bartana, Su Friedrich, Todd Haynes, Sharon Hayes*. Berlin 2017.

Deuber-Mankowsky, Astrid / Hanke, Philipp (eds.): *Queeres Kino / Queere Ästhetiken als Dokumentationen des Prekären*. Vienna 2021.

Duggan, Lisa: The New Homonormativity: The Sexual Politics of Neoliberalism. In: *Materializing Democracy: Toward a Revitalized Cultural Politics*, ed. by Castronovo, Russ / Nelson, Dana D. / Pease, Donald E. New York, NY 2002, 175–194.

Dyer, Richard: *Now You See it: Studies on Lesbian and Gay Film*. London / New York, NY 1990.

Dyer, Richard: *White*. London / New York, NY 1997.

Edelman, Lee: *No Future: Queer Theory and the Death Drive*. Durham, NC / London 2004.

Eng, David L. / Halberstam, Judith / Muñoz, José Esteban: What's Queer About Queer Studies Now? *Social Text* 23/3–4 (Fall/Winter 2005), 1–17.

Ferguson, Roderick A.: *Aberrations in Black: Toward a Queer of Color Critique*. Minneapolis, MN 2004.

Foucault, Michel: *The Order of Things: An Archaeology of the Human Sciences* [French original 1966]. London / New York, NY 2005.

Foucault, Michel: *History of Sexuality*, vol. 1, *An Introduction* [French original 1976], trans. by Robert Hurley. New York, NY 1978.

Freeman, Elizabeth: Time Binds, or, Erotohistoriography. *Social Text* 23/3–4 (2005), 57–68.

Gaber, Jenny / McRobbie, Angela: Girls and Subcultures. In: *Resistance through Rituals. Youth Subcultures in Post-War Britain*, ed. by Hall, Stuart / Jefferson, Tony. London 1976, 209–222.

Goldman, Vivien: *Revenge of the She-Punks: A Feminist Music History from Poly Styrene to Pussy Riot*. Austin, TX 2019.

Grandt Jürgen E.: Prelude: So What? In: *Kinds of Blue. The Jazz Aesthetic in African American Narrative*. Columbus, OH 2005, xi–xix.

Halberstam, J. Jack: *In a Queer Time and Place: Transgender Bodies, Subcultural Lives*. New York, NY / London 2005.

Halberstam, J. Jack: *Gaga Feminism: Sex, Gender, and the End of Normal*. Boston, MA 2012.

Halberstam, Jack: Trans* Feminism and Punk Performance. In: *Fringe of the Fringe. Queering Punk Media History*, ed. by Dreckmann, Kathrin / Semmerling, Linea / Vomberg, Elfi. Berlin 2023, 35–45.

Hall, Stuart (ed.): *Representation: Cultural Representations and Signifying Practices*. London 1997.

Halperin, David M. / Traub, Valerie: Beyond Gay Pride. In: *Gay Shame*, ed. by Halperin, David M. / Traub, Valerie. Chicago, IL / London 2009, 3–40.

Harper, Philip Brian / McClintock, Anne / Muñoz, José Esteban / Rosen, Trisch: Queer Transexions of Race, Nation, and Gender. An Introduction. *Social Text* 52/53 (Fall/Winter 1997), 1–4.

Hawkins, Stan: *Queerness in Pop Music: Aesthetics, Gender Norms, and Temporality*. New York, NY / London 2016.

Hebdige, Dick: *Subculture: The Meaning of Style*. London 1979.

Hebdige, Dick: *Hiding in the Light. On Images and Things*. London 1988.

Hecken, Thomas: *Pop. Geschichte eines Konzepts 1955–2009*. Bielefeld 2009.

Hemmings, Clare: Invoking Affect. Cultural Theory and the Ontological Turn. *Cultural Studies* 19/5 (2005), 548–567.

hooks, bell: *Black Looks. Race and Representation*. Boston, MA 1992.

Horak, Laura. *Girls will be Boys: Cross-Dressed Women, Lesbians, and American Cinema, 1908–1934*. New Brunswick, NJ / London 2016.

Horkheimer, Max / Adorno, Theodor W.: The Culture Industry: Enlightenment as Mass Deception. In: *Dialectic of Enlightenment*, ed. by Schmid Noerr, Gunzelin, trans. by Edmund Jephcott. Stanford, CA 2002, 49–136.

Kaplan, E. Ann: *Women in Film Noir* [1978]. London 1998.

Keeling, Kara: *Queer Times, Black Futures*. New York, NY 2019.

Kühl, Richard: *Der Große Krieg der Triebe. Die deutsche Sexualwissenschaft und der Erste Weltkrieg*. Bielefeld 2022.

Laufenberg, Mike / Trott, Ben (eds.): *Queer Studies. Schlüsseltexte*. Frankfurt 2023.

Leibetseder, Doris: *Queere Tracks: Subversive Strategien in der Rock und Popmusik*. Bielefeld 2010.

Lillvis, Kristen: Introduction. In: *Posthuman Blackness and the Black Female Imagination*. Athens, GA 2017, 11–24.

Lorde, Audre: Eye to Eye: Black Women, Hatred, and Anger. In: *Sister Outsider. Essays and Speeches by Audre Lorde*. Freedom, CA 1984.

Love, Heather: *Feeling Backward: Loss and the Politics of Queer History*. Cambridge, MA 2007.

Malakaj, Ervin: *Anders als die Andern*. Montréal and Berlin 2023.

Maniu, Nicholas: *Queere Männlichkeiten. Bilderwelten männlich-männlichen Begehrens und queere Geschlechtlichkeit*. Bielefeld 2023.

McElroy, Dolores: Camp. In: *Gender: Laughter*, ed. by Papenburg, Bettina. Macmillan Interdisciplinary Handbooks. Farmington Hills, MI 2017, 293–310.

Mercer, Kobena: *Welcome to the Jungle. New Positions in Black Cultural Studies*. New York, NY 1995.

Mercer, Kobena: Skin Head Sex Thing: Racial Difference and the Homoerotic Imaginary. In: *The Masculinity Studies Reader*, ed. by Adams, Rachel / Savran, David. Malden 2002, 188–200.

Muñoz, José Esteban: *Disidentification: Queers of Color and the Performance of Politics*. Minneapolis, MN 1999.

Muñoz, José Esteban: *Cruising Utopia. The Then and There of Queer Futurity*. New York, NY 2009.

Parnaby, Julia: Queer Straits. *Trouble and Strife* 26 (1993), 13–16.

Peele, Thomas (ed.): *Queer Popular Culture: Literature, Media, Film, and Television*. Basingstoke 2011.

Penelope, Julia / Wolfe, Susan J.: Sexual Identity / Textual Politics: Lesbian {De/Com}positions. In: *Sexual Practice, Textual Theory: Lesbian Cultural Criticism*, ed. by Wolfe, Susan J. / Penelope, Julia. Cambridge, MA 1993, 1–24.

Press, Joy / Reynolds, Simon: *The Sex Revolts. Gender, Rebellion and Rock'n'Roll*. Cambridge 1995.

Puar, Jasbir K.: *Terrorist Assemblages: Homonationalism in Queer Times*. Durham, NC / London 2007.
Rehberg, Peter: *Hipster Porn. Queere Männlichkeiten und affektive Sexualitäten im Fanzine Butt*. Berlin 2018.
Savage, Jon: *Teenage. The Creation of Youth Culture*. New York, NY / London 2007.
Sedgwick, Eve Kosofsky: Queer and Now. In: *Tendencies*. ed. by Barale, Michèle Aina / Goldberg, Jonathan / Moon, Michael. London 1994, 1–8.
Sedgwick, Eve Kosofsky / Frank, Adam: Shame in the Cybernetic Fold: Reading Silvan Tomkins. In: *Shame and Its Sisters. A Silvan Tomkins Reader*. Durham, NC 1995, 1–28.
Sedgwick, Eve Kosofsky: *Touching Feeling*. Durham, NC 2003.
Sontag, Susan: Notes on "Camp." *The Partisan Review* (1964), 515–530.
Stryker, Susan: Transgender Studies: Queer Theory's Evil Twin. *GLQ: A Journal of Lesbian and Gay Studies* 10/ 2 (2004), 212–215.
Tomlinson, Barbara: *Feminism and Affect at the Scene of Argument: Beyond the Trope of the Angry Feminist*. Philadelphia, PA 2010.
Tremblay, Sébastien: Review of *The Queer Art of History: Queer Kinship After Fascism*. ed. by Evans, Jennifer V. Durham, NC: Duke University Press. *German History* 41, No. 4 (2023), 632–634.
Tremblay, Sébastian: *A Badge of Injury: The Pink Triangle as Global Symbol of Memory*. Berlin 2024.
von Bose, Käthe / Klöppel, Ulrike / Köppert, Katrin / Michalski, Karin / Treusch, Pat (eds.*): I is for Impasse. Affektive Queerverbindungen in Theorie_Aktivismus_Kunst*. Berlin 2015.
von Bose, Käthe / Klöppel, Ulrike / Köppert, Katrin / Michalski, Karin / Treusch, Pat (eds.): *Queere Männlichkeiten. Bilderwelten männlich-männlichen Begehrens und queere Geschlechtlichkeit*. Bielefeld 2023.
Zilles, Sebastian (ed.): Queer(ing) Popular Culture. Special Issue, *Navigationen: Zeitschrift für Medien- und Kulturwissenschaft* 18/1 (2018). http://dx.doi.org/10.25969/mediarep/1920.

Filmography

Bohemian Rhapsody. Directed by Bryan Singer. 20th Century Fox / Regency Enterprises / GK Films / Queen Films, USA/UK 2018.

Part I: **Queer Aesthetics in Pop Music**

Kathrin Dreckmann

Queer Curls, Gender Power, and Plato: Eclectic Iconographies of Self-Empowerment in Lil Nas X's *Montero (Call Me By Your Name)*

Abstract: In recent years, mega-stars such as Beyoncé, Janelle Monáe, and Sevdeliza have successfully integrated critical academic discourse into the conceptions of their current music video productions. In a way, queer Black superstar Lil Nas X is continuing that tradition. He creates an eclectic, hybrid image between Christian iconography, Greek mythology, and Platonism and has empowered himself in this scenery as a Black queer devil. In doing so, he recapitulates the 2000-year-old exegesis of Plato's Symposium, questioning representational logics of the European cultural history of queer people. This paper traces the connections of media representations of queerness in Christian iconography, Greek mythology, and self-empowerment thematized in the music video *Montero (Call Me By Your Name)*.

Keywords: Lil Nas X, music video, queer pop, Montero, queer representation, queer, Black empowerment, queer iconography, media art

With his debut studio album *Montero (Call Me By Your Name)* and the music video of the same title (both 2021), queer Black artist Lil Nas X presented a production in which he links Christian iconographies with those of the ancient Greeks, negotiating positions from the Bible and ancient philosophy on the "third" gender.[1] In the music video he quotes the story of creation as well as Plato's Aristophanic treatise on the third gender from *The Symposium* (385 and 378 BC). The video can thus be read as an audiovisual representation that mediates between the appropriation of a European canon, the adoption of Christian and ancient iconography, and the exegesis of Platonic male-male relationships. Artistic conceptions dedicated to the appropriation of the European canon from a Black perspective have recently been very successful. There seems to be a tendency in current music productions of adopting a European configuration of the gaze to not only make it visible but also expose it as male, colonial, or patriarchal. These productions thus expose the fact that visual regimes become established under specific historical and cultural circumstances.[2] Lil Nas X takes this as a starting point for reversing centuries-old visual regimes; in doing so, he follows a political program.

---

1 R. E. Allen: *The Dialogues of Plato. Volume II. The Symposium.* New Haven, CT 1991, 130. See also: Markus Hirschfeld: *Berlin's Third Sex*, trans. by James J. Conway, 2017.
2 Kathrin Dreckmann: Black Queen and King: Iconographies of Self-empowerment, Canon, and Pop in the Current Music Video. In: *More Than Illustrated Music: Aesthetics of Hybrid Media between Pop, Art and Video*, ed. by Kathrin Dreckmann / Elfi Vomberg. London 2023, 125–144.

Logics of visibility as well as strategies of enactment become apparent and transform themselves into poignant political visual agendas. How can one describe aesthetic concepts such as these? How are traditional iconographies reconfigured and reflected between the present and the past?

In an interview with TIME magazine he states that "he wanted to deploy this type of iconography and symbolism to draw a connection between ancient and modern-day persecution."[3] He is concerned with taking queerness seriously as a concept that has been around since antiquity. However, perspectives that either label queerness as a heterosexual esoteric fantasy or socially marginalize it through pathologization should be taken into account.[4] Roland Betancourt, art professor at the University of California and author of *Byzantine Intersectionality: Sexuality, Gender, and Race in the Middle Ages* says in an interview with TIME Magazine: "[the video] says that institu-

---

3 Andrew R. Chow: Historians Decode the Religious Symbolism and Queer Iconography of Lil Nas X's "Montero" Video. *Time* (March 2021). https://time.com/5951024/lil-nas-x-montero-video-symbolism-explained/ (last accessed 03 July 2022).
4 Luc Brisson: *Sexual ambivalence: androgyny and hermaphroditism in Graeco-Roman antiquity*. Berkeley / Los Angeles / London 2002, xiii.
In *Sexual Ambivalence*, Brisson consolidates and develops his earlier explorations of sexuality in the ancient Mediterranean. He describes *Sexual Ambivalence* as a "working aid to the study for all those interested in the question of dual sexuality, whether in the domains of psychoanalysis, gay or gender studies, the history of medicine or zoology, the history of ideas, or even the history of art." Especially in chapter two (Dual Sexuality and Homosexuality), Brisson considers another type of simultaneous dual sexuality in humans, displayed by persons with the physical attributes of one sex and gender characteristics of the other, specifically: passive male homosexuals who assumed women's costume, behavior, and submissive sexual role, along with females who acted out aggressive male personas in their relationships with (passive) female partners. Brisson touches briefly on several related issues that have received much recent scrutiny. Current scholarship on the ancient Greek and Roman perceptions of homosexuality and heterosexuality indicates that they were not the same as our own Western ones. The polarized categories of homosexual and heterosexual themselves are relatively modern. In chapter three (Archetypes), Brisson turns to divine paradigms and precedents for simultaneous dual sexuality, considering mythological prototypes, entities not viewed as monsters but as essential contributors to the generation of the universe, gods, and mortals. He begins with Aristophanes' myth of Eros and the androgynes in the *Symposium*, considers possible links with Orphic traditions, and then examines related phenomena in Gnosticism, the Chaldean Oracles, and the Hermetic Corpus. Brisson's full, interpretive discussion provides useful background for an analysis of Aristophanes' vision in the *Symposium*. The Orphic cosmography, with its double-sexed progenitor Phanes, called by a variety of other names, has been considered a parallel for Aristophanes' globe-shaped ur-humans. The connection of Aristophanes' fable with the Orphic tradition of a bisexual proto-being is problematic. Dover has suggested that the *Symposium* may have influenced later versions of the Orphic material and that Aristophanes' androgynes were the inspiration for the subsequent Orphic fragment in which Phanes' genitals are described as projecting from the rear of his body.

tionalization of homophobia is a learned thing – and that there are other origin myths available to us that are not rooted in those ideas."[5]

This thesis implies that the representation of homosexual love in European cultural philosophy is in need of a new reading. To seriously consider this would also mean that in the video *Montero,* the exegesis is brought into a connection with feudal self-dramatization in the style of European monarchies as a strategy of empowerment. This bears the question: Does a music video, which primarily serves the purpose of marketing a product, possess the capacity to question the canon of significant philosophical history on a mass-cultural level?

First, the themes of the music video and its dramaturgy will be deliberated in the following. Subsequently, the thematic spectra hybridized in the music video will be elaborated on and discussed. In the conclusion, the results on the relevance of deconstructivist music video analysis will be discussed.

1 Plato's *Symposium* and Christian Iconography

The music videos scenic opening shows a sky – a sun surrounded by pink clouds. The camera descends from the shots of the sky to another world (00:11); the viewer catches a short glimpse of the remains of ancient-looking columns, broken Greek sculptures (Fig. 1) (00:10), a death mask (00:12), while a snake slithers along an underworld architecture.

From the mountain of the gods ("monte") down into the apparent underworld, which at the same time is not clearly defined, for implied here is a Garden of Eden in the marble ruins of ancient Greece. Right from the start, hierarchies of propositional logic between Christian and ancient iconography are addressed. Inevitably the recipient thinks of Platonic shadow people from the cave allegory formulated in the Politeia.[6] This context is already called upon in the lyrics:

> You live in the dark, boy,
> I cannot pretend
> I'm not fazed, only here to sin
> If Eve ain't in your garden, you know that you can

The figure of Eve, introduced in the text, is perceived as a guardian – only when she is not present does "you" know that he can sin. The boy who lives in the dark does not

---

5 Andrew R. Chow: Historians Decode the Religious Symbolism and Queer Iconography of Lil Nas X's "Montero" Video. See also: Roland Betancourt: *Byzantine Intersectionality Sexuality, Gender & Race in the Middle Ages.* Princeton / Oxford 2020, 121–143.

6 Plato: Republic. In: id: *The Collected Dialogues of Plato,* ed. by Huntington Cairns / Edith Hamilton, trans. by Lane Cooper. Princeton, NJ 1961, 747.

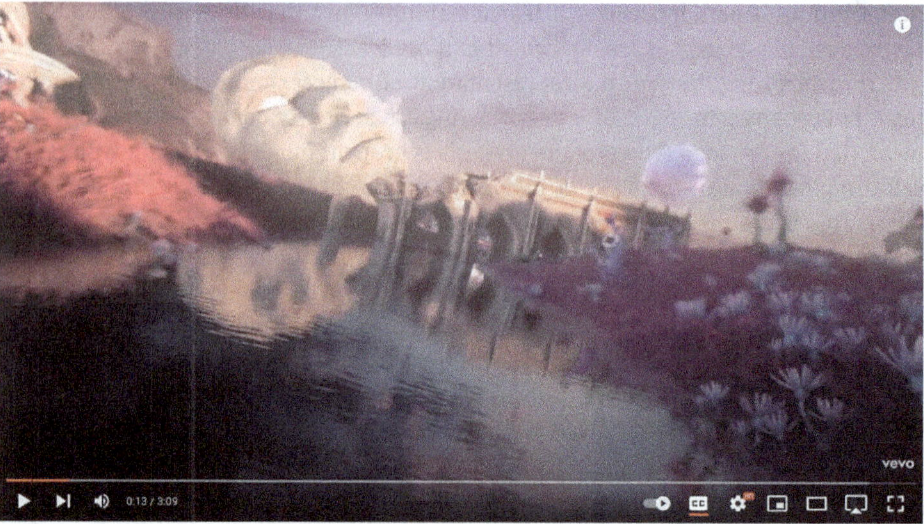

Fig. 1: Ruins of ancient Greek statues and buildings.
Screenshot: Lil Nas X: "Montero (Call Me By Your Name)" (Official Video). Directed by Tanu Muino and Lil Nas X (26 March 2021).

live in the light, he does not show himself and is not visible. Since this scene, which contains Plato's verses from the *Symposium*, focuses on brightness and darkness, the philosophically trained eye inevitably makes an association with recognizing vision, an ontological category of inner knowing established in Plato.[7] For Plato, seeing is not a sensory-physiological process, it is epistemological. With the implied image and gaze aesthetics in the video, the recipient gains the impression that the detachment from Eve in the story of creation here also means the detachment from the heteronormatively determined male-female relationship associated with Eve.

> Romantic talking? You don't even have to try
> You're cute enough to fuck with me tonight
> Looking at the table all I see is weed and white
> Baby, you living the life, but nigga, you ain't livin' right
> Cocaine and drinking with your friends
> You live in the dark, boy, I cannot pretend
> I'm not fazed, only here to sin
> If Eve ain't in your garden, you know that you can

Apparently, the protagonist of the song is living in the shadows, intoxicated and going down the wrong path – unenlightened. As in Plato's verses from the *Symposium* that are directed toward brightness and darkness, the philosophically trained eye inevita-

---

7 Plato: *Republic*, 747.

bly makes the association with cognitive seeing, an ontological category of inner cognition established by Plato. For Plato, seeing is not a sensory-physiological process, it is both ontological and epistemological.

If the lyrics seem simple and uncomplex at first, they merge through the divergence of image and text into a reformulation of the history of Plato's Forms ("Ideas"). Referring back to the cave allegory, Plato's maieutic questioning makes possible the achievement of a state of "the good" by overcoming the darkness and the shadows.

The video's narrative goes even further, hybridizing Christian and Greek imagery with Roman architecture. The shadow existence and the fall of man are formulated with a view to Roman pictorial logics as historicized gestures turned to stone in the video:

> In the background while the serpent is hypnotizing him, the broken hand of a ruined marble colossus is plainly visible. This may be based on the famous colossal hand of Constantine I, the first Christian emperor of the Roman Empire, that is on display in the Musei Capitolini in Rome. This hand, of course, falls at the intersection of the Christian and the classical, thereby further emphasizing both themes, which are important throughout the video. The fact that the hand is broken and lying on the ground also emphasizes the idea of the fall of man.[8]

2 Plato's Spherical Creatures or: When the Bodies Were Separated by Angry Zeus

As mentioned above, the video's citation of Plato's *Symposium* is noteworthy. It poses the first exegetical riddles to the recipients. Inserted in ancient Greek: ἐπειδὴ οὖν ἡ φύσις δίχα ἐτμήθη, ποθοῦν ἕκαστον τὸ ἥμισυ[9] (Fig. 2) ("Now when our first form had been cut in two, each half in longing for its fellow would come to it again"[10]).

This passage from Greek mythology, which Plato has the comic poet Aristophanes narrate in his dialogue *Symposium*, explains the Platonic perspective on the origin of erotic desire. According to Plato, Aristophanes explains his perspective on Eros, the god of love, in an extensively formulated monologue at a banquet.[11] He then formulates it with regard to the origin of man and desire, explaining that there were originally three sexes,[12]:

---

8 Spencer McDaniel: Here's the meaning of the Symbolism in Lil Nas X's Controversial New Music Video. *Tales of times forgotten* (07 April 2021). https://talesoftimesforgotten.com/2021/04/07/heres-the-meaning-of-the-symbolism-in-lil-nas-xs-controversial-new-music-video/ (last accessed 09 June 2023).

9 Gregory R. Crane: Plato Symposium 190a. *Perseus Digital Library.* http://www.perseus.tufts.edu/hopper/text?doc=Perseus%3Atext%3A1999.01.0173%3Atext%3DSym.%3Asection%3D190a (last accessed 09 June 2023).

10 Gregory R. Crane: Plato Symposium 191a. In: *Perseus Digital Library.* http://www.perseus.tufts.edu/hopper/text?doc=Plat.+Sym.+191a&fromdoc=Perseus%3Atext%3A1999.01.0174 (last accessed 09 June 2023).

11 Allen: *The Dialogues of Plato*, 130–134.

12 (190 St3 A) Allen: *The Dialogues of Plato*, 130.

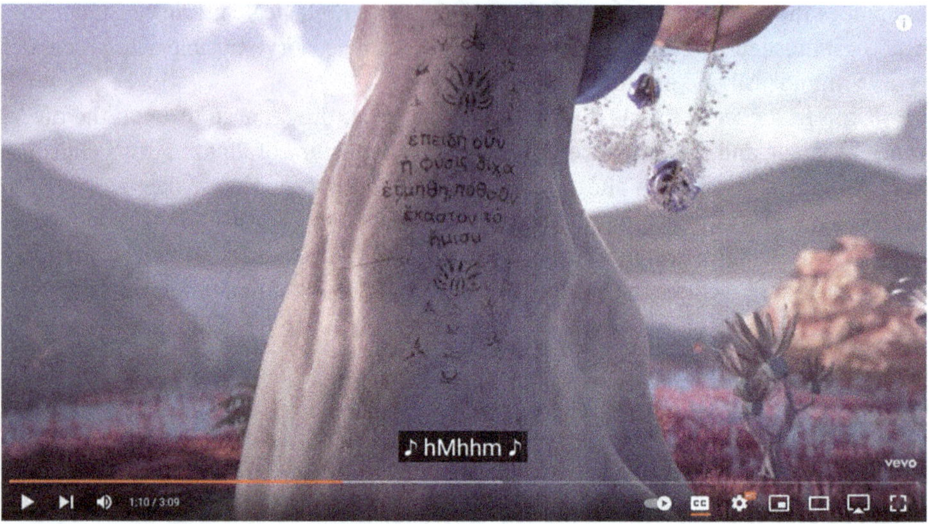

Fig. 2: A tree with ancient Greek enscription.
Screenshot: Lil Nas X: "Montero (Call Me By Your Name)" (Official Video). Directed by Tanu Muino and Lil Nas X (26 March 2021).

> In the first place, there were three sexes among men, not two as now, male and female, but a third sex in addition, being both of them in common, whose name still remains though the thing itself has vanished; for one sex was then derived in common from both male and female, androgynous both in form and name, though the name is now applied only in reproach.[13]

In the exegesis of this passage, inserted by Lil Nas X, there are different positions which essentially have to do with the translation history of this text. Lil Nas X conveys a one-sided perspective in the video, as if the quote from antiquity were already about queer love as it is understood today.[14] However, the quote he stages has a complex exegetical history which is not commonly known. Against the background of this history, one can understand the video as a reference to an interpretive construct of "queer" since antiquity, formulated in terms of the history of science. The history of translation already gives a good indication of the complexities of interpretation and reception. Thus, in 1920, when Sigmund Freud did not deduce desire from the "pleasure principle," he followed a different translation than that of Rudolf Kaßner in 1921.[15] In his interpretation, however, Freud definitely sees heteronormative unions between the halves separated by Zeus.

---

13 Allen: *The Dialogues of Plato*, 130.

14 This scholarly term only came into fashion at the beginning of the 1990s.

15 Sigmund Freud: Beyond the Pleasure Principle. Group Psychology and Other Works [1920–1921]. In: id.: *The Standard Edition of the Complete Psychological Works*, ed. by James Strachey. New York, NY 1962, 57–58.

It becomes clear that "Freud considers only one pair out of three, and not the one favored by Aristophanes. Astoundingly, how the fact of same-sex desire, which is supposed to be explained by the story, becomes even more surprising in the Freudian version."[16]

The interpretation by sexologist Magnus Hirschfeld is remarkable. Philosopher Michael Groneberg, who has dealt extensively with the translation history of Plato's *Symposium* and reconstructed the passage in its reception history, states of Magnus Hirschfeld that he was the one who did an enormous amount of highly differentiated research, both of empirical and historical nature, pursuing the same project of scientific enlightenment and de-criminalization of homosexuality. He developed a rich taxonomy of the empirical phenomena of sexual differentiation and sexuality, e.g. distinguishing hermaphroditism and androgynism by referring to the primary and secondary sexual features respectively. This distinction is useful and has been retained in the scientific literature. Hirschfeld also uses the term of a third sex, with explicit reference to Plato's Aristophanes. He identifies the third sex with his "sexuelle Zwischenstufen" that in English would be called "intersexes." He distinguishes four groups among them: hermaphrodites, androgynes, homosexuals, and transvestites. He criticizes the fact that they were formerly mixed in together, but continues to do this himself by subsuming them under one category: the third sex.[17]

Hirschfeld's achievement, then, was to sexually differentiate and redefine Aristophanic mythology. Aristophanes explains his conception of Eros on the basis of the male spherical men, who become homosexual men after being split by Zeus. Moreover, he finds these spherical men to be the most masculine of all due to their purely male form of origin. Aristophanes deals with male homosexuality in particular detail and with apologetic tendency; with this example (of homosexual men) he explains/ demonstrates his understanding of Eros in further detail. He defends boys who devote themselves to men; they would not be shameless but especially manly and brave, which he considers proven by the following:

> A great proof: actually, it is only men of this sort who, when they grow up, enter on political affairs. When they reach manhood they love boys, and by nature pay no heed to marriage and the getting of children except as compelled to it by custom and law; it suffices them to live out their lives unmarried, with one another. So this sort of becomes wholly a lover of boys or a boy who loves having lovers, ever cleaving to what is akin.[18]

This is now the point at which Aristophanes – starting from the love of a boy – describes the appearance and nature of Eros in more detail. He describes the shock that

---

16 Michael Groneberg: Myth and Science around Gender and Sexuality: Eros and the Three Sexes in Plato's Symposium. *Diogenes* 52/4 (2005), 39–49, 45.
17 Groneberg: *Myth and Science around Gender and Sexuality*, 44.
18 Allen: *The Dialogues of Plato*, 133.

seizes a lover when he meets his corresponding half; the philologist of antiquity Reginald E. Allen writes:

> they are then marvelously struck by friendship and kinship and Eros, and scarcely willing to be separated from each other even for a little time. These are the people who pass their whole lives with each other, but who can't even say what they wish for themselves by being with each other. No one can think it is for the sake of sexual intercourse that the one so eagerly delights in being with the other. Instead, the soul of each clearly wishes for something else it can't put into words; it divines what it wishes, and obscurely hints at it.[19]

It is thus quite possible to read the relevant excerpt from the *Symposium* on the so-called spherical people in a "queer" way. Logics of visibility and strategies of representation of queer Black people correspond at this point with one of the earliest and elitist philosophies between desire and eros, with strong consequences for the definition of social-sexual role concepts.

3 Wigs, Curls, and Power

It is evident that Lil Nas X works intensively on questions of exegesis in the form of a hybrid aesthetic. The deliberate implication and inclusion of sexual and exegetical ambivalence at the beginning of the video sets the tone for further metaphorical and iconographical composition throughout the following scenes.

After the *Symposium* quote fades, a scene follows in which the Lil Nas X can be seen wearing a blue wig (01:16). This is followed by a sequence in which he appears three times as a clone. In the foreground, an alter ego with not-so-highly "toupeed" hair in pink appears, and to his left and right two other versions in blue but with different hair lengths (Fig. 4). The protagonist (i.e. Lil Nas X) can be seen bound by chains in the next scene, Greek sculptures behind him; shortly after (01:49), a scene that quotes the myth of Icarus – or a possible reference to Zeus. A little later, Zeus grasps a staff, which turns into a pole on which he glides down into the underworld (Fig. 3). This scene combines elements from the mythological worlds of Icarus and Orpheus. The hairstyle has changed in this scene. Lil Nas X descends into the depths of the glowing lava. (02:19).

The campy hairstyle could also be deciphered as an interpretative reference point to the television series *Bridgerton* (Fig. 5), which premiered on 25 December 2020.[20] Lil Nas X's album had its release one year later. The references to socially constructed

---

19 Allen: *The Dialogues of Plato*, 133. See also: Groneberg: *Myth and Science around Gender and Sexuality*, 41; Robert Eisner: A Case of Poetic Justice: Aristophanes' Speech in the Symposium. *The Classical World* 72/7 (1979), 417–419. https://doi.org/10.2307/4349087, 417–418. [Own translation, K.D.].
20 References to cultural theory are certainly a possibility, as this can also be seen in the work of Janelle Monáe, cf. Kathrin Dreckmann: "PYNK" beyond forests and thighs. In: *Music Video and Trans-*

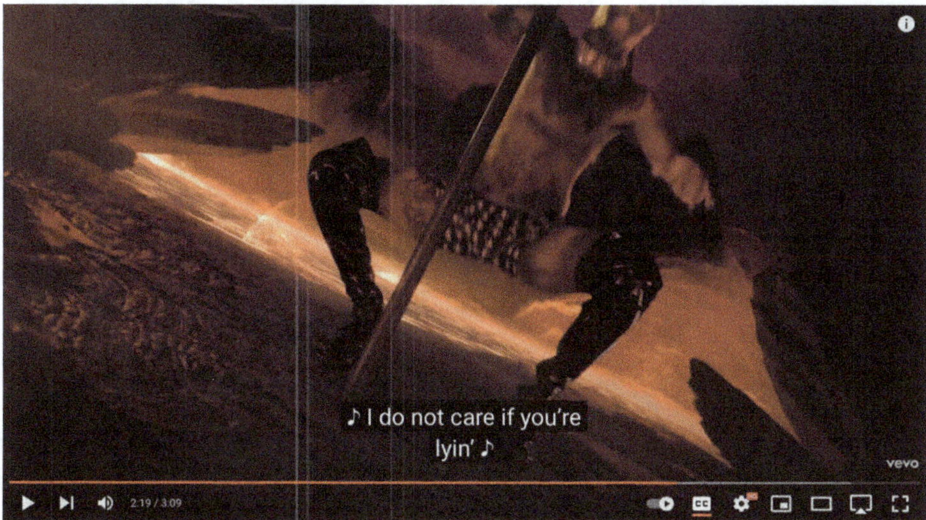

Fig. 3: Lil Nas X pole dancing while wearing tall leather boots.
Screenshot: Lil Nas X: Montero (Call Me By Your Name) (Official Video). Directed by Tanu Muino and Lil Nas X (26 March 2021).

classifications of race, class, and gender in his video are visually so intense that they could have absorbed the affinity to the Baroque wig. Looking at the canon of European art and through royal productions handed down in cultural history, videos like those of the Carters and of Janelle Monáe have developed appropriation as an Afro-diasporic empowerment strategy.[21]

The fact that Lil Nas X views himself as part of this successful tradition and uses it aesthetically can be seen as a very specific practice of citation and reception from a pop-cultural point of view. In any case, the hairstyle plays a special, royal role here.

The fact that Lil Nas X could have drawn on Louis XIV in terms of hairstyle history,[22] and as a man carries this wig code to the outside world, points to a cultural-historical interference: British cultural historian Peter Burke quotes George Collas from 1912, referring to Louis XIV's "glory enterprise" which he views as reminiscent

---

culturality: Manifestations of Social Utopia?, ed. by Kathrin Dreckmann / Christofer Jost / Bastian Schramm. Münster going to press 2024, 2024, as in Beyoncés work *Lemonade* cf. Kintra D. Brooks / Kameelah L. Martin: Introduction. In: *The Lemonade Reader*, ed. by Kintra D. Brooks / Kameelah L. Martin, New York, NY 2019, 3. Or in her current Renaissance tour. Cf. Kathrin Dreckmann: "I'm too classy for this world, forever, I'm that girl". Media hybrids between Pop and Art in Beyoncé's *RENAISSANCE*. In: *Aesthetic Amalgams and Political Pursuits. Intertextuality in Music Videos*, ed. by Agata Handley et al. London going to press 2024, 2024.

21 Kathrin Dreckmann: Black Queen and King, 125–144.

22 Susan Sontag dates the origins of Camp back to Louis XIV. Susan Sontag: *Notes on "Camp"*, In: Fabio Cleto: *Camp: Queer Aesthetics and the Performing Subject: A Reader*. Edinburgh 1999, 56–57.

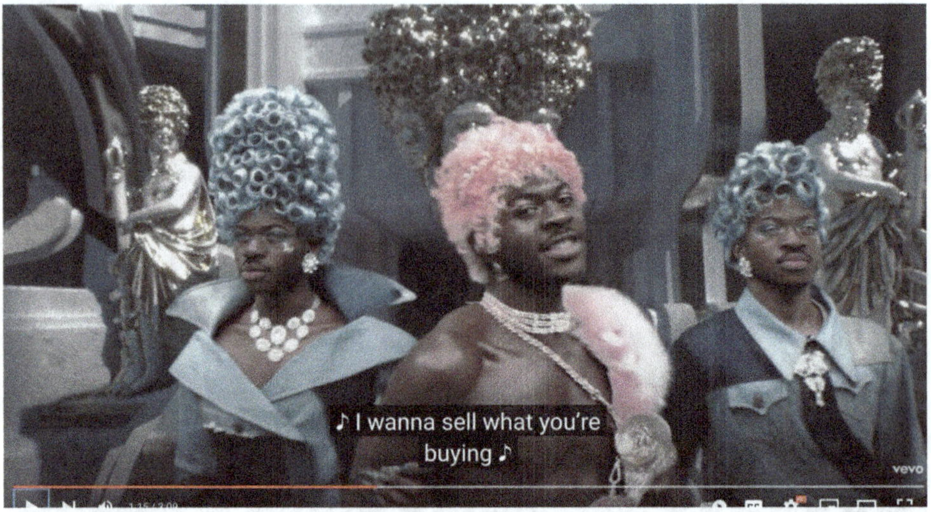

Fig. 4: Three clones of Lil Nas X wearing differently colored wigs.
Screenshot: Lil Nas X: "Montero (Call Me By Your Name)" (Official Video). Directed by Tanu Muino and Lil Nas X (26 March 2021).

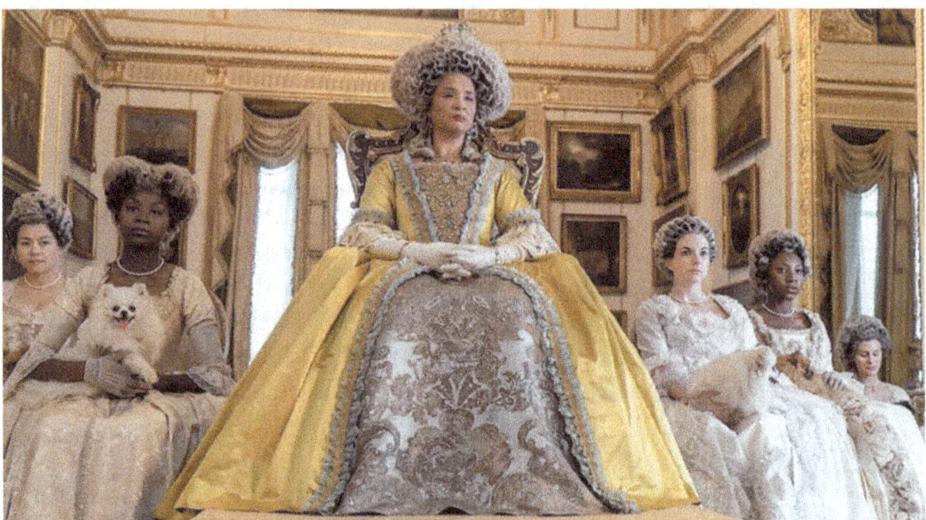

Fig. 5: The Character of Queen Charlotte in Netflix's "Bridgerton". Screenshot from Bridgerton Episode 5, Season 1 "The Duke and I". Directed by Sheree Folkson. Shondaland / CVD Productions, UK 2020.

of "contemporary publicity."[23] The wig played a central role: "integration of the allonge wig into the exaggerated courtly etiquette that developed at the Versailles court under the Sun King made it the culmination of the refined lifestyle of the Baroque."[24] Louis XIV, in particular, introduced the luxuriant allonge as a state wig.[25]

> By 1665, wigs were so common that Louis XIV approved royal wigmakers for Paris. The king, on whose head thick, curly, exceedingly beautiful hair was sprouting, had, however, refused to wear a wig in his youth. If at all, he initially accepted only *wigs à fenetres,* that is, those through whose openings natural curls could protrude. Only after 1672 did he wear wigs *à cheveux vifs,* which presupposed shaved skulls and were later powdered. Perhaps the reason for this was that wearing increasingly large wigs on full head hair resulted in oversized shapes and their fastening caused difficulties. Or perhaps people were looking for a way to ward off troublesome parasites.[26]

The wig became an "expression of status and power" through him: "Louis XIV did not invent the voluminous curly wig, in fact he was not the first to wear it, but during his reign it acquires the rank of an outfit piece."[27]

It becomes clear that the wig was not only used as a social marker but also gained general acceptance as a fashion accessory. The self-staging strategies and advertising campaigns in the self-representation by the Sun King obviously had a direct influence on the era and fashion and social semantics: "Thus, the wearing of an allonge wig directly influences courtly fashion."[28]

The staging of Lil Nas X as a self-empowering person who has appropriated codes of European iconographies becomes evident. The singer rises above cultural history and philosophy and transforms his claim to power (which can be read as a code of hairstyle, fashion, and gesture) into a campy, i.e., ironically condensed, quotation. When mentioning Lil Nas X's reference to the wig from the baroque period, Queen Marie Antoinette

---

23 Peter Burke: *The Fabrication of Louis XIV.* New Haven, 1992, 4.

24 Luckhardt et al: *Lockenpracht und Herrschermacht,* 9. [Own translation, K.D.]. Basically, it is true that wigs were worn in ancient Egypt and Rome, and especially women in Greece and the Roman Empire owned extensive hairpieces. In the Baroque period, the fashion was rediscovered, whether the hair loss to be concealed was due to disease or treatment by quack doctors. Wigs were part of the contemporary fashion.

25 Paas et al: *Liselotte Von Der Pfalz: Madame Am Hofe des Sonnenkönigs; [Ausstellung der Stadt Heidelberg zur 800-Jahr-Feier, 21. September 1996 Bis 26. Januar 1997 im Heidelberger Schloß].* Heidelberg: HVA, 1996, 191.

26 Paas et al: *Liselotte von der Pfalz,* 191. However, there are also other positions on this: "Accessories, especially the wig, also played an important role in the 17th century. This fashion had appeared around 1633, even before Louis XIV took office, after his father, Louis XIII, had lost his hair due to illness and had used this trick to hide his baldness. Soon he found imitators among men who had been deprived by nature of beautiful long hair, as the courtiers were fond of wearing." [Own translation, K.D.].

27 Luckhardt et al.: *Lockenpracht und Herrschermacht,* 9. [Own translation, K.D.].

28 Luckhardt et al.: *Lockenpracht und Herrschermacht,* 11. [Own translation, K.D.].

must be acknowledged as well.[29] Queen Marie Antoinette and the Sun King both placed importance on the imprint and choice in courtly fashion and the associated pose. This concerned not only outward appearance – habitus was also crucial, as distinction required "years of rehearsed body language influencing the entire body language."[30]

4 A Black Gay Man in the Context of Greek Philosophy and Christian Iconography

The now iconic Baroque-looking wigs worn by Lil Nas X were more for royal representation than for pleasure and can certainly be assigned to the fashion style of an old Europe in terms of pictorial history. Lil Nas X thus thematizes the connection between extraordinary festivities and their fashion since the Baroque period, such as accessions to the throne (another example would be the legendary festivities at the court of Louis the XIV). Royal pomp and historical extravagance seem to have been hybridized in this video. Black representational logics thus reveal Lil Nas X as the mastermind of aesthetic staging. As a Black gay man, he interprets himself in the context of Greek philosophy and Christian iconography and crowns himself – just as Napoleon crowned himself emperor. As Lil Nas X simultaneously stages himself on a pedestal as a motionless statue in multiple duplicity – with a wig that seems chiseled in purple hair – he is at the same time referring to Black identity, Baroque fashion history, and basic gender-theoretical questions. It seems as if he is aware that at least one figure is being quoted. Possibly he even makes it particularly clear, since he appears several times as a quasi-clone. He cites the techniques of citation himself by inserting himself as a Black queer man into the condensed gestures and poses of antiquity that have made their way through the Renaissance to pop culture.[31] Lil Nas X's citing techniques might remind one of the intermediary migrations of the Warburg School.[32] Intertextual pop culture strategies are definitely transcended. Statues also usually symbolize power; think of the statues of Augustus of Primaporta, Nike of Samothrace, and the Venus de Milo. Lil Nas X recognizes these gestures of power in

---

29 Luckhardt et al: *Lockenpracht und Herrschermacht*, 9. [Own translation, K.D.].

30 Luckhardt et al: *Lockenpracht und Herrschermacht*, 9. [Own translation, K.D.].

31 As discussed in footnote 20, it is not unlikely that artists hire e.g. ethnomusicologists, religious practitioners, literary scholars, pop culture critics, and historians to conduct research for their artistic projects as evidenced by Beyoncé's visual concept album *Lemonade,* see Kintra D. Brooks / Kameelah L. Martin: Introduction, 3.

32 The term "Warburg School" derives from Aby Warburg's library and writings. He developed his own method of iconography and iconology by using examples of different times and themes with similar motifs. Erwin Panowski's concept of iconography is influenced by this tradition. This discourse is continued, see, for instance, Colleen Becker: Aby Warburg's Pathosformel as Methodological Paradigm. *Journal of Art Historiography,* 9 (2013), 1–25.

the history of white people, and the moment of self-empowerment is revealed in the hybridization of doubling as a statue and thus as a work of art – the statuary thereby acting in the sense of breaking a continuity of history.[33]

5 Lil Nas X: Rise and Fall of Icarus

In the video *Montero (Call Me By Your Name)*, Lil Nas X is tied up in an arena as if a spectacle is about to begin, with identical-looking spectators positioned around him. He is being filmed from above; the camera suddenly shows an Icarus floating in the sky. Lil Nas X abruptly returns to the arena as the Devil. A gun is handed to him out of nowhere. He wears red braids, symbolizing a metamorphosis. He returns to the arena and stages himself as Orpheus descending into the underworld. Here he meets the Devil, who is waiting for him (Fig. 6), thus also returning in turn to an eclectic underworld fantasy between Greek mythology and Christianity; he sits down in front of the Devil and conveys to the viewer that he has just had anal sex with him. This is followed by the writing "Damnant quod non intelligunt." This means "They condemn what they do not understand." Clearly there is an analogy to Jesus' quote as he died on the cross: "Father, forgive them, for they do not know what they are doing."[34]

The response to this quote from Lil Nas X: "If that [i.e., Hell] is where we [i.e., queer people] belong, then let me be the king of that,"[35] possibly alluding to a trip to Hell, since Heaven remains denied to him. This rejection of Heaven and the resulting coronation of the king of Hell seems to be identified here as both an empowerment and liberation strategy.

In the end, he kills the Devil and puts on his own crown. Suddenly he grows wings. This is the ultimate empowerment – which is then no longer precarious, since he has ended up in Hell anyway. Actually, of course, what is meant by this is the detachment from teleologically conceived Christian afterlife concepts of Heaven and Hell. The fact that he imagines himself in Hell wearing a crown engaged in a sexual act that is socially identified as "gay" on the one hand takes up the social constructions of sexual practices

---

33 Eckart Marchand: Aby Warburg on plaster casts. *Sculpture Journal* 28/3 (2019), 401–402, 405.

34 Lil Nas X (2021): "Montero (Call Me By Your Name)" (Official Video). Directed by Tanu Muino and Lil Nas X. 26 March 2021. Music video, 03:09. *YouTube*. Available online: https://www.youtube.com/watch?v= 6swmTBVI83k (last accessed 08 June 2023). In blog posts related to this video, reference is made to the poem "Paradise Lost" by John Milton (1667), who advocated freedom and self-determination, especially in the seventeenth century. It states: "Whom Thunder hath made greater? Here at least / We shall be free; th' Almighty hath not built / Here for his envy, will not drive us hence: / Here we may reign secure, and in my choyce / To reign is worth ambition though in Hell: / Better to reign in Hell than serve in Heaven." John Milton: *Paradise Lost*. England 1667, lines 258–263.

35 Zach Campbell: Lil Nas X "Montero (Call Me By Your Name)" REACTION WITH LIL NAS X!!. YouTube video (8:45–8:50). Available online: https://youtu.be/h2OAuf4G6CI?t=525 (last accessed 21 June 2023).

with gender connotations; on the other hand, aesthetically and culturally historically reflected fantasies of kingship and enthronement are linked from these internalized imaginings of the Devil with the gesture of self-empowerment, which always remains fragile through the figure of Icarus.

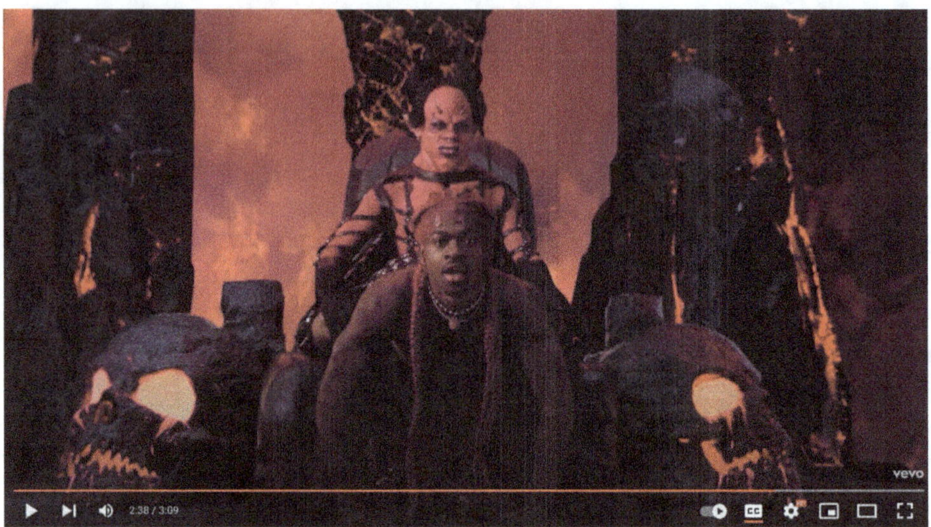

Fig. 6: Lil Nas X giving the devil a lap dance.
Screenshot: Lil Nas X: "Montero (Call Me By Your Name)" (Official Video). Directed by Tanu Muino and
Lil Nas X (26 March 2021).

It is remarkable that a queer Black man adopts white metaphors of queen and king at this point, mediating between gender, race, and class with the help of the phantasmagoria of Heaven and Hell – as well as the appropriation of Platonic philosophical history and fashion theory reworked in terms of the history of clothing. The level of reflection not only refers to a panoramic view of a reflective canonization process narrowed in cultural and philosophical history; the view also adopts a multiplicity of media. Even the title in brackets Call me by your name refers to a 2017 film by Luca Guadagnino of the same name and a 2007 novel by André Aciman, a story about an affair between a 17-year-old Italian and a 24-year-old American man. The criticism is made clear in the video by a re-enacted scene of Brokeback Mountain (2005): gay movies are white.[36] On all levels, including the cinematic, Lil Nas X highlights the exclusion of intersectional or queer gay love in representations of Hollywood cinema, philosophy, art, and Christian iconography.

---

36 Further contributions to this discussion can be found in: Rodrick A. Ferguson: *Aberrations in Black*. Minnesota, MN 2004.

6 Conclusion

In examining the references made in the video, it becomes evident that hybridization processes not only take place between Christian and philosophical iconographies, but also that new image orders are created that indicate cultural and philosophical exclusions without self-victimization. On the one hand, this nobilizes the music video as a cultural form itself within the framework of a conceptually commercially successful spectrum of art media; on the other hand, it designs a new visual language in that the hybrid painting itself – between iconic art language, reflected canon and philosophical history, media critique of representation, and queer self-positioning –becomes an image that corresponds with other images.

It follows that a new image-programmatic video aesthetic has been formed. The reformulation of an (iconic) art history grounded in a classical concept of canon introduces a new perspective of queer Black empowerment which has developed an agency that appropriates without colonizing.

In recent years, mega-stars such as Beyoncé, Janelle Monáe,[37] and Sevdeliza[38] have successfully integrated critical academic discourse into the conceptions of their current music video productions. While doing so, they quote from historical films, make use of canonized iconographies that circulate in art, video, and film, or refer to pop-cultural aesthetics that in turn feed on the field of European popular culture as well as art history. Examples of possible points of reference are Oskar Schlemmer, Fritz Lang, and Walter Ruttmann, whose works have become the starting point for a variety of references in for example Janelle Monáe's videos, among others.[39]

Bibliography

Allen, R. E.: *The Symposium. The Dialogues of Plato Volume II*. New York, NY 1991.
Becker, Collen: Aby Warburg's *Pathosformel* as Methodological Paradigm. *Journal of Art Historiography* 9 (2013): 1–25.
Betancourt, Roland: *Byzantine Intersectionality: Sexuality, Gender & Race in the Middle Ages*. Princeton, NJ and Oxford, 2020.
Brisson, Luc: *Sexual ambivalence. Androgyny and Hermaphroditism in Graeco-Roman antiquity*. Los Angeles, CA 2002.
Brooks, Kintra D. / Martin, Kameelah L.: Introduction. In: *The Lemonade Reade*r, ed. by Brooks, Kintra D. / Martin, Kameelah L. New York, NY 2019.
Burke, Peter: *The Fabrication of Louis XIV*. New Haven, CT 1992.

---

37 See Kathrin Dreckmann: "PYNK" beyond forests and thighs.
38 See Kathrin Dreckmann: Dehumanize your bitch, 211–231.
39 See Kathrin Dreckmann: Black Queen and King, 125–144.

Chow, Andrew R.: Historians Decode the Religious Symbolism and Queer Iconography of Lil Nas X's 'Montero' Video. *Time* (2021). https://time.com/5951024/lil-nas-x-montero-video-symbolism-explained/ (last accessed 03 July 2022).

Crane, Gregory R.: Plato Symposium 190a. *Perseus Digital Library*. http://www.perseus.tufts.edu/hopper/text?doc=Perseus%3Atext%3A1999.01.0173%3Atext%3DSym.%3Asection%3D190a (last accessed 09 June 2023).

Crane, Gregory R.: Plato Symposium 191a. *Perseus Digital Library*. http://www.perseus.tufts.edu/hopper/text?doc=Plat.+Sym.+191a&fromdoc=Perseus%3Atext%3A1999.01.0174 (last accessed 09 June 2023).

Dreckmann, Kathrin: Black Queen and King: Iconographies of Self-empowerment, Canon, and Pop in the Current Music Video. In: *More Than Illustrated Music. Aesthetics of Hybrid Media Between Pop, Art and Video*, ed. by Dreckmann, Kathrin / Vomberg, Elfi. London 2023, 125–144.

Dreckmann, Kathrin: Dehumanize your bitch. Hybridität und Fluidität im Musikvideo. In: *Fluide Mediale. Medialität, Materialität und Medienästhetik des Fluiden*, ed. by Dreckmann, Kathrin / Meis, Verena. Düsseldorf 2022, 211–231.

Dreckmann, Kathrin: "PYNK" beyond forests and thighs: Manifestations of Social Utopia in Current Music Video. In: *Music Video and Transculturality: Manifestations of Social Utopia?*, ed. by Dreckmann, Kathrin / Jost, Christofer / Schramm, Bastian. Münster going to press 2024, 2024.

Dreckmann, Kathrin: "I'm too classy for this world, forever, I'm that girl." Media hybrids between Pop and Art in Beyoncé's *RENAISSANCE*. In: *Aesthetic Amalgams and Polotical Pursuits. Intertextuality in Music Videos*, ed. by Handley, Agata, et al., London going to press 2024, 2024.

Eisner, Robert: A Case of Poetic Justice: Aristophanes' Speech in the Symposium. *The Classical World 72/7* (1979), 417–419.

Ferguson, Rodrick A: *Aberrations in Black*. Minnesota, MN 2004.

Freud, Sigmund: Beyond The Pleasure Principle. Group Psychology and Other Works. In: *The Standard Edition of the Complete Psychological Works*, ed. by Strachey, James. New York, NY 1962, 57–58.

Groneberg, Michael: Myth and Science around Gender and Sexuality: Eros and the Three Sexes in Plato's Symposium. *Diogenes 52/4* (2005), 39–49.

Hirschfeld, Magnus: *Berlin's Third Sex*, trans. by James J. Conway. 2017.

Luckhardt, Jochen: *Lockenpracht und Herrschermacht*. Leipzig 2006.

Marchand, Eckert: Aby Warbung on plaster cats. *Sculpture Journal 28/3* (2019), 401–405.

McDaniel, Spencer: Here's the meaning of the Symbolism in Lil Nas X's Controversial New Music Video. *Tales of times forgotten* (07 April 2021). In: https://talesoftimesforgotten.com/2021/04/07/heres-the-meaning-of-the-symbolism-in-lil-nas-xs-controversial-new-music-video/ (last accessed 09 June 2023).

Paas, See / et. al.: *Liselotte Von Der Pfalz: Madame Am Hofe des Sonnenkönigs*; [Ausstellung Der Stadt Heidelberg Zur 800-Jahr-Feier, 21. September 1996 Bis 26. Januar 1997 Im Heidelberger Schloß]. Heidelberg: HVA 1996.

Plato: *The Collected Dialogues of Plato*, ed. by Cairns, Huntington / Hamilton, Edith, trans. by Lane Cooper. Princeton, NJ 1961.

Videography

Brokeback Mountain. Directed by Ang Lee. River Road Entertainment, USA/Canada 2005.

Call Me By Your Name. Directed by Luca Guadagnino. Frenesy Film Company / La Cinéfacture / RT Features / M.Y.R.A. Entertainment / Water's End Productions, Italy/France/USA/Brazil 2017.

Campbell, Zach: Lil Nas X "Montero (Call Me By Your Name)" REACTION WITH LIL NAS X!!. *YouTube* (March 2021). https://youtu.be/h2OAuf4G6CI?t=525 (last accessed 21 June 2023)

Lil Nas X: *Montero (Call Me By Your Name) (Official Video)*. Directed by Tanu Muino and Lil Nas X. *YouTube*. (March 2021) https://www.youtube.com/watch?v=6swmTBVI83k (last accessed: 08 June 2023).

Franziska Haug

"Work, Work, Work, Work, Work." On the Aesthetic Production of Gender *in* and *through* Pop Music

Abstract: Karl Marx states that the previous materialism has a blind spot in the comprehension of the sensual, the physical, and the subjective on a practical level. Judith Butler agrees with this understanding of materialism by understanding practice as a socially transforming activity. The object – a body, name, gender – practices and produces itself, according to Butler. Gender, then, is not the effect of a simple practice of construction, it is the practice of production itself. If we understand gender in its discursive constitution as sensual, aesthetic, polymorphously perverse, that is, immensely-really material, then it is neither an effect of production nor its precondition; it is above all one thing: labor! "You wanna hot body? You better work bitch!" (Britney Spears). This article analyzes a queer aesthetic of the production of gender through gendered modes of labor in pop songs. Queer is understood less as an identity but rather as a practice that is able to produce gender differently than (hetero)normative production aesthetics can.

Keywords: Pop songs, music video, queer, capitalism, neoliberalism, labor body, gender, femininity, consumer culture

Britney Spears: "You wanna hot body? You better work bitch!". Madonna: "'Cause we are living in a material world and I am a material girl". Rihanna: "Work, work, work, work, work". All of these foreshadow what it means to have a gender in neoliberal capitalism: It means work. In other words, in order to have a gender, a desire, and a sexuality, work must be done – sex, gender, and desire are not just there. And although the thesis of gender as socially constructed seems to be philosophically and sociologically accepted on the one hand, many queer and feminist discourses regarding visibility and representation in aesthetic considerations currently often assume that when Britney, Madonna, and Rihanna perform in their videos or appear as characters, they already have a gender that can be assigned. What seems clear is that they sing, speak, rap there *as* women. These discourses group under the label Female Pop, Female Rap – the future is female as an aesthetic program. However, in my understanding, this does not say anything about the aesthetics of this pop music in general or the aesthetics of the production of gender in particular. For example, the discourse around Beyoncé's song *Formation* from the album *Lemonade* revolved around a rhetoric – prominent in intersectional queer feminism – about the liberation of a woman *as* a woman. In the reception, something is already presupposed here that is first produced *in* and *through*[1] aesthetic and sociocultural practice. When Beyoncé sings and raps: "Ladies now let's get in formation, 'cause I slay"[2] and occupies and appropriates various sites of colonization and racialization of female People of Color in the video, it is not only her womanhood and blackness or its representation in art that is shown off; rather, the conditions of production, the struggles for the materializing interpretive sovereignty over gender, sexuality, and the body are negotiated aesthetically. The ladies only become ladies *through* aesthetic and material formation, which is tied to a productive, appropriating activity such as work, according to the thesis developed in the following.

The meaning of "becoming gendered", the question of which work processes precede this and at what limits queer-feminist representational politics first become apparent *in* and *through* the aesthetic form of art, for example pop music – not through the *correct* or *incorrect* representation of what is apparently already fixed in its material meaning. "Gender becoming", for example "becoming-woman",[3] is a term by Deleuze (in the original French "devenir femme"), who thus explicitly focuses on gender becoming in the sense of producing and making. In the following, then, I am basically concerned with the materialization of gender *through* aesthetic modes of formation. With Susan Sontag's *Against Interpretation*, the interpretation of art – pop music here – is not seen as a detective search for meaning in or behind the content of the object;[4] rather, form or a particular aesthetic of production in this respect first determines the semantics of production: it (form) is prior to it in a fundamental sense. At this point, pop music, following Diedrich Diederichsen, means the "context of images,

---

1 My use of the term pair *in* and *through* refers to a movement that I use as a code for a literary procedure of materialization following Judith Butler (among others) in *The Psychic Life of Power*: Theories in Subjection and Michel Foucault (among others) in *Histoire de la sexualité* and *Surveiller et punir*. For Butler's and Foucault's theory of subjectivation, the subject is dependent on so-called submission to the dominant symbolic order in order to equally be or become a subject in the first place. This movement into and through the structure that the subject necessarily goes through in order to be a subject can be described as a movement of negative dialectics. For aesthetic procedures of producing gender, the code *in* and *through* stands for the mediating relationship between form and content, or aesthetic form and material object: both presuppose and condition each other, without a temporal causal logic. In addition to Butler and Foucault, this movement is equally found in Louis Althusser's idea of invocation, explicitly in *Idéologie et appareils idéologiques d'État*, wherein he describes the said double movement on the basis of the French sujet as follows: as subject and subject at the same time. Althusser's invocation within capitalist orders thus means that the subject is/becomes in and through the invocation simultaneously free and subject (French assujettisment).
2 Beyoncé: 'Formation' from the album *Lemonade*, Columbia Records 2016.
3 Gilles Deleuze / Félix Guattari: *A Thousand Plateaus. Capitalism and Schizophrenia* [2005], trans. by Brian Massumi. Minneapolis, MN / London 1987, 134, 248, 268, 272, 276.
4 Susan Sontag: "What is needed, first, is more attention to form in art". In: id.: *Against Interpretation*. New York 1966, 8. For more recent connections to the queer theory used here in relation to pop and its genre-specific historicity, see especially Jack Halberstam: *Trans*. A Quick and Quirky Account of Gender Variability*. Oakland, CA 2018.

performances, (mostly popular) music, texts, and narratives tied to real people."[5] How, then, does gender become what it apparently is: a given; something that seems fixed and rigid; something that seems unchanging and identical to itself? This question prefaces the aforementioned thesis that gender has no natural ontology (in the sense of *first nature*), that it is supposedly there unprocessed as mere passive matter, and that its existence in this or that way – that is, in a certain way – is dependent on cultural, social, and economic factors. Gender is, above all, a practice bound to certain conditions of production.[6] For this reason, to ask how gender is made *in* and *through* a pop culture aesthetic is to ask about the means of this production. In what ways is gender produced, and with what aesthetic tools? Franco Moretti assumes, in relation to literature, that "[the story] speaks to us, only through the medium of form."[7] That is, the objects – for example, the feminine or the woman that pop singers like Britney Spears seem to appeal to – only produce themselves *in* and *through* their aesthetic formation. Silvia Bovenschen refers to the "feminine as a form"[8] in this consequence. It is not, then, a pre-existing content to which one could simply refer in an aesthetic process, or which could be properly mapped, depicted, or represented. The matter of gender only comes to its social-real form or, in other words, to its material meaning in the formation of the same: *bodies that matter*.[9]

If a gender is a form, then it is a constantly producing, moving, something that is necessarily remade with every pop cultural staging and performance. Whether intended or not: it – the gender – is therefore the "production of production."[10]

1 "I am a material girl". The Relationship between Gender and Economy

They can beg and they can plead, but they can't see the light (that's right). 'Cause the boy with the cold hard cash is always Mister Right. 'Cause we are living in a material world and I am a material girl. You know that we are living in a material world and I am a material girl.[11]

---

5 Diedrich Diederichsen: *Über Pop-Musik*. Cologne 2014, XI. "Zusammenhang aus Bildern, Performances, (meist populärer) Musik, Texten und an reale Personen geknüpfte Erzählungen." [Own translation; F.H].
6 Judith Butler: *Bodies That Matter. On the discursive limits of "sex."* New York, NY 1993.
7 Franco Moretti: *The Bourgeois. Between History and Literature*. London / New York, NY 2013, 15.
8 Silvia Bovenschen: *Die imaginierte Weiblichkeit. Exemplarische Untersuchungen zu kulturgeschichtlichen und literarischen Präsentationsformen des Weiblichen*. Frankfurt 1979, 56. "Das Weibliche [...] ist eine Form." [Own translation; F.H.].
9 This formulation comes from Judith Butler's book of the same name *Bodies That Matter*.
10 Gilles Deleuze / Félix Guattari: *Anti-Oedipus. Capitalism and Schizophrenia* [2000], trans. by Robert Hurley / Mark Seem / Helen R. Lane. Minneapolis 1983, 12.
11 Madonna: "Material Girl" from the album *Like a Virgin*. Sire / Warner Brothers Records 1984.

. . . sings Madonna in 1984 and thus shows that capital and labor are not only somehow connected with love, sexuality, and gender but are in a necessary relationship of dependence.[12] Because even within the heterosexual romantic understanding of love of the one "mister right," which Madonna sings here, the capitalist production relation seems to find itself necessarily also in *sexus* and love: In a "material world" lives a "material girl" and therefore the "mister" with the "cold hard cash" is also the right one.[13] The "mister right" is therefore not simply the perfect man but must first be produced in a process of normative manhood. Thus, in a tightly woven syntax, the "boy" from the beginning of the sentence becomes a man through "cold hard cash" at the end of the sentence; the "mister right." The truth about being a man is thus derived here from having "cold hard cash." Or to put it another way: to be in possession of the means of production, to have capital, means here to be a real man, the "mister right".[14] The capitalist production process and gender, in a sense, produce each other at this point. The material world of "cash" and that of material masculinity as such exists only when it is worked out, that is, when it is in the permanent process of production.

The production of economic commodities in the contradiction between capital and labor is thereby not prior to the production of erotic/sexual commodities in the contradiction of the sexes. In this, only the "production of production"[15] is initial or original. If the beginning and origin of each sex is production, this negative-cyclic movement abolishes primordiality as the possibility of the one, single beginning. Thus, with these examples, the talk of major and minor contradictions is already mistaken in the beginning. When Judith Butler determines gender as a way of mattering in which "matter is always materialized,"[16] Butler thereby marks a specific characteristic of Marx's understanding of materialism – namely that matter is always historically concrete, that is, it has become, it has thus been made, produced, and elaborated. Part

---

12 What is interesting at this point is the interpretation of the public discourse: instead of recognizing that "Material Girl" is an analysis and illustration of material conditions in capitalism, the press portrayed Madonna as the female embodiment and advocate of hypercapitalism, which is why she herself later regretted the song. Similar misinterpretations can be found in anti-capitalist songs by, for example, the Pet Shop Boys (for instance with "Opportunities" or "Shopping"). Following on from this, it could be examined here whether there is a difference in the interpretation of anti-capitalist pop songs and artistic expressions depending on the gender of the artists.

13 What is striking here is how the attributes of "cash" ("cold" and "hard") also gender (in the sense of an active verb) the economic, in that not only is being a man determined by the possession of capital, but also, conversely, capital is determined by adjectives with masculine connotations.

14 Compare the movement of how the "boy" uses his "cold hard cash" to buy labor power and the accompanying transformation into a man with the movement of the "transformation of money into capital" described by Marx and Engels in: id.: *Das Kapital. Kritik der politischen Ökonomie*. Vol. I, Book I, MEW 23. Berlin 1962, 161–191. [Own translation; F.H.].

15 Deleuze / Guattari: *Anti-Oedipus*, 12.

16 Butler: *Bodies That Matter*, xviii.

of the social enforcement of gender relations in everyday capitalist life is that the status of the procured is aesthetically invisibilized in everyday processes of production and reproduction. Thus, the point of the fetish character of the commodity, according to Marx, is that the specific social relation of the capitalist mode of production appears as a "social natural property"[17] of things, matter, bodies, etc. Capitalist everyday life is characterized by the aesthetic experience of gender as a self-contained natural property rather than the aesthetic experience of the social productions of gender.

2 The Aesthetic Procedures of Gender Productions

Pop music is a good entry point to being able to grasp the aesthetic and normative production of natural properties in their essence as produced; this is due to the fact that it consists – as Diedrich Diederichsen states in *Über Pop-Music* – of heterogeneous "products (or product parts)"[18] that "do not [form] the environment or the decor of pop music, but are part of it."[19] For it is precisely as "indexical art,"[20] as an art that must permanently negotiate the dialectic of aesthetics and reality *in* and *through* its media-specific indexicality, and as an art that visibly consists of queer principles of form such as sampling, mixing, repetition, rearrangement, collage, appropriation, etc., that pop music can be used to trace the process of production, manufacture, and compilation. It becomes clear that the body or sexual identity that appears as given in relation to gender is produced through processes of repetition and appropriation that have to be permanently generated. Because in pop music, a certain sound, a suitable body, a certain makeup, and the like exist only in and through an infinite intertextual context of reference. And even if the product of pop music exists as an object/matter in its own right, the "unity of pop music is a combination of heterogeneous media, archives, and distribution channels that are localized and localizable in different ways. This unity is […] not addressable as an institution, but is handled in the life-world as if it were one."[21] The unity of pop music, then, is its multiplicity of aesthetic productions. In this, it shows how many places are produced and worked in order to

---

17 Karl Marx / Friedrich Engels: *Das Kapital*, 86. "gesellschaftliche Natureigenschaft" [Own translation; F.H.].

18 Diedrich Diederichsen: *Über Pop-Musik*, xx. "Produkten (oder Produktteilen)" [Own translation; F.H.].

19 Diedrich Diederichsen: *Über Pop-Musik*, xx. "[…] nicht etwa die Umwelt oder den Dekor der Pop-Musik [bilden], sondern […] ihr Teil [sind]." [Own translation; F.H.].

20 Diedrich Diederichsen: *Über Pop-Musik*, xix, "indexikalische Kunst." [Own translation; F.H.].

21 Diedrich Diederichsen: *Über Pop-Musik*, xxi. "Einheit der Popmusik […] [eine] Verbindung aus heterogenen und auf unterschiedliche Weise lokalisierten und lokalisierbaren Medien, Archiven und Distributionskanälen. Diese Einheit ist […] nicht als Institution adressierbar, wird aber in der Lebenswelt so gehandhabt, als wäre sie eine." [Own translation; F.H.].

produce products such as the following songs, which also negotiate on the level of the phenomenon of work and gender: Missy Elliott *Work it* (2002), Kelly Rowland *Work* (2007), Ciara *Work* (2009), JME *Work* (2013), A$AP Ferg *Work* (2013), Iggy Azalea *Work* (2014), Omarion *Work* (2014), Stella Mwangi *Work* (2016), Rihanna *Work* (2016), Fifth Harmony *Work from Home* (2016), Britney Spears *Work B**ch!* and many more. The latter expresses in her song *Work B**ch!* what it means to come into the world today: That is, to become a commodity through work, ergo a physical/sensual subject:

> You wanna hot body? You want a Bugatti? You want a Maserati? You better work bitch! You want a Lamborghini? Sip martinis? Look hot in a bikini? You better work bitch! [...] Ring the alarm. Don't stop now. Just be the champion. Work it hard like it's your profession [...].[22]

Here, it is not only the imperatives ("you better") that make it clear that it takes work to be a woman. The aesthetic linking of work and gender in the video also does not follow an antecedent logic of identity but rather exposes the production process of gender identity itself. For example, in the line that accompanies "You wanna hot body? [...] you better work bitch", the body is first trained in fitness movements in order to be able to advertise it later in the video as an erotic commodity ("hot body") in a red-tinted small room with the neon sign "Bitch". By presenting herself as a dominatrix (she has three different whips and several types of whips with which she chains other women), Britney Spears also shows herself as a capitalist ("be the champion") who can dispose of the labor of others because she has worked hard to achieve the status of "fancy living in a big mansion" with Bugatti and Maserati. Through the suggestion that her chained subordinates can only free themselves from their state of bondage through work ("work it hard like it's your profession"), she embodies the capitalist production process in neoliberalism per excellence ("be the champion") because all the work is also supposed to be fun ("Sippin' martinis. Party in France").

3 Work Hard, Play Hard

David Guetta's, Ne-Yo's and Akon's song *Play hard* – as a remix of the 1999 Euro dance hit Better *Off Alone* by Alice Deejay – also talks about how the production of gender, especially masculinity, works in capitalism: "We work hard, play hard. [...] keep partyin' like it's your job."[23] The video tells of the classist, racist (e.g. a stereotypical image of Mexicans), and sexist lines along which the production of gender in neoliberal labor processes is arranged. Contrary to the seemingly primitive text, the aesthetics of the video are surprisingly unavailable, even exaggerated, and a bit queer. The simultaneity of different scenes in which work and celebration take place (money

---

22 Britney Spears: "Work B**ch" from the album *Britney Jean*, RCA Records 2013.
23 David Guetta: "Play Hard" from the album *Nothing But the Beat*, Virgin Records 2012.

deals in prison, beauty contest, housewives who don't do housework, rodeo on Warhol's banana, pink horses, money games, etc.) first of all shows in how many places supposedly "only" working takes place. And on the other hand, demonstrates in how many places where supposedly "only" partying takes place that work is also represented in the classical sense and vice versa (exemplified by the scene in a traditionally pastiche living room featuring a man ironing in his underpants with a poodle on the ironing board, a gender-unassignable person dancing in a tiger body, and a person with pointy boots chilling in an armchair).

A similar parallelization of work and sexuality or the production of goods and bodies is pursued in the song *Work* by Rihanna (feat. Drake). In it, work is paralleled with a sexual or erotic sensation in that "working" and "being dirty" take place simultaneously: "He said me haffi work, work, work, work, work! He see me do mi dirt, dirt, dirt, dirt, dirt!".[24] "Work" and "dirt" not only rhyme (impurely), they later even blur into a new word. Thus, "work" and "dirt" are eventually followed only by a merged "uaäh". Linguistically, what already functions together visually in the video in the form of the simultaneity of a party in the club, flirting, erotic dancing, and the designation of this as work, comes together in the song. Drake asks Rihanna: "You need to get done, done, done at work, come over, we just need to slow the motion" to which she replies: "he said me haffi work, work, work, work, work."[25] In the song it is sung in endless repetitive figures that work is being done (the word "work" occurs 80 times).

Work in the sense of recognizable wage labor, however, is not to be seen – except for one person who works in the kitchen of the club but dances and laughs even there. Not only dancing in the club is aesthetically described as work here but above all the mode of producing gendered bodies: "You see me doing dirt" means here, you see me doing my gender, producing my desire through practice ("doing"). The bodies – read as female or male – are only produced by repeating in a producing way what already seems to be present: the gender of *the* bodies. In the case of both Rihanna and Britney Spears, these repetitions in the video are also performed in front of a mirror. Looking at oneself in the mirror while working could here represent the self-reference of pop, that is, the identification of art as work. This stands in contrast to an autonomy-aesthetic conception of art, which precisely veils or denies its status as work, or must deny it in order to function.

At the same time, the neoliberal ideology of the subject that is necessarily permanently working on itself is also always negotiated. In Rihanna's repetitive movements, in dancing and performing ("doing work"/"doing dirt"), the body itself becomes active: the object becomes a "transformative activity",[26] as Judith Butler states in their queer

---

24 Rihanna feat Drake: "Work" from the album *Anti*, Westbury Road/Roc Nation 2016.
25 Rihanna: Work. The word "haffi" is Caribbean/Jamaican slang, which Rihanna uses throughout the song, for the English "have to".
26 Butler: *Bodies That Matter*, 192.

understanding of materialism. Thus, following Karl Marx's Feuerbach thesis, they defines materialism as something "[...] which can affirm the practical activity that structures and inheres in the object as part of that object's objectivity and materiality."[27] Marx states that "[t]he main defect of all materialism up to now [is] that the object is reality, sensuousness, conceived only under the form of the object *or of the Anschauung*; but not as *sensually human activity, praxis*; not subjectively."[28] Judith Butler prescribes to this very practical and producing activity when she describes performative language processes as well as bodily processes of working on the body as somatically materializing. Therefore, "[...] for to be material means to materialize [...]"[29] in the constant process of "transformative activity":

> If materialism were to take account of praxis as that which constitutes the very matter of objects, and praxis is understood as socially transformative activity, then such activity is understood as constitutive of materiality itself. [...] In either case, according to this new kind of materialism that Marx proposes, the object is not only transformed, but in some significant sense, the object is transformative activity itself [...]. The materiality of objects, then, is in no sense static, spatial, or given, but is constituted in and as transformative activity [...].[30]

Thus, by attributing changing activities to the objects themselves, Karl Marx and Judith Butler deconstruct the materiality of biological gender, which appears as static, as changeable. At the same time, they point to the dialectics of a social practice in capitalism that produces the appearance of gender as unchangeability, rigid etc. Last but not least, they thus open up a view of materiality that makes it possible to think queer interventions and subversions into what *has always been there*, because matter that is processually determined has gaps and ruptures. Those gaps and ruptures could become usable for a subversive intervention into the matter of gender, which appears to be fixed and unchanging.

For a queer feminist aesthetics and a queer reception of pop music, this could mean that it is not enough as queer feminists to aim at the recognition of identities, their participation, and the *right* representation. The logic of recognition by the *Big Other* (see Jacques Lacan) always implies an affirmation of the power of the *Big Other*.[31] The *Big Other* is the other of the subject. The *Big Other* is the non-self (in German the so-called *Nicht-Ich*), which, however, always already structures and aligns this subject. Certain identity politics strategies, as popular in parts of queer theories and movements

---

27 Butler: *Bodies That Matter*, 191.
28 Karl Marx / Friedrich Engels: *Thesen über Feuerbach*. MEW 3. Berlin 1958, 5. "Der Hauptmangel alles bisherigen Materialismus [] ist, daß der Gegenstand die Wirklichkeit, Sinnlichkeit nur unter der Form des *Objekts oder der Anschauung* gefaßt wird; nicht aber als *sinnlich menschliche Tätigkeit*, Praxis; nicht subjektiv." [Own translation, F.H.].
29 Butler: *Bodies That Matter*, 7.
30 Butler: *Bodies That Matter*, 191–192.
31 Matthias Haase / Marc Siegel / Michaela Wünsch (eds.): *Outside. Die Politik queerer Räume*. Berlin 2005, introduction.

aim to create ever new categories for "erotic identities",[32] as Sedgwick puts it, into the aesthetic regime of representation. They come much too late, should they aim at subversive entries into and accesses to the dominant order. For they can only criticize at the point where production has already taken place and subsequently demand that the regime of production now also include other, better, supposedly non-normative and exclusionary positions. They thus always remain a critique in the Future II (Simple) tense. By Future II I mean that this critique behaves as if the gender of the present and future is already completed or finalized. Such an identity-political conception of aesthetics has no concept of the aesthetic procedure as a production procedure of matter in general and gender in particular.

4 Conclusion

Accordingly, aesthetic procedures are not only part of the production process of gender, they are themselves genuinely producing in their forms as well as, in the best case, aesthetically reflecting on their own production. However, this can only be understood with a precise and detailed look at the aesthetic form of production. If queer strategies look exclusively at the fact that bodies in videos or advertising are "misrepresented" and not diverse enough, they do not change the aesthetic and political structure that is supposed to *correctly* render these non-normative bodies. On the contrary, the likelihood is high that the queer that is fought to be included in the representational regime becomes identical to the existing. For "society in its existing form", sociologist Karin Stögner aptly writes, "is [...] not a good place for those who represent the non-identical. [...] Identity compulsion and total integration are predominant."[33] For this very reason, then, the question should be asked whether the queer fight against ideologies of origin of the self-identical is not the essential starting point for a better understanding of the fight against a conservative, heteronormative aesthetic – that is, one that is hostile to everything queer.

Bibliography

Bovenschen, Silvia: *Die imaginierte Weiblichkeit. Exemplarische Untersuchungen zu kulturgeschichtlichen und literarischen Präsentationsformen des Weiblichen.* Frankfurt 1979.
Butler, Judith: *Bodies That Matter. On the discursive limits of "sex."* New York, NY 1993.

---

32 Eve Kosofsky Sedgwick: *Epistemology of the Closet.* California 1990, 81.
33 Karin Stögner: *"Jenseits des Geschlechterprinzips": Zum Problem von Gender und Identifikation in der Kritischen Theorie. sans phrase. Zeitschrift für Ideologiekritik* 9 (2016), 130. "Gesellschaft in ihrer bestehenden Form ist kein guter Ort für diejenigen, die das Nicht-Identische repräsentieren." [...] Identitätszwang und totale Integration sind vorherrschend." [Own translation, F.H.].

Deleuze, Gilles / Guattari, Félix: *Anti-Oedipus. Capitalism and Schizophrenia* [2000], trans. by Robert Hurley / Mark Seem / Helen R. Lane. Minneapolis, MN 1983.

Deleuze, Gilles / Guattari, Félix: *A Thousand Plateaus. Capitalism and Schizophrenia* [2005], trans. by Brian Massumi. Minneapolis, MN / London 1987.

Diederichsen, Diedrich: *Über Pop-Musik*. Cologne 2014.

Haase, Matthias / Siegel, Marc / Wünsch, Michaela (eds.): *Outside. Die Politik queerer Räume*. Berlin 2005.

Marx, Karl / Engels, Friedrich: *Thesen über Feuerbach*. MEW 3. Berlin 1958.

Marx, Karl / Engels, Friedrich: *Das Kapital. Kritik der politischen Ökonomie*. Vol. I, Book I, MEW 23. Berlin 1962.

Moretti, Franco: *The Bourgeois. Between History and Literature*. London / New York, NY 2013.

Sontag, Susan: *Against Interpretation*. New York, NY 1966.

Stögner, Karin: "Jenseits des Geschlechterprinzips". Zum Problem von Gender und Identifikation in der "Kritischen Theorie." *sans phrase. Zeitschrift für Ideologiekritik* 9 (2016).

Song Directory

Beyoncé: "Formation" from the album *Lemonade*. Columbia Records 2016.

Britney Spears: "Work B**ch" from the album *Britney Jean*. RCA Records 2013.

David Guetta: "Play Hard" from the album *Nothing But the Beat*. Virgin Records 2012.

Rihanna feat Drake: "Work" from the album *Anti*. Westbury Road / Roc Nation 2016.

Daniel Baranowski

Getting-into. Queerness at Work in Early Pet Shop Boys

Abstract: Especially in the early phase of their work, the Pet Shop Boys often address queer aspects only casually, hidden and on the sidelines. This supposed renunciation of an offensive, direct political statement, however, goes hand in hand with discrete hermeneutics through which queer topics are marked as an "excentric center." This essay brings together numerous references of queerness at work in the work – especially from their early years (1984 to 1990).

Keywords: Queerness, pop music, Pet Shop Boys, masculinity, gender, subversion, close reading, deconstruction, mainstream, sexuality

> I'm just a failed flaneur / Looking for a gadabout / But where that life is lived / I have
> yet to figure out /
> There's no one to tell me / No one to catch my eye / Living in slow motion / It's a
> long goodbye /
> I'm looking for someone / To help me get into here
> *In Slow Motion* (2017)

At the beginning of their career in the mid-1980s, the Pet Shop Boys were seldomly regarded as a decidedly queer (or simply a gay) band, especially outside the UK. It is only since the early 1990s – the songs *Being Boring* and *Go West* play a crucial role here – that queer perspectives of the band's work have received more attention. But where are traces of queerness to be found in the early years and how do these traces address their discussion of queerness? The following text focuses on these questions. The video for the single *Domino Dancing* marks an interesting turning and starting point, so I will begin with a close reading of this song.

After the Pet Shop Boys had reached the No. 1 spot in the British charts with their two previous singles *Always on My Mind* and *Heart*, they released *Domino Dancing* in September 1988 as a teaser for their third album *Introspective* with high expectations of a corresponding chart position. Judging by the previous releases, however, their hopes were disappointed.

1 Practical Introduction. *Domino Dancing*: Everything Is as It Seems

In the music video for *Domino Dancing*, directed by Eric Watson, two young men compete for the favor of a young woman. However, since the woman does not want to choose either the one or the other suitor, a quarrel ensues between the men. It is instructive to watch the Extended Version of the video based on the *Disco Mix* of the song. Although the plot of this version, which is three and a half minutes longer, is ultimately identical to the 7-inch version, the queer shift that occurs on the narrative and visual level is exemplified musically through a passage that only occurs in the *Disco Mix*: About two-thirds of the way through the running time, we hear a 26-second drum break that references, in an astonishing way, a passage of nearly the same length from the 2013 song *Love Is a Bourgeois Construct*, which musicologist Stan Hawkins once called "the 24 seconds of queering the bourgeoisie."[1] In the latter song, there is a striking break "where the word bourgeoisie is released and looped, phased, flanged and technologically 'screwed up,'"[2] which idiosyncratically points to the rejection of a bourgeois understanding of love in order to quite literally and, indeed, musically perform a queer conception of relationship.[3] Similarly, in the video for *Domino Dancing* nothing (or everything, depending on how you look at it) is as it seemed after the break. From then on, the two men are no longer in interaction with the young woman but instead perform – at least during the last two minutes of the video – a lustful brawl on the beach with bare upper bodies: On the surface, it is about the favor of the desired woman, but the bodies of the men are staged in such a way that a queer reading is almost mandatory and we are thus actually witnessing a homosexual love scene.[4]

There are other, more hidden references to the character of the relationship being negotiated here (for example, one of the young men and the young woman are reflected in the sunglasses of keyboardist Chris Lowe at the beginning of the video, while at the end we watch the beach scene with the two men in those same glasses). But this did not stop Neil Tennant, the band's singer, from making an astonishing statement about the content of the video. In the 2006 documentary A LIFE IN POP he remarks:

---

1 Stan Hawkins: *A Very Queer Construct. The Pet Shop Boys in Retrospect.* Unpublished lecture at the conference *Pet Shop Boys Symposium.* Edinburgh (24 March 2016).
2 Stan Hawkins: *Queerness in Pop Music. Aesthetics, Gender Norms, and Temporality.* New York, NY 2016, 38.
3 This paper is based on a lecture that consisted mainly of a detailed analysis of *Love Is a Bourgeois Construct* and traced a queer reading of the song by playing it from beginning to end. Since this is not possible in the context of a written text, I focus here more extensively on the examples only briefly touched upon in the lecture.
4 The two young men are taken away by the police at the end of the video. For what reason? Because of the scuffle? Or because of something else?

People say, "The video for *Domino Dancing* is very homoerotic." Well, yeah, I guess, you can look at two guys fighting and think it's homoerotic. It wasn't the intention. The script is simply following the story of the song. The boy's in love with the girl, but she's going off with someone else. That's it. That's what the video is.[5] Eric, obviously, had the idea that the two boys would romp in the sea. They're actually fighting each other. But that imagery is then translated through the modern filter of sort of Calvin Klein ads and things to be homoerotic. I don't believe the intention behind it was to be homoerotic. But I know no one will ever believe I would say that.[6]

Starting with this example, Tennant then speaks more generally about the queer view on their music, which he does not want to embrace entirely:

Chris and I have a strange naivety [. . .] in that we do things and don't necessarily think them through that much. [. . .] But people, if they know you're gay, they will see everything through a gay prism. And I don't think, I or we look at things through a gay prism. I don't honestly think we do.[7]

2 Theoretical Introduction. An Invitation to "Get into": Addressing Queerness on the Side

Thus, the following is certainly not about proving an *intentional* omnipresence of queer topics in the work of the Pet Shop Boys. At the same time, we should not believe the creators unconditionally and underestimate the fact that beyond their status as LGBTIQ* musicians, which manifests itself in the general public primarily through the sexual orientation of the singer, queer topics play a prominent role.[8] In particular, I will explore *how* these issues are dealt with and will try to understand the fact that they achieved their pop-superstar status as part of a staging that transcends music and text and performs a specifically queer form of masculinity. I focus on the band's early work from 1984 until the release of the song *Being Boring* (1990), which "became, for many, a song of a lifetime, and for a generation of LGBT people an essential and

---

5 However, it should be noted that contrary to Tennant's statement, the video actually does not end with the image of a heteronormative relationship and thus does not "follow the story of the song": the woman is alone; the men are taken into police custody.

6 PET SHOP BOYS: *A LIFE IN POP*, Directed by George Scott. UK 2006.

7 PET SHOP BOYS: *A LIFE IN POP*.

8 The sexual orientations of the band members are certainly irrelevant for the considerations outlined here. Nevertheless, it should be mentioned that Tennant had his public coming-out in 1994. Lowe has never publicly commented on his sexual orientation, which music critic Wayne Studer comments on reservedly and shrewdly: "[I]f Chris is indeed heterosexual, he's certainly done a magnificent job of hiding it all this time." (Wayne Studer: *Don't you know that the Pet Shop Boys aren't really gay? Commentary. Interpretation and Analysis of Every Song by Pet Shop Boys.* http://www.geowayne.com/newDesign/extras/faq/notgay.htm [last accessed 23 May 2022]).

early monument to a senseless tragedy."[9] During this period, the Pet Shop Boys were most successful for a mainstream audience although they abandoned spectacular stage shows and live concerts for most of the time and in television appearances usually stood motionless on stage. This is all the more astonishing when you consider their exhibited grumpiness – the iconic cover of the album *Actually* (1987) immediately comes to mind – the perception of Tennant's voice as distant, deadpan, even cold, and their age, which is almost suspicious to a teenager audience. Hawkins writes: "All in all, the surplus value of their signature is found in a collision of meaning that contravenes norms as they depoliticize identity categories with great panache."[10] While Hawkins' study deals with queerness within a discourse-analytic framework and theories of opacity and temporality, treating the Pet Shop Boys as merely one of many dozens of artists and with songs from only one creative period, I am concerned with a more detailed queer close reading of their early work.

The fact that queer topics have been at stake from the beginning but are nevertheless only visible at the margins and with a certain (unexcited) casualness demonstrates in the theoretical horizon of the essay just how significant the treatment of queerness is for the overall work of the band. Queerness appears in the Pet Shop Boys as an "excentric center."[11] It is not the focus of the work but (especially in their early phase) is mostly incidental and peripheral. At the same time, however, it inscribes a queer shift in the work that cannot be overlooked. So instead of directly addressing and exploiting queerness as a subject and thus adopting a one-dimensional perspective, the Pet Shop Boys allow it to enter it into their work subcutaneously and, thus, to slowly unfold its effectiveness. They enable the audience familiar with queer themes to recognize and classify it as such. However, this discreet coming-out may at the same time for an uninitiated audience serve as an invitation to a getting-into to engage with queer issues.[12]

---

9 Fergal Kinney: Time Would Come To An End. Pet Shop Boys' Behaviour at 30. *The Quietus* (26 October 2020). https://thequietus.com/articles/29089-pet-shop-boys-behaviour-review-anniversary (last accessed 23 May 2022).

10 Hawkins: *Queerness*, 37.

11 Jacques Derrida: *Memoires for Paul de Man* [1986], trans. by Cecile Lindsay / Jonathan Culler / Eduardo Cadava / Peggy Kamuf. New York 1986, 73.

12 Of course, the fact that queer traces are the focus of this essay does not mean that the work lacks other topics and readings. Regarding this point German music journalist Jan-Niklas Jäger states: The music of the Pet Shop Boys "takes world- and socio-political events into account, portrays the people affected by them, knows about the history of ideas and the most diverse discourses, deals with identity and sexuality, comments on (mass- as well as sub-) cultural developments [. . .]. The amazing thing is that this complex image is transported in an art form whose quality is defined to a significant extent by simplicity." (Jan-Niklas Jäger: *Factually. Pet Shop Boys in Theorie und Praxis*. Mainz 2019, 14 [Own translation, D.B.].) An examination of queer aspects of the band in the context of his own biography is provided by Kristof Magnusson: *Pet Shop Boys. Kristof Magnusson über die Pet Shop Boys, queere Vorbilder und musikalischen Mainstream*. Cologne 2021.

In this essay, I deal in more detail with that period of the Pet Shop Boys' career, going on now for more than forty years, which Tennant once described as their "imperial phase," "when they can seemingly do no wrong, when everything they release proves hugely successful and is widely accepted by the public."[13] It may well have significance for the topic of this essay that he conflates the end of that phase with the song *Domino Dancing*:

> I remember driving back from my house in Rye and listening on the radio when it entered the charts at number nine and I thought, "That's that, then – it's all over." I knew then that our imperial phase of number one hits was over.[14]

3 1984 to 1986. Queerness, *Please*

West End Girls, released in 1984 as the band's first track and again a year later in a drastically altered version re-produced by Stephen Hague as its fourth single that would make them famous worldwide, is already full of queer traces. The paratactic association of the band's name Pet Shop Boys with the song title *West End Girls*, the fact that the B side of the first *West End Girls* release is a largely instrumental song called *Pet Shop Boys*, and also that the band was originally to be called West End may be just the obvious clues to an ongoing, production- and distribution-related oscillation between male and female, between "boys" and "girls," which continues to materialize vocally, especially in the album version, in the breathy evocations of the "West End girls" and the "East End boys" during the long fadeout. *West End Girls* is a song about social and sexual tensions in mid-1980s London; the West End, particularly Soho, was a district with numerous sex stores at the time and remains an LGBTIQ* center to this day. Numerous lines of the lyrics suggest ambisexual (exchange) acts: "Too many shadows, whispering voices / Faces on posters, too many choices [. . .] Which do you choose / A hard or soft option? / (How much do you need?)" The protagonists have "got no future / We've got no past" and are on their way, "Running down underground / To a dive bar in a West End town," a not-at-all-coincidental allusion to The Dive Bar in Gerrard Street, which actually existed at the time[15] – one of those places of a gay bar scene that they were to sing about in the 1993 track *To Speak is a Sin* shortly before it largely disappeared.

Released after the success of *West End Girls*, the single *Love Comes Quickly* (1986) is a straightforward love song but its initially banal-seeming lyrics take on a much

---

13 Studer: Terms and phrases coined by the Pet Shop Boys that have been adopted by writers. *Commentary*. http://www.geowayne.com/newDesign/lists/coined.htm (last accessed 23 May 2022).

14 Pet Shop Boys with Chris Heath. *Introspective. Further Listening 1988–1989 (Sleeve Notes)* [2001]. EMI Parlophone 2018.

15 Pet Shop Boys: *Annually 2018*. London 2018, 22–23.

more yearning undertone when we read them in light of anti-homosexual legislation and a societal mood that largely associates the advent of AIDS with homosexuals:

> You can live your life lonely / Heavy as stone / [. . .] Say this is all you want / But I don't believe that it's true / 'Cause when you least expect it / Waiting round the corner for you / [. . .] Taste forbidden pleasures / Whatever you want / [. . .] 'Cause just when you least expect it / Just what you least expect

– as well as the oft-repeated ambiguous line "You can't stop falling." This reading of *Love Comes Quickly* is underlined by the record cover: It shows only the head of Chris Lowe, who wears a baseball cap from the London fashion company *Boy* with just this inscription. Lowe's eyes are covered by the visor of the cap and are shaded, which allows a remarkable reference back to the lines "Too many shadows, whispering voices / Faces on posters, too many choices" from *West End Girls*.

To read the cover of the first studio album *Please* (1986) as *not* being queer also seems rather absurd. In our context, however, it is more revealing that the image showing the musicians with towels draped over their shoulders, as well as the title of the album and the band name, appear only very tiny in the middle of a huge white space. We can read this design, unusual for the debut album of a pop band, rather as a concealment of the image's clearly homoerotic aesthetics – a concealment, however, that was made visible (involuntarily?) not only by EMI Parlophone's German distribution: Since they obviously didn't trust the original artwork by designer Mark Farrow, who realizes almost all of the band's record sleeves to this day,[16] they inflated the image of the two men with towels to record size.

Five of the ten full-fledged songs on *Please* are open to queer readings.[17] Besides the aforementioned singles, this is the case with the opening song *Two Divided By Zero*, albeit in a more conceptual way: The album follows a loose storyline, at the beginning of which two people set out on a path that brings them together as a couple at the end. The fact that the two call themselves two divided by zero at the beginning implies, on the one hand, of course, their universal bond and the potential infinity of their relationship (in the end, the mathematical operation $2 \div 0$ is not defined, does not result in a quantifiable value, and is thus infinite in a figurative sense). Beyond that, however, the zero of the title (precisely because it is recited by the machine voice of a pocket calculator) may also refer to the radical, anonymous, and all-encompassing totality of the threat to the (in this reading non-heterosexual) couple's relationship – by a society that forces those two to leave: "I think they heard a rumour / (Divided by, divided by) / Or someone tipped them off / (Divided by, divided by) / It's better to go sooner / (Divided

---

16 Cf. Hoare/Heath: *Pet Shop Boys*, 42–43.

17 Furthermore, *Violence* partly deals with binary gender models. In addition, the songs *Tonight Is Forever* and *Why Don't We Live Together?* also deal with gender-ambiguous relationships and even make this a topic themselves: "The woman in me shouts out / The man in me just smiles."

by, divided by) / Than call it all off." That one of the two left a farewell letter that "explained everything" may further support this reading.

While *I Want a Lover* blatantly and hedonistically promotes quick sex adventures ("This is us doing gay disco [. . .]. [I]t was totally a pre-Aids song"), Tennant's observations about the reception of the ballad *Later Tonight* are highly revealing here: "This is the most gay song we've ever written, and no one noticed at the time."[18] In addition to the refrain that is repeated three times, *Later Tonight* contains only the following verse:

> That boy never cast a look in your direction / Never tried to hook for your affection / Dresses like the mod of your invention, tall and proud / He is the head boy of a school of thought / That plays in your intentions, night and day.

It does not make sense to equate the gender of the singer with the gender perspective of the narrator, but in this case, as with the record cover, it is more than obvious to assume a homosexual, in this case impossible, denied, and secret desire in *Later Tonight*.

One of the 7-inch B sides from that period contains the first of countless literary references in the Pet Shop Boys' oeuvre.[19] Also released in 1986, *Jack the Lad*, a song about empowerment, includes the lines "To feast with panthers every night / You must be careful, Jack," referencing Oscar Wilde's remark about his dinners with both politicians and male prostitutes: "It was like feasting with panthers; the danger was half the excitement."[20] The importance of Oscar Wilde for the LGBTIQ* movement and its relationship to mainstream society, especially in the UK, was immense.[21] Additionally, *Jack the Lad* explicitly features Officer Thomas Edward Lawrence and Double Agent Harold Adrian Russell "Kim" Philby, who were presumably gay, and thus illustrates furthermore the specifically queer orientation that the issue of empowerment takes here.

4 1987–1989. *Introspective* Queerness, *Actually*!

"LGBT people [. . .] dominated the disco era."[22] As is well known, the end of the heyday of disco as an independent music genre in the early 1980s also had to do with

---

18 Pet Shop Boys with Chris Heath: *Please. Further Listening 1984–1986 (Sleeve Notes)* [2001]. EMI Parlophone 2018.

19 Studer: PSB songs with literary references. *Commentary.* http://www.geowayne.com/newDesign/lists/literary.htm (last accessed 23 May 2022).

20 Oscar Wilde: De Profundis [1913]. In: id.: *The Complete Works of Oscar Wilde.* Vol. 2: *De Profundis.* "*Epistola: In Carcere et Vinculis,*" ed. by Ian Small. Oxford 2005, 130. The positive reference to Oscar Wilde becomes even clearer some years later in the lyrics and video for *DJ Culture* (1991).

21 Didier Eribon: *Insult and the Making of the Gay Self,* trans. by Michael Lucey. Durham 2004, 141–244.

22 Darryl W. Bullock: *David Bowie Made Me Gay. 100 Years of LGBT Music.* London 2017, 3. See also 205–225.

anti-queer sentiments. That the Pet Shop Boys titled their first remix album *Disco*, released in late 1986, was at least regarding to the mainstream market, an unusual move. According to Hawkins, the explicit reference to disco not only provides a link to their "queer utopianism" but also points to the moment of critical and crisis-like masculinity addressed here and pervading the entire work:

> The kind of practices adopted within disco culture involved a queer utopianism, and the Pet Shop Boys' style has turned to this pleasure principle with gender modifications. Tennant's flamboyant singing style and Lowe's low-key presence as keyboardist on stage vividly depicted a unique class of male-ness. The experiences of young white men in the UK during the 1980s and 1990s are framed by discourses on "masculinity in crisis", something the Pet Shop Boys' narratives address. By promoting aspects of queerness, they contributed to new trends in male expression.[23]

One of the classic disco songs is undoubtedly Gloria Gaynor's *I Will Survive* (1978), a worldwide anthem of the LGBTIQ* movement like no other. The Pet Shop Boys included *I Will Survive* in their program during three concert series: in 1994, as part of the *DiscoVery* tour limited to Australia, North and South America; in 1997, at the *Somewhere* shows at the Savoy Theatre; and finally, on the *Nightlife* world tour (1999/2000), later released on DVD under the title MONTAGE. In all these cases, *I Will Survive* functions as a brief opening and/or closing of a medley with another song they first presented in June 1987: *It's a Sin.*

Mainstream audiences in particular had mostly missed that behind the bombastic musical façade of one of the band's biggest hits, indeed of the 1980s in general, is the deeply sad story of a young man who, because of his homosexuality, fails with regard to the demands of the (Catholic) Church and his own life. In some respects *It's a Sin* is the negative mirror to *I Will Survive*: While in the latter song the survival, the victory over the circumstances is at its center, the Pet Shop Boys song ends clearly more downbeat with the lines of the confession of guilt "Mea culpa, mea culpa, mea maxima culpa" performed in Latin, an "Amen" performed by a choir, and a machine-voiced "Zero" (compare the reference to *Two Divided By Zero*). The narrator's entire existence is overshadowed by "Everything I've ever done / Everything I ever do / Every place I've ever been / Everywhere I'm going to / It's a sin" and holds no redemption even in retrospect: "So I look back upon my life / Forever with a sense of shame / I've always been the one to blame." The burning of the singer at the stake in the video for *It's a Sin* may be an overly drastic representation of the topic – what is more decisive, however, is that the director of the video is British filmmaker and artist Derek Jarman, who had made a name for himself as an LGBTIQ* rights activist and whose films, especially CARAVAGGIO (1986), released shortly before *It's a Sin*, clearly had homosexual issues as their content. Thus, in *It's a Sin* at the latest, a mosaic of different levels of meaning, production, distribution, and reception is assembled that does not directly name queerness

---

23 Hawkins: *Queerness*, 42.

per se but circles it so closely that it confronts even the uninformed recipient with an artistic web, with traces of non-heteronormative points of view.[24]

In this context, it may also be interesting to know which artists the Pet Shop Boys collaborated with in the early years of their career, when they were often still perceived as an unambitious, typical 1980s pop phenomenon: In addition to Jarman, who was later also responsible for the video for *Rent* (1987) and parts of the set design for the *MCMLXXXIX* tour (1989), these include, for example, producer Bobby "O" Orlando, music manager Tom Watkins, singers Dusty Springfield and Liza Minnelli, and DJs and producers François Kevorkian and Frankie Knuckles, all of whom have close ties to the LGBTIQ* community or at least a high standing among queer recipients.[25]

In addition to *It's a Sin* and the collaboration with Dusty Springfield on *What Have I Done to Deserve This?* which, admittedly, deals with a clearly heterosexual subject on the textual level, there are further songs that can be read as queer on the second studio album *Actually* (1987). The songs the lovesick protagonist listens to in *I Want to Wake Up* clearly identify their desire as homosexual: "I stood at the kitchen sink, my radio played / Songs like 'Tainted Love' and 'Love Is Strange' / As I listened and the words hit my ears / I cried sudden tears." They are joined not only by the largely unknown track *Hit Music*, but also by *Rent*, released as a single in October, the fan-favorite and critically acclaimed *King's Cross*, and *It Couldn't Happen Here*, which gave the title to their 1988 feature film. While *Rent* (also largely unnoticed at the time of its release) deals with male prostitution, the other three tracks take up the AIDS pandemic and address the deaths caused by the HIV virus and its effects on social cohesion, especially in *King's Cross*, even in an intersectional perspective.[26]

Always on My Mind, released as a single at the end of the year, also contains a shift that may be typical because it happens incidentally, but offers a queer reading in the Pet Shop Boys version. The song, made famous by Brenda Lee (1972), Elvis Presley (1972) and Willie Nelson (1982), is the Pet Shop Boys' first ever cover version. "In the early version by Brenda Lee, she sang 'Boy, I'm sorry I was blind,' and when Elvis Presley and Willie Nelson covered the song, they sang 'Girl, I'm sorry I was blind.' All three of these cases are indisputably heterosexual."[27] In contrast, the corresponding lyrics in the Pet Shop Boys version, analogous to the original but lesser known version by Gwen McCrea (1972), simply read: "I'm so sorry I was blind."

---

24 After the 2021 broadcast of the Channel 4 series IT's A SIN about young gay men in 1980s London, perceptions of the Pet Shop Boys song have admittedly changed.

25 These are only names from up until 1989. The list could be completed to include countless people: David Bowie, Elton John, Lady Gaga, Madonna, Kylie Minogue, Wolfgang Tillmans, Rufus Wainwright, Bruce Weber, Years & Years, to name just a few of the better known.

26 Studer: Songs by PSB that were inspired by AIDS. *Commentary.* http://www.geowayne.com/newDe sign/-lists/aids.htm (last accessed 23 May 2022).

27 Studer: Always on My Mind / In My House. *Commentary.* http://www.geowayne.com/newDesign/-introspective/mind.htm (last accessed 23 May 2022).

For more than twenty years, American music critic Wayne Studer has been running the extensive website "Commentary," where he presents analyses of every single song by the Pet Shop Boys. He cannot go into detail about every aspect of the songs (and does not deal specifically with queerness) but provides countless, often overlooked minutiae, and his website has become a comprehensive encyclopedia, a kind of handbook on the band's work. In reference to *Always on My Mind*, he interprets the aforementioned passage as "an instance of altering gender-specific language in order not to identify the gender of the person being addressed [. . .], thereby avoiding any specific suggestion of the sexual orientation of the singer",[28] more precisely the narrator. It's just a nice side story that *Always on My Mind* held the traditionally most important Christmas number one spot in Great Britain and denied this place to *Fairytale in New York* by The Pogues feat. Kirsty MacColl, which is repeatedly criticized because of its partly homophobic lyrics.[29]

Domino Dancing is not only open for queer readings through its video, but on the textual level it contains the recurring lines "Watch them all fall down," which can be read as a discussion on AIDS.[30] *I'm not Scared*, which immediately follows on the third album *Introspective* (1988), contains numerous lines that address the difficulties of openly queer lives: "What have you got to fight? / What do you need to prove? / You're always telling lies / And that's the only truth / [. . .] What have you got to hide? / Who will it compromise? / Where do we have to be / So I can laugh and you'll be free." Sometimes, it takes Tennant's voice to read such lines queerly – *I'm not Scared* had initially been given by the Pet Shop Boys to the band Eighth Wonder and their singer Patsy Kensit, who were the first to release the song – which is also firmly demonstrated by the track *In Private*, which the band wrote for Dusty Springfield, who released it as a single in 1989. The lines

> Take your time and tell me / Why you lied / I realise that we've been found out / This time / We should stand together if we can / But what you've planned / Means there's a difference between / What you're gonna say in private / You still want my love / We're in this together / And what you're gonna do in public / Say you were never in love / That you can remember / [. . .] And what you gonna say / When you run back to your wife / I guess that's just the story of my life

unfold a more overtly queer scenario in the song's 2006 duet released by the Pet Shop Boys together with Elton John. Not so incidentally, a little later in *It Must Be Obvious* (1990) the Pet Shop Boys tell of a friendship whose queer expression can only be kept secret from the environment (and in the plot of the song even from one of the two

---

28 Studer: *Always on My Mind / In My House.*

29 Patrick Strudwick / Luke Turner / Alex Hood: Should the BBC have censored Fairytale of New York? *The Guardian* (19 November 2020). https://www.theguardian.com/music/2020/nov/19/should-the-bbc-have-censored-fairytale-of-new-york (last accessed 23 May 2020).

30 The instrumentation of the original version obscures the depressing and sad quality of the song, which comes out more clearly in the *Alternative Mix* released with the 12-inch record.

people) with difficulty. The refrain "Everyone knows when they look at us / Of course they do it must be obvious" is also a thinly veiled self-reference.

The last point of the "imperial phase" is certainly marked by the album *Introspective*, whose last single release in 1989 was the Sterling Void cover *It's Alright.* One of its bonus tracks, in turn, is not entirely coincidentally the last song released before the striking break that will occur in the Pet Shop Boys' career in 1990. The sparely orchestrated short track *Your Funny Uncle* is somewhat reminiscent of the earlier ballad *Later Tonight* and autobiographically recounts the funeral of the singer's very good friend, who died of AIDS.

5 1990 and Onward. Addressing Queerness

The memory of that friend precisely marks the beginning of a new creative phase, which is also characterized by the much more explicit addressing of queer content in lyrics, music, and performance. The fourth album *Behaviour* (1990) is introduced by a song almost seven minutes long, with which the Pet Shop Boys "gave voice to an entire generation of gay men who to that point and afterward had managed to survive the AIDS epidemic"[31] – *Being Boring*, "a melancholic review of the past and all the things and close people that got lost along the way,"[32] "looks at the biggest of themes – friendship, loss, the passage of time [and] allows people to hear themselves, and to see their lives reflected back at them."[33] This elegy to a friend, also at issue again in 2019's *An Open Mind* ("When you don't belong there / You don't care what they think / But you know what you want"), is at the start of a series of more explicit queer references:

The sexually charged interpretation and linking of U2 and Frankie Valli in *Where the Streets Have No Name (I Can't Take My Eyes Off You)* (1991), the swan song to a gay utopia *Go West* (1993), the remix of David Bowie's *Hallo Spaceboy* (1996), the coding of bisexuality on the album *Bilingual* (1996),[34] the coming-out song *Metamorphosis* (1996), the dialogue performed with Kylie Minogue between a gay father and his daughter in *In Denial* (1999), the Village People pastiche *New York City Boy* (1999), the storyline of the musical *Closer to Heaven* (2001), the Eminem-goes-gay-fantasy *The Night I Fell in Love* (2002), the openly bisexual orientation in the *Possibly More Mix* of

---

31 Studer: Being Boring. *Commentary.* http://www.geowayne.com/newDesign/behaviour/boring.htm (last accessed 23 May 2022).

32 Norman Fleischer: "Behaviour" Turns 30. Reflections On The Legendary Pet Shop Boys Album. *Nothing But Hope And Fashion* (21 October 2020). https://nbhap.com/sounds/pet-shop-boys-behaviour-anniversary (last accessed 23 May 2022).

33 Kinney: *Time.*

34 Cf. a literary adaptation Thomas Meinecke: Pet Shop Boys. In: id.: *Feldforschung. Erzählungen.* Frankurt 2006, 27–45.

Did You See Me Coming? (2009), the depiction of the situation of homosexual men in the early 1960s in *Odd Man Out* (2013), the song-cycle about Alan Turing *A Man from the Future* (2014), the addressing of homophobia disguised as freedom of expression in *Oppressive (The Best Gay Possible)* (2014), the gay and lesbian setting around Berlin's subway line U1 in *Will-o-the-wisp* (2020), and the queer marriage in *Wedding in Berlin* (2020) are indeed only the most obvious traces of queer topics on the textual level. In addition, there are adaptations and quotations of works by LGBTIQ* artists, such as the new soundtrack to Sergei Mikhailovich Eisenstein's *Battleship Potemkin* (2005), the inclusion of a motif from Pyotr Ilyich Tchaikovsky's *The Nutcracker* in *All Over the World* (2009), and the paraphrasing of Marcel Proust in *Memory of the Future* (2012). The cover versions of *Girls & Boys* (1994), *If Love Were All* (1994), and *Try It (I'm in Love with a Married Man)* (2003) as well as the videos for *Was It Worth It?* (1992), *Paninaro '95* (1995), *A Red Letter Day* (1997), and *Winner* (2012) would be as worthy of mention here as almost the entire album *Very* (1993).[35]

A wide variety of queer traces and queer readings culminate, so to speak, in the first one-and-a-half minutes of the single *Love Is a Bourgeois Construct*, a song I briefly dealt with at the beginning of this essay. Here, different musical levels already overlap, all of which more or less can be read in a queer way. The production very obviously bears the signature of British producer Stuart Price, who had previously worked with Kylie Minogue and Scissor Sisters. However, his most famous and commercially successful collaboration was probably with Madonna on her 2005 album *Confessions on a Dancefloor*, whose lead single *Hung Up* he produced, among others, and which is immediately invoked by the musical entry. The melody is a direct quote from Michael Nyman's piece *Chasing Sheep is Best Left to Shepherds*, which Nyman wrote for the soundtrack to Peter Greenaway's THE DRAUGHTMAN'S CONTRACT (1982) – a film that (among many other things) deals with the inversion of gender roles and sexual frustration. Very early after its release, *Chasing Sheep is Best Left to Shepherds* was used in the soundtrack of Jean Daniel Cadinot's gay porn movie STOP SUNRISE (1984). Nyman's piece, in turn, is based on Henry Purcell's opera *King Arthur, or The British Worthy* (1691), from the third act prologue, which has gained some pop cultural relevance because another piece from it, *What power art thou . . .,* based on the same bass line as here, has become known as *The Cold Song* (1981) by Klaus Nomi. This is the cultural and pop-historical background of the first ninety seconds of the song that appeared on the 2013 album *Electric*. Hawkins notes of this accumulation of disparate tracks: "Indeed, [the Pet Shop Boys'] idiolect comprises a range of musical criteria that encompass attitude, generation, ethnicity, and class. It is the accumulation of such ingredients that defines the Pet Shop Boys' act."[36] This musical foundation

---

35 Ramzy Alwakeel: *Smile If You Dare. Politics and Pointy Hats with the Pet Shop Boys.* London 2016. See also Jäger: *Factually*, 97–117.

36 Hawkins: *Queerness*, 40.

is then followed by a five-minute swan song to bourgeois, heterosexual desire, ending with that queering of the word bourgeoisie already mentioned at the beginning of this text. The German singer Andreas Dorau published the song *Liebe ergibt doch keinen Sinn* in 2017, which states: "Liebe ist, wenn man genau hinguckt / Nichts weiter als ein bourgeoises Konstrukt."[37]

Finally, I would like to refer to an interesting conclusion drawn by Studer, who has already been quoted several times here. He collects *10 things the Pet Shop Boys did to commit career suicide in the U.S.*, and lists, among others, the release of the *Disco* album, the topic of the song *Rent*, and finally the video for *Domino Dancing*: "Now we're really getting down to it – the final days of the Pet Shop Boys' tenure as major U.S. hit makers. [. . .] [D]espite its heterosexual veneer, the video's blatant homoeroticism [. . .] was just too much for the bulk of their American fan-base to handle."[38] Studer's list ends with Neil Tennant's coming-out. Certainly, these are pure speculations, but it cannot be denied that with increasing visibility of queer references, the mainstream success of the Pet Shop Boys begins to wane, not only in the United States of America.

6 Conclusion: Queerness as an "Excentric Center" in Early Pet Shop Boys

The overarching subject of most of these passages can be described as a crisis of masculinity in a heteronormative sense: "This is achieved by employing the musical codes of dance-pop and sewing them into a style that offsets queer masculinity against the more conventional male representation found in the music industry."[39] The easily accessible surface, the mainstream sound, the at times militaristic beat, the extensive lack of emotion and expression of the musicians, especially at the beginning of their careers, only allow the queer view of masculinities to gleam.[40] Hawkins points out that one "might say that the Pet Shop Boys' songs depict a Dionysian sonic universe that indexes a desire that undercuts normative and naturalized stereotypes" and that "their queer aesthetic is spatially organized in studio productions that reference a cultural context that exudes incandescence."[41]

---

37 "Love is, if you look closely / Nothing more than a bourgeois construct." [Own translation, D.B.].
38 Studer: 10 things the Pet Shop Boys did to commit career suicide in the U. S. *Commentary*. http://www.geowayne.com/newDesign/lists/suicide.htm (last accessed 23 May 2022).
39 Hawkins: *Queerness*, 38–39.
40 Jäger: *Factually*, 16: "Their multidimensionality makes them a band for the masses as well as a band for the minority." [Own translation, D.B.].
41 Hawkins: *Queerness*, 42.

In this essay, I have attempted to gather the many traces and references to queer-ness in the work of the Pet Shop Boys in order to demonstrate the apparent obvious-ness of the band's status as queer beyond the sexual orientation of the musicians *in the work itself*. In doing so, I have focused in more detail on the early period, in which there is comparatively less direct addressing of the issue. These rather incidental, hidden figurations, which are sometimes not recognizable at first glance and do not want to proclaim a direct socio-political message, nevertheless fulfill a hermeneutic and, in a broader sense, utopian function in their marginalization: They are that "defective cornerstone" which, according to French philosopher Jacques Derrida, is "always already at work in the work," "not at the center but in an excentric center, in a corner whose eccentricity assures the construction of the system."[42]

To understand themes and traces as an excentric center means, on the one hand, to grant them a character constituting the work as a whole. It is essential, in the words of American literary critic Paul de Man, that one also listens

> [. . .] to what is being said obliquely, figurally, and implicitly (though not less compellingly) in less conspicuous parts of the corpus. Such a way of reading is by no means willful; it has its own constraints, perhaps more demanding than those of canonization.[43]

On the other hand, the rather indirect way in which these topics are performed is a departure from a one-sided, logocentric readability. By constantly circling queer topics, they invite one to venture a getting-into (rather clandestinely and cautiously, in deliberate contrast to publicly coming out) without being pinned down to it.

It is all the more ambiguous when, in (presumed) cluelessness, their last real hit single to date, *Go West* (1993), has now been lustily intoned for decades in the world's soccer stadiums, of all places: "Who would have thought that an obscure Village People song covered by the Pet Shop Boys would become the song of football. It's fantastic. I think it's our greatest achievement."[44]

Bibliography

Alwakeel, Ramzy: *Smile If You Dare. Politics and Pointy Hats with the Pet Shop Boys*. London 2016.
Bullock, Darryl W.: *David Bowie Made Me Gay. 100 Years of LGBT Music*. London 2017.
Derrida, Jacques: *Memoires for Paul de Man* [1986], trans. by Cecile Lindsay / Jonathan Culler / Eduardo Cadava / Peggy Kamuf. New York, NY 1986.
Eribon, Didier: *Insult and the Making of the Gay Self*, trans. by Michael Lucey. Durham 2004.

---

42 Derrida: *Memoires*, 72–73.

43 Paul de Man: Reply to Raymond Geuss. *Critical Inquiry* 10 (1983), 375–382, 380.

44 Pet Shop Boys with Chris Heath: *Very. Further Listening 1992–1994 (Sleeve Notes)* [2001]. EMI Parlophone 2018.

Fleischer, Norman: "Behaviour" Turns 30. Reflections On The Legendary Pet Shop Boys Album. *Nothing But Hope And Fashion* (October 2020). https://nbhap.com/sounds/pet-shop-boys-behaviour-anniversary (last accessed 23 May 2022).

Hawkins, Stan: *Queerness in Pop Music. Aesthetics, Gender Norms, and Temporality*. New York, NY 2016.

Hawkins, Stan: *A Very Queer Construct. The Pet Shop Boys in Retrospect*. Unpublished lecture at the conference *Pet Shop Boys Symposium*. Edinburgh (24 March 2016).

Hoare, Philip / Heath, Chris: *Pet Shop Boys. Catalogue*. London 2006.

Jäger, Jan-Niklas: *Factually. Pet Shop Boys in Theorie und Praxis*. Mainz 2019.

Kinney, Fergal: Time Would Come To An End. Pet Shop Boys' Behaviour at 30. *The Quietus* (October 2020). https://thequietus.com/articles/29089-pet-shop-boys-behaviour-review-anniversary (last accessed 23 May 2022).

Magnusson, Kristof: *Pet Shop Boys. Kristof Magnusson über die Pet Shop Boys, queere Vorbilder und musikalischen Mainstream*. Cologne 2021.

de Man, Paul: Reply to Raymond Geuss. *Critical Inquiry* 10 (1983), 375–382.

Meinecke, Thomas: Pet Shop Boys. In: id.: *Feldforschung. Erzählungen*. Frankfurt 2006, 27–45.

Pet Shop Boys: *Annually 2018*. London 2018.

Pet Shop Boys with Chris Heath: *Introspective. Further Listening 1988–1989 (Sleeve Notes)* [2001]. EMI Parlophone 2018.

Pet Shop Boys with Chris Heath: *Please. Further Listening 1984–1986 (Sleeve Notes)* [2001]. EMI Parlophone 2018.

Pet Shop Boys with Chris Heath: *Very. Further Listening 1992–1994 (Sleeve Notes)* [2001]. EMI Parlophone 2018.

Strudwick, Patrick / Turner, Luke / Hood, Alex: Should the BBC have censored Fairytale of New York? *The Guardian* (November 2020). https://www.theguardian.com/music/2020/nov/19/should-the-bbc-have-censored-fairytale-of-new-york (last accessed 23 May 2020).

Studer, Wayne: *Commentary. Interpretation and Analysis of Every Song by Pet Shop Boys*. http://www.geo wayne.com/newDesign/extras/faq/notgay.htm (last accessed 23 May 2022).

Wilde, Oscar: De Profundis, [1913]. In: *The Complete Works of Oscar Wilde. Vol. 2: De Profundis. 'Epistola: In Carcere et Vinculis'*, ed. by Ian Small. Oxford 2005.

Videography

Domino Dancing. Extended Version. Directed by Eric Watson, Pet Shop Boys Partnership / EMI Records Ltd., UK 1988.

Montage. The Nightlife Tour 99/00. Ed. by Meneely, Warren, Pet Shop Boys Partnership / EMI Records Ltd., UK 2001.

Pet Shop Boys. A Life In Pop. Directed by George Scott. Isis Productions, UK 2006.

Part II: **Homonationalism and Homonormativity
in Television**

Katharina Wiedlack

Russian Bodies We Can Laugh About? Ethnic Drag in Race Conscious Gay US Media

Abstract: This article problematizes ethnic drag in the popular US-American reality TV-series *RuPaul's Drag Race*. Building on prior works that address the racialization of Black contestants and Contestants of Color, it critically investigates the representation of white female Russianness through the *Drag Race* season seven and *Drag Race All Star* season two contestant Katya. It makes visible how Russian femininity becomes meaningful through performance, style and mannerisms. Reading Katya's embodiment of Russianness against the context of *RuPaul's Drag Race* and liberal gay progressive discourses around the concept and artistic form of drag in general, the article aims to demonstrate that although Katya's performance is a form of ethnic drag that could have the potential to unmask racialized signification as cultural construct, it ultimately fails to do so. Moreover, by employing the concepts of orientalism and racialization as well as homonationalism the case study of Katya shows the covert racialization of (female) Russian bodies as one aspect of homonationalism that depends on the very visible and widespread critique of Russian homophobia.

Keywords: Drag Queen, queer, racialization, whiteness, Russianness, comedy, East/ West divide, homonationalism, racial commodification

1 Introduction

This essay investigates the potential of comedy and ethnic drag to critically interrogate prejudice and stigma through the reiteration of racialized social stereotypes in *RuPaul's Drag Race*. *RuPaul's Drag Race* is the most popular representation of drag queens in popular culture and arguably one of the most successful reality competition shows in the history of US television and beyond. RuPaul – the show's host, head judge, and contestant mentor for the series, is one of the most famous African American drag performers. As of 2024, the show has 16 seasons and several spin-offs, such as the *All Star* series; RuPaul has won numerous awards for her role in the show, among them several Emmys.[1]

---

1 Sandra Gonzalez: RuPaul makes Emmy history. *CNN* (September 2021). https://www.cnn.com/2021/ 09/19/entertainment/rupaul-emmys/index.html (last accessed 15 August 2022).

American feminist media theorists such as Sabrina Strings and Long T. Bui[2] have long pointed out that *RuPaul's Drag Race* is a space that signifies American national belonging and queer neoliberalism, and where race, racialization, and American racial politics are negotiated. They criticize the uneasy place of race and racialization within *RuPaul's Drag Race.* Public critics such as the popular bloggers Jason Flores[3] and Grace John[4] as well as YouTube commentators such as Kevin O'Keeffe and Mathew Rodriguez[5] have equally publicly criticized the racist and classist baseline of *RuPaul's Drag Race,* which confines Contestants of Color to a limited set of "queens" they are allowed to impersonate as well as the blunt racism of the fan community. Most recently, researchers have discussed racialized gender performances, particularly with regards to trans* contesters, and the show's struggles with issues on the intersection of racialization and transphobia.[6]

While most of these discussions seem to debate Black and People of Color representation, sentiments against LatinX and Asian performers as well as anti-Black racism, this article focuses on the representation of white female Russianness through ethnic drag in the example of the *Drag Race* and *Drag Race All Star* contestant Yekaterina Petrovna Zamolodchikova, Katya for short. It analyzes the relationship between the bodily performance of Katya's Russian femininity as expressed through style and mannerisms and liberal gay progressive discourses around the concept and artistic form of drag.

Analyzing Katya against the context of *RuPaul's Drag Race,* this article tests the thesis that although Katya's performance is a form of ethnic drag that could have the potential to show racialized signification as cultural construct, it ultimately fails to do so. It employs the concepts of orientalism and racialization to analyze the construction of white Russian bodies through ethnic drag. The Palestinian American postcolonial scholar Edward Saïd[7] coined the concept of orientalism to describe how philosophers of the European Enlightenment constructed the "East" or "Orient" as a distinct sphere to distinguish it from a white civilized superior "West." These mostly male white Euro-

---

2 Sabrina Strings / Long T. Bui: "She Is Not Acting, She Is." The conflict between gender and racial realness on RuPaul's Drag Race. *Feminist Media Studies* 14/5 (2014), 822–836.

3 Jason Flores: No Matter How Much You Like "RuPaul's Drag Race," It's Still Problematic. *Pride* (April 2016). https://www.pride.com/firstperson/2016/4/07/no-matter-how-much-you-rupauls-drag-race-its-still-problematic (last accessed 10 April 2018).

4 Grace John: *"RuPaul's Drag Race" Often Displays Racial Bias to Favor White Queens.* March 2018. https://studybreaks.com/tvfilm/rupauls-drag-race/ (last accessed 10 April 2018).

5 Kevin O'Keeffe / Mathew Rodriguez: Racism in RuPaul's Drag Race. The Kiki Ep 3. *YouTube.* (August 2018). https://www.youtube.com/watch?v=T3Gj2wUgKpI (last accessed 16 August 2022).

6 Lore/tta LeMaster / Michael Tristano: Performing (Asian American Trans) Femme on RuPaul's Drag Race: Dis/orienting Racialized Gender, or, Performing Trans Femme of Color, Regardless. *Journal of International and Intercultural Communication* 16/1 (2023), 1–18.

Marcos Gonsalez: Fantasies of Valentina. *TSQ: Transgender Studies Quarterly* 9/4 (2022), 587–608.

7 Edward Saïd: *Orientalism.* New York, NY 1978.

peans connected a presumed lack of civilization among inhabitants of the "Orient" to bodily phenomena, such as skin color. This process of assigning meaningful racial markers or characters to peoples is a specific form of othering, generally referred to as racialization. Using the concept of racialization highlights the artificiality and constructedness of "race" – as visual phenomena and meaning – and its contested relationship to biological bodies. Although Saïd did not discuss the position of Russians or Slavic peoples in his text, scholars such as American historian and European Studies professor Larry Wolff[8] and Scandinavian international relations professor Iver Neumann[9] have argued that the (white) inhabitants of Eastern Europe and Eurasia were produced through the same orientalist discourses. Because of their signification as white and their geographic location in-between the presumably civilized West and the presumably uncivilized Orient, they were understood to be a group of half-civilized or transitional people who were only in the process of becoming as civilized as the modern West.

This article proposes that Russian embodiment and characteristics are still imagined through orientalist discourses, and that the identification of such bodies as white plays a significant role for how Russianness becomes represented and evaluated in popular culture. It argues that while Russian whiteness is a privilege within the racist white supremacist Western context of the United States and Europe, it is a kind of whiteness that is classed and gendered in a way that signifies embodied difference as slow, not-yet modern, not-yet civilized, or even backward. This embodied difference will be identified by building on the findings of critical whiteness studies, decolonial studies, and the orientalization of Russia as a geo-political location. Moreover, current methodological tools of queer theory that were developed in a US-American decolonial and anti-racist context will be adapted in order to make them applicable to white Russian bodies. In particular, the concept of homonationalism, developed by American gender, queer, and decolonial studies scholar Jasbir Puar,[10] will be adopted to analyze the place and function of Russian bodies in liberal pro-gay discourses. Homonationalism describes how Western national and supranational discourses include gay and lesbian minorities and claims to minoritarian civil rights into ideas of progress and civilization in order to distinguish themselves favorably from racialized Others. This allows nationalists for example to identify racialized migrants as a threat to sexual minorities or reject entire nations' rights to sovereignty because of their alleged homophobia. It will be argued that the contemporary covert racialization of (female) Russian bodies is one aspect of a form of homonationalism that depends on the very visible and widespread critique of Russian homophobia in mainstream discourses.

---

8 Larry Wolff: *Inventing Eastern Europe. The Map of Civilization on the Mind of the Enlightenment.* Stanford, CA 1994.
9 Ivar Neumann: *Russia and the Idea of Europe.* New York / London 1996.
10 Jasbir Puar: *Terrorist Assemblages. Homonationalism in Queer Times.* Durham, NC 2007. Jasbir Puar: Rethinking Homonationalism. *International Journal of Middle East Studies* 45/2 (2013), 336–339.

2 Katya: Ethnic Drag or Racialized Commodification?

In 2006, American actor, author, and comedian Brian McCook created the Russian drag character Yekaterina Petrovna Zamolodchikova or Katya for short, to work as the hostess of a monthly drag show called "Perestroika" at a cabaret club in Boston.[11] McCook is from Massachusetts and of Irish Catholic ancestry.[12] He is neither Russian nor a Russian heritage speaker, although he speaks some Russian and his pronunciation is quite authentic.[13]

In his first appearance on *RuPaul's Drag Race* in March 2015, McCook said that the Russian-based aspect of his persona was inspired by one of his female professors at the Massachusetts College of Art and Design who "never left the house without a full face of makeup [with] six-inch stilettos in the snow."[14] On other occasions he stated that the stage name is a reference to one of his favorite gymnasts, Elena Zamolodchikova.[15] After her participation in *RuPaul's Drag Race* in 2015 and 2016, Katya hosted the drag comedy YouTube series *UNHhhh*[16] and later became co-host of a similar comedy format called *The Trixie & Katya Show* on Viceland.[17] Additionally, she recently featured in the comedy movie HURRICANE BIANCA: FROM RUSSIA WITH HATE[18] and co-authored "a parody of self-help and [women's] etiquette" book;[19] she frequently tours with her own live performance show.

Katya represents many American stereotypes about Russian women throughout *Drag Race* season seven. An entire bundle of stereotypes is mentioned in the first episode of the video series *RuFLECTIONS* dedicated to her character. Each character gets her own *RuFLECTIONS* series which consists of several one-and-a-half minute long professionally produced YouTube videos where the show's contestants have the chance to develop and explain their characters in more depth than the TV episodes allow for. The

---

11 Maria Oliver: Night Watch. Perestroika. *Boston Globe* (29 April 2011). http://archive.boston.com/ae/music/articles/2011/04/29/night_watch_perestroika/ (last accessed 06 April 2018).

12 RuPaul: What's the Tee? SoundCloud Episode 76 – Katya. *SoundCloud.* (2017). https://soundcloud.com/rupaul/episode-76-katya (last accessed 15 December 2016).

13 Stephan Lee: RuPaul's Drag Race Miss Congeniality winner Katya speaks! *Entertainment Weekly's EW.com.* (02 June 2015). https://ew.com/article/2015/06/02/rupauls-drag-race-miss-congeniality-winner-katya-speaks/ (last accessed 31 January 2022).

14 "Katya Gets To Work." RuPaul's Drag Race S7 E1. Video Clip. *LOGOTV.com* http://www.logotv.com/video-clips/b84pew/rupauls-drag-race-katya-gets-to-work (Retrieved 18 April 2016).

15 Andre Akimov: His name is Katya. *Russian Chicago Magazine* 125 (May 2015) https://russianchicagomag.com/katya_zamo_eng/.

16 UNHhhh episode 01. Directed by Trixie Mattel and Katya Zamolodchikova. *YouTube* (25 March 2016). https://www.youtube.com/watch?v=uSwY31GMqY0&t=20s (last accessed 15 August 2022).

17 The Trixie & Katya Show. Viceland 2017–2018. *IMDb.* https://www.imdb.com/title/tt7557336/ (last accessed 15 August 2022).

18 Hurricane Bianca: From Russia with Hate, directed by Matt Kugelman. *IMDb. 2018.* https://www.imdb.com/title/tt6113122/ (last accessed 15 August 2022).

19 Trixie Mattel / Katya Zamolodchikova: *Trixie and Katya's Guide to Modern Womanhood.* London 2020.

RuFLECTIONS videos are presented on individual YouTube channels, and Katya's was titled "We Love Katya." In episode one,[20] Katya introduces herself to the audience in an inner monologue. In heavily accented English, she tells the audience that she came to the US in the 1990s in search of a better life; that she works as a sex worker; that she loves money and decadence. Her sentences frequently start with "In Russia, we / no one / everyone . . ." indicating that her character – her melancholy, sex- and body-positive attitude, her ruthlessness and shamelessness etc. – are cultural and not individual aspects. Katya's look is also stereotypical. She wears tight clothes, very short tight-fit dresses, a lot of animal print, fur hats, and (fake) diamonds.

While Katya is so far unprecedented within the genre of commercial drag, she is by far not the only Russian sex worker within the recent US comedy media landscape. Katya appeared approximately at the same time as Svetlana Maximovksaya,[21] an LA-based Russian brothel owner and elite sex worker played by Jewish American comedian Iris Bahr. Other examples of similar representations are several female Russian characters performed by American comedian Kathryn McKinnon in recent episodes of the late-night live television sketch comedy and variety show *Saturday Night Live* as well as the wrestling persona Zoya the Destroyer played by Jewish American actress Alison Brie Schermerhor.[22]

None of these representations are meant to be taken seriously since they are all deeply embedded into different forms of comedy. Yet, their jokes rest on the embodiment of stereotypical and essentialist ideas about Russian women. Since none of the mentioned performers and comedians is of Russian descent, yet their embodiment is distinctly signified as Russian, they can be understood as ethnic drag.

Performance studies and queer theory scholar Brian Herrera defines "ethnic drag" as performance strategy that brings forward "attributes of racial and ethnic distinction in order to highlight the poignancy, absurdity, artifice, and/or politics of a particular culture's history of racialized difference."[23] Ethnic drag, according to German theater studies scholar D.C. Katrin Sieg,[24] is based on the theories of parody and performativity developed by American rhetoric and gender studies scholar Judith Butler. Additionally, Sieg builds on theories on the perpetual process of the social construction of race, theorized by Asian American ethnic studies scholar Michael Omi together with American sociologist and race theorist Howard Winant.[25] It shows race

---

20 RuFLECTIONS: episode 01. We Love Katya. *YouTube* (04 March 2015). https://www.youtube.com/watch?v=Saq6zLJ1GLE (last accessed 15 August 2022).

21 *Sventlana*, HDNet 2010–2011.

22 *GLOW*, Netflix 2017.

23 Brian Herrera: Ethnic Drag. In: *Reading Contemporary Performance*, ed. by Meiling Cheng / Gabrielle H. Cody. London / New York 2015, 114–115.

24 Katrin Sieg: *Ethnic Drag. Performing Race, MEMOIRS Nation, Sexuality in West Germany*. Ann Arbor, MI 2002.

25 Michael Omi / Howard Winant: *Racial Formation in the United States. From the 1960s to the 1990s*. New York 1994.

as "masquerade,"[26] thereby drawing attention to the workings of race and ethnicity as continually re-produced significations on the stage and beyond.

Ethnic drag underscores the artificiality of performances of ethnic or racial distinction through accents, physical gestures, and postures or costumes, as well as through social behavior or character traits. Often, ethnic drag performances center on the racial masquerade itself. No matter if ethnic drag is intended to be a celebration of cultural difference or an anti-racist critique, "it exploits the performance event to highlight the theatrical and aesthetic conventions that construct race and/or ethnicity within a given culture,"[27] states Herrera.

While I agree with Herrera that ethnic drag can have the potential to critique the construction of race in contemporary culture, I am not entirely convinced that every ethnic drag manages to perform anti-racism. Queer Asian American performance artist Tina Takemoto cautions against an all too optimistic view on ethnic drag as anti-racist critique. Reacting to Herrera's definition and based on her own experience as a performer she points "to the instability of interventionist art practices and the risk that [ethnic drag] can also be read as reinforcing the stereotypes that are under scrutiny."[28]

I want to argue that ethnic drag that performs Russianness is in particular danger of becoming racialized ethnic commodification because, as already pointed out, there is little public discourse on the Orientalization of Russian bodies. This is despite the fact that Katya, much like all the other fictional characters I just mentioned, emerges within a decidedly liberal, pro-gay, and occasionally feminist context. Considering this, my intuition towards these figures is that there is a connection between the emergence of Russian women we can laugh about, and core ideas of what Asian American queer theorist David Eng[29] calls queer liberalism. In fact, I argue that their co-appearance is not coincidental but a consequence of queer liberalism's unwillingness to deal with racial and class-based inequalities.

To deconstruct McCook's performance as racialized ethnic commodification, his embodiment of Russian womanhood and femininity need to be understood as racializing practices in the first place. Identifying white bodies as racialized is difficult. Although Jamaican-born British Marxist, postcolonial and cultural theorist Stuart Hall established an understanding of race as denoting essentialized bodily attributes, mindsets, and cultural aspects beyond phenotypes, the concept is still strongly connected to forms of discrimination based on skin color, hence to Black and People of Color. Accordingly, the application of the concept and term of racialization to mark forms of othering of white populations runs the risk of denying white privilege and accordingly anti-black sentiments and colorism. Yet, Eastern European historians

---

26 Sieg: *Ethnic Drag*, 2.

27 Herrera: *Ethnic Drag*, 115.

28 Tina Takemoto: Memoirs of Björk-Geisha. In: *Reading Contemporary Performance*, ed. by Meiling Cheng / Gabrielle H. Cody. London / New York 2015, 115–117.

29 David L. Eng: *The Feeling of Kinship. Queer Liberalism and the Racialization of Intimacy*. Durham 2010.

such as Joseph Rouček have long shown that twentieth century America had a concept and category of Slavic people that signified "'inferior' nations and 'races.'"[30] This concept was applied through pre-WWII immigration laws; but beyond the legal, it was also very much part of the general discourses on Western civilization and progress. Although the racist language of eugenics is no longer in use today, the signification of Russians, Eastern Europeans, and Eurasians as latecomers to or outside of modernity and progress is still persistent. Moreover, while it might seem that "Slavic" is today understood to be rather a cultural than a racial category, the construction of Russians and especially Russian women within US media suggests that embodied racial difference is still part of the concept.

3 Western Modernity, Gay Liberalism, and Russian Otherness

Katya's Russianness is constructed through several visual, bodily, and psychological characteristics: her exaggerated and *cheap* style and makeup, which includes her big blond hair, immediately evoke a Russian identification in the Anglophone audience, (see Fig. 1).

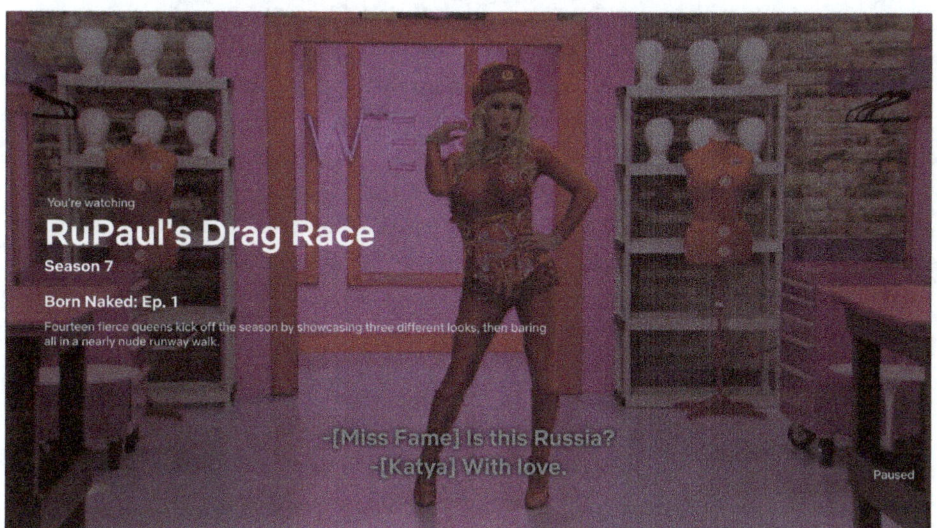

Fig. 1: Katya in her Signature Stage Costumes.
Screenshot: *Drag Race* Season Seven, Episode One. Born Naked. (min 2:57). Netflix.

---

30 Joseph S. Rouček: The Image of the Slav in U.S. History and in Immigration Policy. *The American Journal of Economics and Sociology* 28/1 (1969), 29–48.

Her exaggerated embodiment of Russian signifiers is complemented through her dark, disillusioned, slightly depressed yet ruthless character, and of course her thick Russian accent, together with a general *slowness*. These characteristics signify her low-class status, expressed through her choice of kitschy, over-the-top costumes, accessories and make-up, her whiteness, her blond hair, only mitigated through her slowness in comprehension and speech as well as her thick rolling "R," and her dark moody little sad character. Additionally, Katya is defined as Russian through her wish or aspirations and her belief in the American Dream.

In fact, all of Katya's characteristics, and particularly her stereotypically aggressive sexuality, go back to the Enlightenment's orientalist ideas of Russia as almost modern, almost progressive, almost, but not quite Western, or civilized as delineated by the mentioned historians Wolff[31] and Neumann.[32] The project of Western Enlightenment structurally enclosed Eastern Europe and Russia, and Eastern bodies in-between, Western European civilization and the "barbarian Orient": they are to be seen as similar, but not the same. Building on Wolff's and Neumann's work allows one to account for the signification of Russian female bodies such as Katya's fictional body as old-fashioned, developmentally delayed, overtly sexualized and commodified. The concept of orientalism allows the Russian body to be identified as the *similar Other* to the white European (American). Yet, neither Saïd's original iteration nor Wolff's and Neumann's adaptations provide language to describe the specific demarcation of otherness on white Eastern or Slavic bodies. Placing orientalist understandings of the Russian body as *not-quite-modern* within critiques of current liberal US-American sexual politics as well as discourses that address the construction of American races on the intersection of class and gender might help to understand Katya as racialized embodiment of Russianness.

Building on the assumption that *RuPaul's Drag Race* is a space that signifies American national belonging and queer neoliberalism, and that it negotiates race and racialization, previously mentioned feminist media theorists Sabrina Strings and Long T. Bui argue that the show fashions racialized and class-based caricatures to satisfy market demands and to expand the brand. Adapting "minority subculture for mass consumption and mainstream titillation," season three of the show for example increasingly pushed contestants into "stereotypical racial identities" under the innocent label of "giving 'personality.'"[33] Demanding *authenticity*, People of Color characters on the show are required to perform what is understood to be their off-stage racial identity. "This policing of racial identity for certain minority characters re-inscribes them as fundamentally 'Other' [. . .], re-instating race as 'natural' or 'real' at the same moment as it undermines gender's 'realness.'"[34] Thus, *Drag Race* contributes

---

31 Wolff: *Inventing Eastern Europe.*
32 Neumann: *Russia and the Idea of Europe.*
33 Strings / Bui: *She Is Not Acting, She Is,* 824.
34 Strings / Bui: *She Is Not Acting, She Is,* 823.

to the naturalization of stereotypes through the signification and demand of "racial 'realness'" as "avant-garde."[35] This had the unfortunate effect of not only commodifying or stereotyping, but effectively re-essentializing race.

Katya's Russianness needs to be understood within this arena of essentialized racialized drag queens on the one hand and white individualism on the other. Following Strings and Bui, and their argument that People of Color performers are limited to their heritage, it can be said that Irish American McCook's embodiment of a Russian sex-worker is allowed because he is white, which means not reduced to his heritage. However, given the progressive liberal audience of the show, blackface or any other clearly racist racial impersonations would be forbidden. Since Slavic people are understood as white, the same does not apply to the Russian drag.

3.1 Queer Liberalism, Homonormativity, and Homonationalism

Two further aspects made any contestations of McCook's embodiment of Russian femininity unlikely and furthered its success: the connotation of drag shows as progressive on the one hand and the looming *New Cold War* between the US and Russia on the other. Queer theorist Matthew Goldmark argues convincingly that *Drag Race* is a "tale of gay integration and social mobility"[36] that "performs a fiction of national improvement wherein the contestant's body serves as a metonym for the national one."[37] He reveals what he calls a "critical paradox" at the heart of US gay integration into the imaginary national body: "though contestants must work to prove their desire for the United States, the United States presented by Drag Race is imagined to have embraced its gay subjects already."[38]

Goldmark shows that *Drag Race* follows a model of social progress where certain sexual identities are granted the possibility to enter the concept of the nation. To do so, however, racial and class-based inequalities need to be negated. Only if racial and economic divisions are ignored can the US queer community appear as a coherent group that can be integrated, "based on individualism and merit."[39]

One strategy to create notions of unity and racial equality is to focus on questions of sexual freedom globally. "Contestants perform for a 'world' that looks to the United States as a social trendsetter,"[40] to use Goldmark's words. Although he does not refer to Puar, he describes homonationalism, a nationalism that uses "'acceptance' and 'tol-

---

35 Strings / Bui: *She Is Not Acting, She Is,* 823.

36 Matthew Goldmark. NATIONAL DRAG. The Language of Inclusion in RuPaul's Drag Race. *GLQ* 21/4 (2015), 501–520.

37 Goldmark: National Drag, 510.

38 Goldmark: National Drag, 510.

39 Goldmark: National Drag, 507.

40 Goldmark: National Drag, 508.

erance' for gay and lesbian subjects [as] a barometer"[41] to evaluate other nations and people. Homonationalism is "a facet of modernity and a historical shift marked by the entrance of (some) homosexual bodies as worthy of protection by nation-states."[42] Within homonationalism, gays and lesbians are put forth as visible signs of modernity and progress. The inclusion of gay subjects in the idea of the nation and their construction as signs of modernity, however, demands the exclusion of racialized Others, who used to be seen as having achieved progress but are now among the uncivilized or half-civilized.[43] In other words, the positive progressive attitude is constructed in opposition to racialized populations, who allegedly threaten its endurance.

Puar developed her concept to understand how US xenophobia and Islamophobia structure racialized Muslim subjects as (homophobic, misogynist) terrorist subjects.

Researchers working on discourses concerning Russia, however, have long pointed out that Russia and Russians are being evaluated according to the same standards of gay liberation and gay rights, with the same effect of supporting Western hegemony. Some, such as Helen Jefferson Lenskyj[44] and Fred LeBlanc,[45] use the framework of homonationalism to signify the current evaluation of Russia. They show that US and Western European national discourses refer to homophobia in law and society to *Other* Russia and Russians as intolerant, backward, and uncivilized, and confirm themselves as highly progressive and modern nations and people. LeBlanc goes as far as to say "in 2013 Russian homophobia seems to have momentarily trumped Arab homophobia in the media's discussion."[46]

Although the drag persona Katya does not signify Russian homophobia or its victims on the surface, it does so within the context of *Drag Race,* which stands – as shown – for gay liberalism and the US progress itself. In this context, Katya's Russianness evokes discourses about Russian homophobia without having to explicitly verbalize it. In turn, any mentioning of Russia – which is also known for hating drag queens[47] – helps to elevate *Drag Race* as national sign for US superiority, progress, and tolerance. Hence the critical framework of homonationalism can shed light on the construction of her racialized body and personality.

---

41 Puar: *Terrorist Assemblages*, 4.

42 Puar: Rethinking Homonationalism, 337.

43 Puar: Rethinking Homonationalism, 337.

44 Helen Jefferson Lenskyj: *Sexual Diversity and the Sochi 2014 Olympics. No More Rainbows.* New York, NY 2014.

45 Fred Joseph Leblanc: Sporting Homonationalism. Russian Homophobia, Imaginative Geographies & The 2014 Sochi Olympic Games. *Sociology Association of Aotearoa New Zealand Annual Conference 2013* (2013), 1–14.

46 LeBlanc: Sporting Homonationalism, 7.

47 Yulia Yurtaeva: Ein Schwarzer Rabe gegen Conchita Wurst oder: Wovor hat Russland Angst? In: *Eurovision Song Contest. Eine kleine Geschichte zwischen Körper, Geschlecht und Nation,* ed. by Christine Ehardt / Georg Vogt / Florian Wagner. Vienna 2015, 111–135.

3.2 Gendered Racialization and Classed Whiteness

Kaya's physical features, her style, and her mannerism and speech are unmistakably Russian: her (fake) blond mane, over-the-top style that looks "cheap," her ruthlessness, and sadness; her simple mind and character; her athletic, hourglass-shaped body, with long legs and big tits. In their combination, all these markers differentiate her from other contestants and are at the same time unmistakably ethnically and culturally specific.

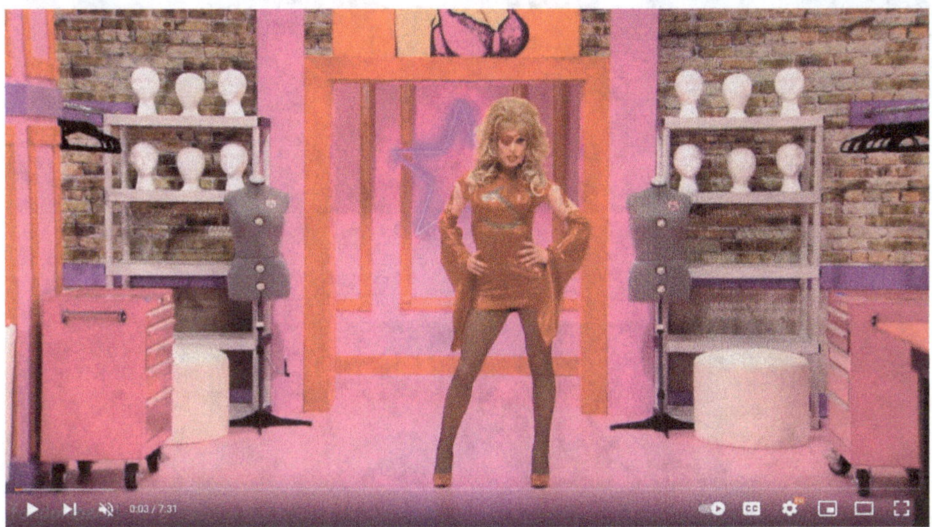

Fig. 2: Katya's big, artificially blond hair, her glowing eyes with exaggerated make-up.
Screenshot: *All Star* Season Two, Episode One – Introducing Katya. (min 3:00). Netflix.

Katya's working-class or low-class status, heterosexuality, her physical appearance, style and (body) language together signify her as Slavic. The combination of her whiteness, her big, artificially blond hair, her glowing eyes with exaggerated make-up (Fig. 2), her big fur hats (Fig. 1), and her occasional Teeth Grillz (Fig. 3 and Fig. 4) – a not-so-subtle reference to the gold teeth dental prostheses that were still common among Russians during the 1990s – and the usage of screaming colors, especially the communist red, creates the meaning of Russianness. These physical and visual aspects correspond to her naiveté and sexual promiscuity. Since these features are not all and not primarily understood to be a result of socialization and culture but seem to emerge from and reside within her body and mind, they can be understood as racialized aspects.

Using the notion of racialization in reference to white bodies is not without risk. It risks the essentialization and naturalization of cultural signifiers. However, I argue that in understanding Katya as embodiment of essentialized ideas of Russianness, the

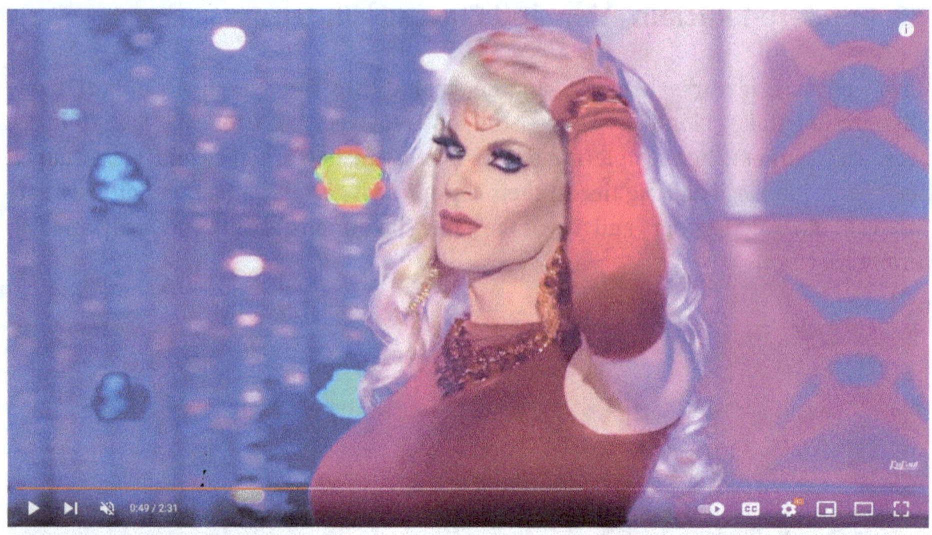

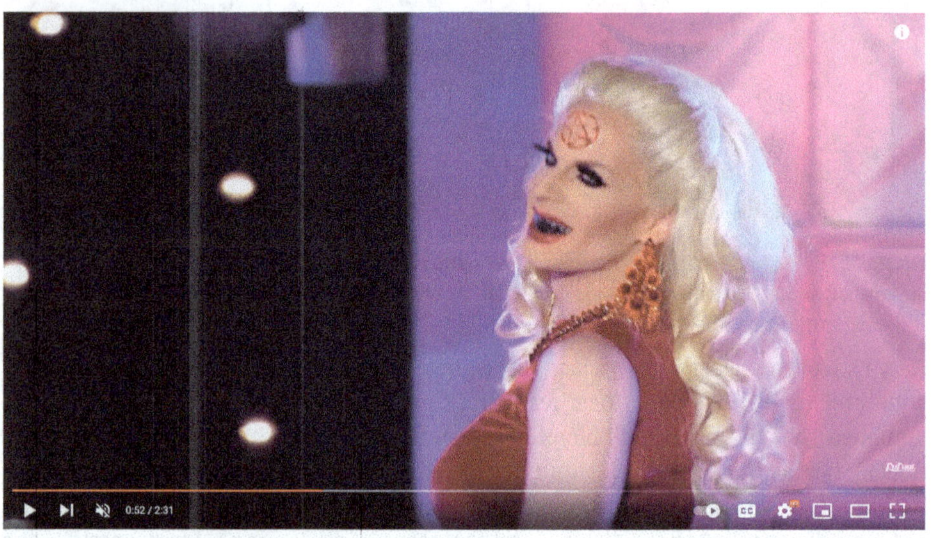

Fig. 3 and Fig. 4: Her occasional Teeth Grillz.
Screenshot: *All Star* Season Two, Episode Four, YouTube. https://www.youtube.com/watch?v=wSSudLKIkkk (min 0:49 und min 0:51) (last accessed 15 August 2022).

general artificiality and constructed character of processes of racialization through sexualized and classed physical and cultural (personality) aspects becomes clear. Race, according to Stuart Hall, is a "badge, a token, a sign, [. . .] a signifier, and [. . .] racialized behavior and difference needs to be understood as a discursive, not necessarily as a genetic or biological fact."[48] Signifiers such as race need to be understood as unstable and in flux. Yet, their meaning is neither arbitrary nor random. The "stratification insignia"[49] that racially determine Slavic women are subtle and there are no analytical tools to identify and name "racialized physical characteristics like hair, teeth, body type, and clothing styles as well as education, religion, and 'values.'"[50]

I argue that these insignia can be read exclusively in contrast to the backdrop of the surroundings in which they appear. *RuPaul's Drag Race* is the perfect platform to make Katya appear as a Russian figure, and the Russian figure Katya is the perfect other to make US-American homonationalism effective.

Although Katya's performance of bodily differences is highly stereotypical and based on an assemblage of problematic ideas of physical and cultural difference, they are not censured, because this form of othering does not manifest itself in discourses around color and race. Since it is commonly agreed that Russians are white, orientalist impersonations of Russian figures can appeal to racist ideas about Slavs in general, and white Russian women specifically, yet are not seen as hateful.

I argue that the contemporary covert racialization of (female) Russian bodies is not an unlucky occurrence but one aspect of a form of homonationalism that depends on the very visible and widespread critique of Russian homophobia in mainstream discourses. The usage of Puar's concept of homonationalism for the US view on Russians runs the risk of mitigating or relativizing the violence against Black people and People of Color, if the nuances of racialization are all lumped together into discourses around phenotypes. Yet, I argue that homonationalism operates through the racialization of multiple and different racial others, and positions those others, although in different ways, in a hierarchical relation to the white norm. Moreover, the categories or aspects applied to racialize these multiple others vary from phenotype to dis/ability, mannerism, bodily and cognitive movements and functions etc. Importantly, the white others are constructed in relation to Black bodies and Bodies of Color. To put it bluntly, the orientalism within current neoliberal homonationalism signifies white developmentally delayed Russian bodies and Brown Chechen bodies on a scale between the white superior (American) people and the utterly barbaric Brown and Black oriental others, whose developmental location is even further removed from the Western hegemonic centers. Importantly, they are inherently classed.

---

48 Stuart Hall: *Race, the Floating Signifier.* A Lecture Given at Goldsmiths College in London, 1997. Transcript: Sut Jhalley, Media Education Foundation. http://www.mediaed.org (last accessed 21 June 2015).

49 Hall quoted in Anca Parvulescu: *The Traffic in Women's Work. Eastern European Migration and the Making of Europe.* Chicago / London 2014, 14.

50 Parvulescu: *The Traffic in Women's Work,* 14.

Gender studies scholar Anca Parvulescu argues that class determines the racialized hierarchy of migrants from the global South and East within the global West.[51] Russian or Ukrainian women, Parvulescu continues, become racialized in the context of migration through their low-class status and a low-class status signifies their racialized otherness in this context. Although Parvulescu notes that skin color is not the determining factor for the racialization of Eastern European women within North Western contexts, she argues that these women are nevertheless hierarchically positioned or labelled as "not quite white."[52] She arrives at this interpretation because she rightly notices that skin color corresponds uncomfortably with the economically produced hierarchy in Europe (like in the US), where Brown and Black people get the lowest wages. She further supports her argument by referring to Rosi Braidotti, who shows that "[p]eople from the Balkans, or the South-Western regions of Europe, in so far as they are not yet 'good Europeans,' they are also not quite as 'white' as others."[53] With this reference Parvulescu suggests that all Central Eastern, South Eastern and Eastern European women are equally racialized. This generalization, however, is highly debatable. I agree with Parvulescu and Braidotti that economic factors play a crucial role in the racialization of Eastern European and Russian women in the context of Western Europe as well as the USA. However, I disagree with Parvulescu's proposal that the racialization necessarily signifies a less white skin color. Based on the works of critical whiteness studies scholars,[54] I argue that very specific forms of racialization mark Russian, Ukrainian, Belarussian, Serbian and Polish immigrants despite or in correspondence with their assessment as white, while very different tropes of Southernness mark the bodies of some people from the Balkans. Building further on the findings of feminist scholar Kimberly Williams[55] and her study on US discourses on Russian women during the 1990s and early 2000s, I claim that although white, Russian women are constructed as bodily different through factors such as style, body language, bodily affect, mental capacities and features, and sexuality, which are all connected to class (Fig. 5a and Fig. 5b are a good example of the cheap glamor – plastic jeweler, high fringe boots, fake flowers, thick black eye make-up – that signifies lower classness and Katya's clumsy failure to mimic female elegance).

The racialization of Slavic women is a "class-occupational stratification," which "does not overlap with familiar patterns of racial stratification."[56] This fact does not

---

51 Parvulescu: *The Traffic in Women's Work*.

52 Parvulescu: *The Traffic in Women's Work*, 14.

53 Rosi Braidotti: On Becoming European. In: *Women Migrants from East to West. Gender, Mobility and Belonging in Contemporary Europe*, ed. by Luisa Passerini et al. New York 2007, 23– 44, 34.

54 David R. Roediger: *Colored White. Transcending the Racial Past*. Berkeley / Los Angeles / London 2002, 139–186; Matthew Jacobson: *Roots Too. White Ethnic Revival in Post-Civil Rights America*. Cambridge, MA 2006.

55 Kimberly Williams: *Imagining Russia. Making Feminist Sense of American Nationalism in U.S.-Russian Relations*. Albany, NY 2012, 4.

56 Parvulescu: *The Traffic in Women's Work*, 14.

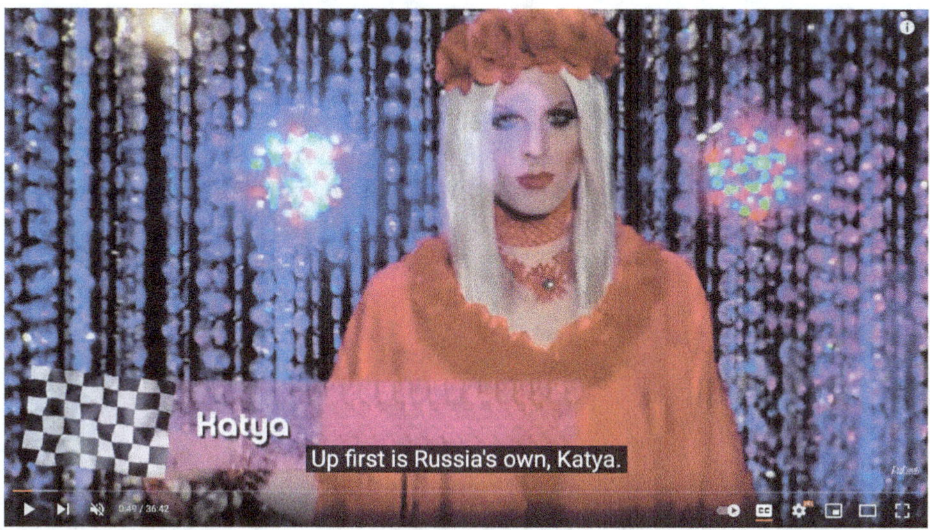

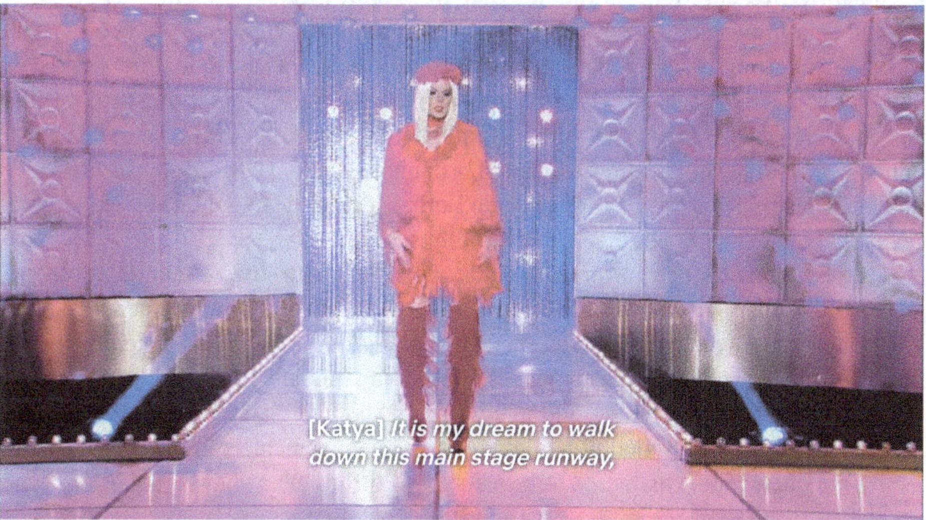

Fig. 5a and Fig. 5b: Plastic jeweler, high fringe boots, fake flowers, thick black eye make-up.
Screenshot: *Drag Race* Season Seven, Episode One, Born Naked Challenge (min 24:07). Netflix.

make Slavic bodies less white. On the contrary, white Russian and other Slavic women's whiteness is particularly visible within US popular culture. However, class-occupational stratification denominates the Slavic body as *Other*. Katya's Slavic body is constructed through her working-classness and her self-definition as a sex worker (she uses the term *prostitute*). Katya lacks the sophistication, politeness and other manners of a bourgeois lady because she is a sex worker and being Russian predetermines her to become one. She is loud and direct, and her behavior seems unpolished and crude (see Fig. 3 and Fig. 4). Within the context of Drag Race we understand these aspects as belonging to a low class but we also easily identify all of them as emerging from her Russian heritage.

3.3 Sex(y)

Her racial stratification is accomplished through her whiteness and her Russianness makes her so appealing to the Western gaze. A feminist scholar working on Eastern European representation, Roumiana Deltcheva states that the whiteness of Slavic women is an important factor for why they "have become a favorite and convenient site for the accumulation of stereotypical images feeding Western lust for the exotic and fear of the 'barbaric.'"[57] Through their whiteness, they "are not drastically Other and thus are endowed with an aura of familiarity, [. . .] and yet they are not fully familiar [. . .], perceived as almost Oriental, as almost exotic, yet not fully so."[58] Whiteness, the position between familiarity and otherness, and the emphasis on (hetero)sexuality together complete Katya's Russianness.

The Eastern European woman is generally often pictured as a femme fatale, "alluring, slightly Oriental or exotic temptress with an edge of vampirism"[59] in North Western media. Especially Russian female bodies are doubly signified as (dangerously) female – first through the imagination of Russia as a feminine (or emasculated) country of bad-tempered white women and drunk incapable men[60] and, second, through the imagination of the celebration of femininity by Russian women. These highly sexualized figures are often willing to use sex as a weapon and means to an end.[61]

---

57 Roumiana Deltcheva: Eastern Women in Western Chronotypes. Representation of East European Women in Western Film after 1989. In: *Vampirettes, Wretches and Amazons. Western Representations of East European Women*, ed. by Valentina Glajar / Domnica Radulescu. New York, NY 2004, 161–185, 162.
58 Deltcheva: *Eastern Women*, 162.
59 Valentina Glajar / Domnica Radulescu: Introduction. In: id.: *Vampirettes, Wretches and Amazons. Western Representations of East European Women*. New York, NY 2004, 1–11, 6.
60 Williams: *Imagining Russia*, 116–118.
61 Williams: *Imagining Russia*, 123.

Katya's whiteness, her low-class status as a sex worker, her sexualization and her style in combination with the fact that she appears as slow or developmentally delayed (her slow speech and logical errors etc.) signify her as a pre-modern, pre-enlightened Russian body. This depiction is not only misogynist, classist and Orientalizing, but also inherently ableist.

Moreover, this embodiment of Russian femininity needs to be read against McCook's public denouncing of Russian and particularly Chechen homophobia.[62] Katya is the bad joke that emerges on the surface of queer liberalism and its homonationalism.

4 Conclusion

McCook's ethnic drag fails to make the construction of race visible and highlight the violence of racial and cultural prejudice. His comedy rests on the backwardness, slowness and brazenness of Katya's character, without a reference to anti-racist and anti-orientalist politics that address specifically Russianness, hence it is ultimately not only misogynic, but also orientalizing. Through this lack of a critical discourse on the Orientalization of Russianness within liberal progressive and anti-racist discourses, the comedy and drag can take up and confirm derogatory discourses about Russian women without being questioned or criticized. Tracing Katya's body performance and style back to earlier comedic versions of ethnic drag, I was able to show that the *RuPaul's Drag Race* contestant is just one – albeit very successful – iteration of an earlier version of the classist, orientalist and racialized impersonation of Russian femininity and womanhood, performed to joke about Eastern backwardness and to affirm the moral and cultural superiority of Western liberalism. Katya's version of Orientalizing ethnic drag is particularly interesting since it emerges in the context of contemporary female drag performances, which are semantically connoted as highly progressive formats that celebrate LGBTIQ+ existence. Within and against the genre of gender drag, Katya's embodied performance shows how the devaluation or even abjection of Russian femininity and womanhood in the form of comedy and drag emerges in the wake of Western liberal pro-gay agendas and discourses that can be framed with Jasbir Puar as homonationalist.

Importantly, Katya appears as a racialized Slavic woman through gendered and classed markers: her strong Russian accent, a cheap 90s under-class style. In the context of the show, Katya's Russianness, her racialized body and character emerge against liberal progressive discourses that condemn Russian homophobia. Hence, her figure becomes a venire to preserve the narrative of a progressive American gay-positive culture and negate racial and class-based inequality. Katya embodies the de-

---

62 Katya and Milk at the Voices 4 Chechnya March NYC. *YouTube.* (October 2017) https://www.youtube.com/watch?v=1gQM9M6e2X8 (last accessed 16 August 2022).

velopmental delay of Russia in a comical way and offers Americans the opportunity to care for the victims of Russian homophobia and affirm their belonging to an in comparison progressive nation. Importantly, the lack of critical discourse on the Orientalization of Russian and other white, non-European bodies in combination with the unwillingness to address class inequality within American gay culture inhibit the understanding of figures such as Katya as critical commentary on ethnic signification. Understanding Katya's ethnic drag as a common form of embodied performance that makes ethnic difference visible and understandable through class-based bodily performances highlights the urgency to mainstream a class-critical self-reflection of gay media culture and beyond. Moreover, it amplifies the necessity to develop analytical tools that allow to think of ethnicity and racialization as issues that are not only or exclusively signified through assigned differences in skin color. In other words, it prompts the development of critical methodologies that are able to address racialized difference in other terms than a scale of whiteness, and a reevaluation of how ethnicity, race, class, gender and ability on the intersection create certain non-European bodies as *Others*.

Bibliography

Akimov, Andre: His name is Katya. *Russian Chicago Magazine* 125 (May 2015). https://russianchicagomag.com/katya_zamo_eng/ (last accessed 05 April 2018).

Braidotti, Rosi: On Becoming European. In: *Women Migrants from East to West. Gender, Mobility and Belonging in Contemporary Europe*, ed. by Passerini, Luisa et al. New York, NY 2007, 23–44.

Deltcheva, Roumiana: Eastern Women in Western Chronotypes. Representation of East European Women in Western Film after 1989. In: *Vampirettes, Wretches and Amazons. Western Representations of East European Women*, ed. by Glajar, Valentina / Radulescu, Domnica. New York, NY 2004, 161–185.

Eng, David L.: *The Feeling of Kinship. Queer Liberalism and the Racialization of Intimacy*. Durham 2010.

Flores, Jason: No Matter How Much You Like RuPaul's Drag Race, It's Still Problematic. *Pride* (April 2016). https://www.pride.com/firstperson/2016/4/07/no-matter-how-much-you-rupauls-drag-race-its-still-problematic (last accessed 10 April 2018).

Glajar, Valentina / Radulescu, Domnica: Introduction. In: id.: *Vampirettes, Wretches and Amazons. Western Representations of East European Women*. New York, NY 2004, 1–11.

Goldmark, Matthew. NATIONAL DRAG. The Language of Inclusion in RuPaul's Drag Race. *GLQ* 21/4 (2015), 501–520.

Gonzalez, Sandra: RuPaul makes Emmy history. *CNN*. (September 2021). https://www.cnn.com/2021/09/19/entertainment/rupaul-emmys/index.html (last accessed 15 August 2022).

Gonsalez, Marcos: Fantasies of Valentina. *TSQ: Transgender Studies Quarterly* 9/4 (2022), 587–608.

Hall, Stuart: *Race, the Floating Signifier*. A Lecture Given at Goldsmiths College in London, 1997. Transcript: Sut Jhalley, Media Education Foundation. http://www.mediaed.org (last accessed 21 June 2015).

Herrera, Brian: Ethnic Drag. In: *Reading Contemporary Performance*, ed. by Cheng, Meiling / Cody, Gabrielle H. London / New York, NY 2015, 114–115.

Jacobson, Matthew: *Roots Too. White Ethnic Revival in Post-Civil Rights America*. Cambridge, MA 2006.

Jefferson Lenskyj, Helen: *Sexual Diversity and the Sochi 2014 Olympics. No More Rainbows*. New York, NY 2014.

John, Grace: 'RuPaul's Drag Race' Often Displays Racial Bias to Favor White Queens. https://studybreaks.com/tvfilm/rupauls-drag-race/ (last accessed 10 April 2018).

LeBlanc, Fred: Sporting Homonationalism. Russian Homophobia, Imaginative Geographies & The 2014 Sochi Olympic Games. *Sociology Association of Aotearoa New Zealand Annual Conference 2013* (2013), 1–14.

Lee, Stephan. 'RuPaul's Drag Race': Miss Congeniality winner Katya speaks! *Entertainment Weekly's EW.com*. (June 2015). https://ew.com/article/2015/06/02/rupauls-drag-race-miss-congeniality-winner-katya-speaks/ (last accessed 31 January 2022).

LeMaster, Lore/tta / Michael Tristano: Performing (Asian American Trans) Femme on RuPaul's Drag Race: Dis/orienting Racialized Gender, or, Performing Trans Femme of Color, Regardless. *Journal of International and Intercultural Communication* 16/1 (2023), 1–18.

Neumann, Ivar: *Russia and the Idea of Europe*. New York / London 1996.

Oliver, Maria: Night Watch. Perestroika. *Boston Globe* (April 2011). http://archive.boston.com/ae/music/articles/2011/04/29/night_watch_perestroika/ (last accessed 06 April 2018).

Omi, Michael / Winnant Howard: *Racial Formation in the United States. From the 1960s to the 1990s*. New York, NY 1994.

Parvulescu, Anca: *The Traffic in Women's Work. Eastern European Migration and the Making of Europe*. Chicago / London 2014.

Puar, Jasbir: Rethinking Homonationalism. *International Journal of Middle East Studies* 45/2 (2013), 336–339.

Puar, Jasbir: *Terrorist Assemblages. Homonationalism in Queer Times*. Durham, NC 2007.

Roucek, Joseph S.: The Image of the Slav in U.S. History and in Immigration Policy. *The American Journal of Economics and Sociology* 28/1 (1969), 29–48.

RuPaul: *What's the Tee?* SoundCloud, episode 76 – Katya. https://soundcloud.com/rupaul/episode-76-katya (last accessed 15 December 2016).

Saïd, Edward: *Orientalism*. New York, NY 1978.

Sieg, Katrin: *Ethnic Drag. Performing Race, MEMOIRS Nation, Sexuality in West Germany*. Ann Arbor, MI 2002.

Strings, Sabrina / Bui, Long T. "She Is Not Acting, She Is." The conflict between gender and racial realness on RuPaul's Drag Race. *Feminist Media Studies* 14/5 (2014), 822–836.

Takemoto, Tina: Memoirs of Björk-Geisha. In: *Reading Contemporary Performance*, ed. by Cheng, Meiling / Cody, Gabrielle H. London / New York 2015, 115–117.

Williams, Kimberly: *Imagining Russia. Making Feminist Sense of American Nationalism in U.S.-Russian Relations*. Albany 2012.

Wolff, Larry: *Inventing Eastern Europe. The Map of Civilization on the Mind of the Enlightenment*. Stanford, CA 1994.

Yurtaeva, Yulia: Ein Schwarzer Rabe gegen Conchita Wurst oder: Wovor hat Russland Angst? In: *Eurovision Song Contest. Eine kleine Geschichte zwischen Körper, Geschlecht und Nation*, ed. by Ehardt, Christine / Vogt, Georg / Wagner, Florian. Vienna 2015, 111–135.

Videography

Katya and Milk at the Voices 4 Chechnya March NYC. *YouTube*. https://www.youtube.com/watch?v=1gQM9M6e2X8 (last accessed 09 April 2018).

Katya Gets To Work. *RuPaul's Drag Race S7 E1*. Video Clip. LOGOTV.com. http://www.logotv.com/video-clips/b84pew/rupauls-drag-race-katya-gets-to-work (last accessed 18 April 2016).

Katya Zamolodchikova. *RuPaul's Drag Race Wiki*. http://rupaulsdragrace.wikia.com/wiki/Katya_Zamolodchikova (last accessed 09 April 2018).

O'Keeffe, Kevin / Rondriguez, Mathew: Racism in RuPaul's Drag Race. The Kiki Ep 3. *YouTube*.
(August 2018). https://www.youtube.com/watch?v=T3Gj2wUgKpI (last accessed 16 August 2022).
The Trixie & Katya Show. Viceland 2017–2018. *IMDb*. https://www.imdb.com/title/tt7557336/ (last accessed
15 August 2022).
RuFLECTIONS – episode 01 – We Love Katya. *YouTube*. https://www.youtube.com/watch?v=Saq6zLJ1GLE
(last accessed 15 August 2022).
UNHhhh episode 1, Directed by Trixie Mattel / Katya Zamolodchikova. *YouTube*. https://www.youtube.com/
watch?v=uSwY31GMqY0&t=20s (last accessed 15 August 2022).

Sarah Rüß

"We Want the Right Kind of Gay" – Homonormative Representation of Lesbian Characters on Television

Abstract: In recent years, television series increasingly include representations of lesbians. This supposedly positive development, which enhances the public visibility of lesbians, however, is tethered to demands for assimilation into the heterosexual model, resulting in a homonormative lifestyle. Media representations, among other things, foster demands for a lifestyle centered around monogamy and reproduction, through establishing, supporting, and disseminating a normative framework on which social tolerance and acceptance rest. This framework provides a model for a desirable lifestyle that focuses on marriage, monogamy, and raising children. Television series focusing on lesbian characters enact this normative framework through narrative by utilizing the sense of shame to invalidate non-homonormative lifestyles. This article will engage with this current, taking as its case studies the US American television series *The Fosters* and *The L Word*.

Keywords: Shame, affect, homonormativity, normativity, *The L Word, The Fosters*, television, lesbian

"We want the right kind of gay," states the producer of a talk show in the series *The L Word* during an off-stage conversation with Alice, one of the lesbian main characters of the series, and thus formulating a social presupposition at the same time. This implies a correct, i.e. normative form of gayness. Yet what is this assumed norm based on? In the Foucauldian sense, it is precisely the dispositive that constitutes an order of norming through jurisprudence, the theological apparatus of power, and intervening social processes of negotiation, which are positioned in between. The "right kind" of queerness thus becomes a requirement which is formulated from a position that is contingent on an inherently heteronormative discourse. More specifically, "the right kind of gay" implies that there is a "right" way of living in the "wrong"[1] way, and that this "right" life must be derived from (hetero-) normative principles of exclusion, as can be argued in terms of common theories of homonormativity.[2]

---

1 This dichotomy of good/bad; right/wrong in regard to a group consisting of a minority has been thoroughly discussed in Stuart Hall (ed.): The Spectacle of the Other. In: *Representation: Cultural Representation and Signifying Practices*. London 1997, 225–277.
2 For an elaboration of the concept of "homonormativity," see Lisa Duggan: *The Twilight of Equality? Neoliberalism, Cultural Politics, and the Attack on Democracy*. Boston, MA 2009; Michael Warner: *The*

It is precisely this tension between the logic of media representation, heteronormativity, and the "normalization" of homosexuality that this chapter addresses. Which discourses generate the normative, which apparatuses of normativity can be identified, and which regulative forces impact this process? Which norms are utilized in the process? Which representational logics do media representations of lesbian characters apply and renegotiate? How can the representation of a certain queer lifestyle lead to the shifting of hierarchies and the division of communities through the use of affects? In the following article, I will argue that affect economies based on normative structures regulate the media staging of lesbianism. This article focuses particularly on lesbian visibility, utilizing two TV series as case studies, namely *The L Word* (2004–2009) by Ilene Chaiken for Showtime and *The Fosters* (2013–2018) by Peter Paige and Bradley Bredeweg for ABC Family. I identify different modes of standardization of lesbian lifestyles, such as the promotion and advocacy for marriage and reproduction, in the narratives of the series *The L Word* and *The Fosters*. With a cumulative duration spanning from 2004 to 2018, the extensive runtime of both series facilitates a comprehensive analysis and comparative examination of the evolving dynamics and transformations that has occurred throughout the twenty-first century. In the following, I will elaborate upon the previous mentioned modes of enforcing a normative lifestyle through shame by means of some selected examples from both series.

1 Theoretical Preconception: Homonormativity and Queerness

Looking at the two series, two modes of operation for the depiction of lesbians become apparent. These are predominantly oriented towards heteronormative role models such as marriage, family life, and idyllic, suburban lifestyle.[3] For instance, heteronormativity and/or homonormativity is expressed in both chosen series through the pursuit of a monogamous relationship with the goal of marriage and a shared desire to have children. The series *The Fosters*, for example, depicts the ideal of a family consisting of two parents, children, and a single-family house in the suburbs. The two women Stef and Lena live in the suburbs of San Diego, where they raise their five children (some of which are biological, some are adopted, and some are foster-children) together. Stef works as a police officer, while Lena is an assistant principal

---

Trouble with Normal: Sex, Politics, and the Ethics of Queer Life. Cambridge, MA 2000; Jonathan Katz / Lisa Duggan: *The Invention of Heterosexuality*. New York, NY 1995; David Paternotte and Manon Tremblay (eds.): *The Ashgate Research Companion to Lesbian and Gay Activism*. Farnham 2015; Noreen Giffney / Michael O'Rourke: *The Ashgate Research Companion to Queer Theory*. Farnham 2009.

3 For an elaboration of the assimilation into the family-oriented heteronormativity, see David L. Eng: *The Feeling of Kinship: Queer Liberalism and the Racialization of Intimacy*. Durham, N.C. 2010, 27.

at her children's private school. Both move in a predominantly heterosexual environment in which they rarely see themselves as "different" or hardly question the hegemony of heterosexuality in the first seasons.

It is evident that the characters lead predominantly privileged lives, therefore departing from previous depictions of tragically suffering homosexual subjects. This change in the portrayal of living to a focus on a fulfilled (upper-)middle-class life, as is the case in *The Fosters*, is often showcased through the highly respected and well-paid professions of the protagonists such as professor, director of museums or schools, the police force, etc., and their living conditions characterized by the inhabitation of luxurious apartments, houses in the suburbs or wealthy neighborhoods of US metropolitan areas. The intention behind this change is to achieve acceptance through the staging of normality in the media. In contrast to *The Fosters*, the first episodes of *The L Word* were produced almost a decade earlier than the former and deal with concepts of *queer* life considerably more distant from the mainstream.[4] For instance, the series addresses topics such as the pregnancy of a trans*man[5] as well as concepts like the one of a chosen queer family. The aforementioned mode of operation becomes evident in *The L Word* through its particular focus on the interpersonal relationships of a group of friends of young, successful, predominantly lesbian women in Los Angeles.

Bette and Tina, a museum director (and later professor) and a film producer, are a couple living in a big house with a pool, trying to have a child together at the beginning of the series. Dana is a successful tennis player who tries to hide her homosexuality out of fear of losing her career and her advertising deals. Meanwhile, Shane lives in a house next door to them and is known for sleeping with (not committing to) a variety of women. She becomes a world-famous hairstylist as the series progresses. Similar to Shane, Alice also gains fame after she goes through a variety of jobs in the entertainment industry and eventually lands her own radio show – and later a talk show. Jenny, who lives with Shane, publishes a book, which then proceeds to become a bestseller and is subsequently made into a movie by Tina. The plot keeps revolving around the friends' problems, which often have to do with jealousy, breakups, and love. Bette and Tina are staged as a dream couple who, throughout the series, always get back together, even after a multitude of separations. The social status of the women is clearly marked as successful, charismatic, and rich. At the same time, *The L*

---

4 As these series deal with other representations of queer life besides lesbians, I have chosen to use the term "queer" when referring to the mentioned series. I have highlighted my understanding of "queernesss" on the following pages.

5 Even though the treatment of the character Max Sweeney has been criticized for "perpetuating harmful stereotypes about transmasculine people and transition." (Quispe López: Max Is Back: The L Word's Daniel Sea and Leo Sheng Discuss the Infamous Trans Character's Return. *Them* (09 December 2022). https://www.them.us/story/daniel-sea-leo-sheng-the-l-word-generation-q-interview-max-return[last accessed 18 June 2023]).

Word challenges the heteronormative narrative of the few queer people in a heterosexual environment through its multitude of queer characters and their relationships of various kinds. There is still no other series that features so many lesbian women as main characters. On one hand, it becomes evident that there is an intentional presentation of particularly heteronormative lifestyles to achieve social acceptance; on the other hand, there is also an implementation of radical concepts of queer life. These concepts however, are ultimately always tied to normatives.

Taking a closer look at this tension between queer and homonormative television concepts in individual scenes, a pattern emerges that limits the repertoire of representations. In this context, it appears that the life goals the characters pursue hardly differ from one another. The previously mentioned norms of marriage with the desire to have children signal a successful, positive representation which, however, does not permit any alternatives. Such depiction in popular TV formats in relation to queer concepts of representation can certainly be described as homonormative. Established in the 1990s by US social- and cultural theorist Lisa Duggan, this term refers to the adaptation of queer people to heterosexual ideals with the goal of normalizing homosexual realities of life.[6] Undoubtedly, the representation of lesbian identities in these television productions appear as deviating from heterosexual norms, by showcasing non-heterosexual lifestyles. However, taking queer concepts seriously and examining lesbian productions in the early 2000s critically leads one to the realization that representation consistently organizes itself in a homonormative manner. What emerges is that in lesbian series, queer role models, family structures, and identity politics are not thwarted, subverted, or even overcome. In fact, it seems that queer productions can hardly be reconciled with the portrayal of lesbian women.

Queer not only serves as a collective term that unites everything that is not cis-, i.e. heterosexual; it embodies changeability and ambivalence, which associates it with "an identity category, political positionality, methodological framework, or system of knowledge production."[7] One of the founders of queer theory, Eve Sedgwick describes the power of the term: "Queer is a continuing moment, movement, motive – recurrent, eddying, *troublant*."[8] The concept is understood to be in a constant state of evolution and change, reflecting its fluidity in its conceptualization and, at the same time, allowing for a broader approach and applicability of the notion.

Furthermore, especially considering the history of the term *queer*, it is important to note that it had long been used as a derogatory term and was reclaimed both academically and socially in the 1990s. According to queer theorist Annamarie Jagose, the term *queer* can be seen as part of a broader cultural and political shift toward a fluid

---

6 Lisa Duggan: The New Homonormativity: The Sexual Politics of Neoliberalism. In: *Materializing Democracy: Toward a Revitalized Cultural Politics*, ed. by Russ Castronovo et al. New York, NY 2002, 175–177.

7 Noreen Giffney: *Queering the Non/human*. Aldershot 2008, 4.

8 Eve Kosofsky Sedgwick: *Tendencies*. New York, NY 1993, XII.

and diverse understanding of sexuality and gender.[9] However, it is important to recognize that queerness as a category is still considered to be predominantly occupied by whiteness and lesbian/gay identity. US trans rights activists and social theorists Dave Spade and Morgan Bassichis demonstrate this by drawing parallels between homonormativity and racism. They describe this as follows: "White gay and lesbian politics must remain silent on anti-black racism, must position itself as anything but black, to keep its place in line for the future."[10] They illustrate that achieving equal rights requires assimilation, which tends to abandon marginalized groups within the LGBTQ+ movement. Their article is not only a rallying cry for the relevance of intersectionality, it also highlights the requirements for tolerance and acceptance of non-normative subjects in society, specifically that the success of queer progress is inevitably tied to processes of hierarchization and demarcation.[11]

One of the main theoretical concepts applicable for a queer analysis of heteronormativity at the intersection of social reality and media representations is Foucault's theorization of normative discourses of order and power.[12] In *The History of Sexuality*, Foucault still identifies homosexuality as a sexual practice and highlights that the practice of homosexuality leads to the formation of an identity through institutions, i.e. through the interaction with clergy, doctors, elected officials, etc., and in this way the "artificial unity" of a homosexual identity was only created by its orientation towards "public authority" with the subject of "sexuality."[13] According to Foucault, these are the norms that exclude homosexuals and incriminate and pathologize them in the first place.[14] This allows the locking up of or shunning away from those identified as homosexuals according to the law. Hence, homosexuals always operate outside of the norm from which they are excluded. The norm that is enforced through exclusion is certainly to be understood here, drawing upon Foucault and Butler, as the heteronormative order. However, a lot has changed since then, such as the increased visibility of people who identify with the LGBTQ+ community, as well as the landmark decision of the US Supreme Court in Lawrence vs. Texas in 2003,[15] essentially decriminalizing homosexuality nationwide.

Through the classification of sexualities in the late nineteenth century, namely that "[t]he sodomite had been a temporary aberration; the homosexual was now a

---

9 Jagose: *Queer Theory: An Introduction.*

10 Morgan Bassichis / Dean Spade: Queer Politics and Anti-Blackness. In: *Queer Necropolitics*, ed. by Jinthana Haritaworn et al. London 2014, 196.

11 For an elaborate discussion, see Roderick Ferguson: *Aberrations in Black: Toward a Queer of Color Critique.* Minnesota, MN 2003.

12 Michel Foucault: *The History of Sexuality. 1: An Introduction*, trans by. Robert Hurley. New York 1990, 144.

13 Foucault: *The History of Sexuality. 1: An Introduction*, 152.

14 Foucault: *The History of Sexuality. 1: An Introduction*, 144.

15 Lawrence v. Texas, 539 U.S. 558 (2003).

species,"[16] Foucault defines the constructivist framework of discourse, since the classification into sexualities enables the formation of a deviant identity in the first place.[17] Thus, it can be stated with and against Foucault that, on the one hand, there are social norms of exclusion against the homosexual, but on the other hand, in the last twenty years, the media visibility of lesbian "homosexuals" has developed its own, independent norms in contrast to heteronormative structures.

Eve Sedgwick had already criticized the existence of the identity-based categorization of heterosexuality and non-heterosexuality, as described by Michel Foucault.[18] She argues that binary dualisms are characterized by a power imbalance. As a result, the identities are in an imbalance, which brings an instability and thus a constant change, because "the question of priority between the supposed central and the supposed marginal category of each dyad is irresolvably unstable an instability caused by the fact that term B is constituted as at once internal and external to term A."[19] Sedgwick outlines deconstruction as an important tool to break down and intersect these categories so that new, more fluid identities and possible enactments of sexuality emerge. She argues the process of queering, i.e. "to queer something," as examining a work through a queer lens in order to discern the underlying subtexts of identity, desire, and longing that challenge the normative.[20] US queer theorist Jack Halberstam considers the power of queering to be attacking, destabilizing, and rejecting normative structures. In his book *Queer Art of Failure* he engages with the rejection of the norm through failure.[21] He further describes this as transformative and productive in enabling and preserving alternative realities of life.[22] As noted by Sedgwick and Halberstam, destabilization can occur through media visibility, as film and television reveal alternative forms of identification and belonging that counteract the exclusionary consequences of heteronormativity.[23]

These representations are certainly tied to patterns of reception and viewing habits, as well as to neoliberal conditions of production.[24] The staging of queer life concepts is always oriented towards heterosexual values and ideals and explicitly marks deviations as negative. That precisely such theoretical considerations played no or

---

16 Foucault: *The History of Sexuality. 1: An Introduction*, 43.

17 Annemarie Jagose: *Queer Theory: An Introduction.* New York 1996, 23–27.

18 Foucault: *The History of Sexuality. 1: An Introduction*, 43.

19 Eve Kosofsky Sedgwick: *Epistemology of the Closet.* Berkeley, CA 2008, 10.

20 Sedgwick: *Tendencies*, 4.

21 Jack Halberstam: *The Queer Art of Failure.* London 2011.

22 Halberstam: *The Queer Art of Failure*, 3.

23 See also Deborah A. Fisher et al.: Gay, Lesbian, and Bisexual Content on Television: A Quantitative Analysis across Two Seasons. *Journal of Homosexuality* 52/3 (2007), doi:10.1300/J082v52n03_08; Kate McNicholas Smith: *Lesbians on Television – New Queer Visibility & The Lesbian Normal.* Bristol 2020, 8.

24 Of course, this is also related to the airing sites which additionally control the content. *The Fosters* ran on primetime Fox, while *The L Word* was primarily available on DVD or aired on the much smaller Showtime channel.

only a marginal role in the production of the series *The L Word* and *The Fosters* will be demonstrated in the following. In particular, linking queer-theoretical models of analysis will substantiate the thesis that lesbian visibility on TV in the 2010s was rather closely tied to normatives, i.e. to a "right kind of gay." Subsequently, this chapter will focus on queer theory in combination with affect theory, in particular with regard to the affect of shame. I will elaborate on the connection between reception models and the balance of affects, as well as the influence on normative structures. Additionally, I will examine the interplay of shame and the goal of obtaining acceptance through reproducing normative social patterns. The goal of this investigation is to find out where and how affect ecologies lead to a perpetuation or reproduction of norms in media contexts and how they negotiate a new representation of lesbians and simultaneously regulate its reception.[25]

2 New Queer Visibility

As a concept rooted in the intentional assimilation to the prevailing system characterized by unequal power dynamics, homonormativity can be regarded as being diametrically opposed to the subversive practice of rejecting identity categories. It aims to regulate and contain the non-normative force through deliberate preferences for specific lifestyles.[26] The German queer theorists Sabine Hark and Mike Laufenberg describe this alleged obtaining of acceptance as an "[i]nvitation of secondary order, [. . .] which leaves the 'heterosexual dominance' untouched."[27] Arguing for a queer feminist perspective that allows for "[s]exuality, not only to be understood as a field of regulation and normalization, but at the same time as a field in which structural relations meet the practices of subjects and thus become negotiable and transformable."[28] The focus on the effects of neoliberalism, which Lisa Duggan highlights in her analysis of homonormativity, implies a connection between sexual orientation and a

---

25 Thomas Peele: *Queer Popular Culture: Literature, Media, Film, and Television.* New York, NY 2011; Fisher et al.: Gay, Lesbian, and Bisexual Content on Television; McNicholas Smith: *Lesbians on Television.*

26 This shift in normativity and the resulting division of the LGBTQ+ community was already discussed and critically examined in 2000 in Warner: *The Trouble with Normal: Sex, Politics, and the Ethics of Queer Life*, 47.

27 "Einladung zweiter Klasse, [. . .] die die 'heterosexuelle Dominanz' unangetastet lässt." Mike Laufenberg: Sexualität in der Krise. Heteronormativität im Neoliberalismus. In: *Gesellschaft. Feministische Krisendiagnosen,* ed. by Erna Appelt / Brigitte Aulenbacher / Angelika Wetterer. 37 (2013), 227–245, 229. [Own translation, S.R.].

28 "Sexualität nicht lediglich als Feld der Regulierung und Normierung begriffen wird, sondern zugleich als Bereich, in dem strukturelle Verhältnisse auf die Praktiken von Subjekten treffen und so verhandel- und transformierbar werden." Laufenberg: *Sexualität in der Krise*, 229. [Own translation, S.R.].

neo-liberal worldview and the ideals attached to it. It is evident that homonormative lifestyles, Duggan argued when she introduced the concept of "homonormativity" in 2003, proclaim a deviation from (hetero-)normative lifestyles, but that normativity itself is at the same time linked to the heterosexual matrix. The expectation appears to be that promiscuity and non-monogamy should be avoided in exchange for acceptance of seemingly non-conforming realities of life. By surrendering to ideals derived from heteronormative ways of living and to normative socio-political concepts, i.e. adapting to the ideal of a stable monogamous relationship and valuing the concept of the family, the marginalized individual can achieve tolerance and recognition.[29] Undeniably, the required staging of (homo)normativity in regards to economic success applies to the representation of marginalized groups such as lesbians. The objective of gaining advantages for the marketing and economic profitability of the respective series leads to the consequence that certain marginalized groups are excluded from the mainstream ideal, which, in turn, is influenced by audiovisual productions. Representations of idealized lifestyles in media productions not only reproduce the common idea of cohabitation, they also organize feelings and affects that can range from the pleasant to the shameful. A lesbian mode of representation also depends on discursive acts along social norms and operates through ecologies of affect that influence spectators not identifying as queer.

Especially since the new millennium, the visibility of queer individuals in different media products increased noticeably.[30] This development is referred to as "new queer visibility" by British media and queer scholar Kate McNicholas Smith.[31] She describes this process as follows: "[N]ew queer visibility emerges through complex politics that encompass (homo)national discourses of democracy and progress, heterosexist and racialized media cultures, and queer and feminist challenges to sexual norms and hierarchies."[32] In her dissertation, she addresses the "lesbian normal" and describes the adaptation of lesbian life to heterosexual ideals.[33] McNicholas also situates the problem of the concept of "new queer visibility" as restricting "for queer women of colour, butch, older, disabled, gender non-conforming or non-binary subjects."[34] This means that representation does not include all lesbian women and a renewed exclusion from representation occurs. Media logics of representation are, as established earlier, shaped by normative desires and, especially in the mainstream, guided by neo-liberal ideals strictly focused on economic success.

---

29 Duggan: *The Twilight of Equality?*
30 GLAAD: *Where We Are on TV 2010 – 2011.* https://www.glaad.org/sites/default/files/wherewear
eontv2010-2011.pdf, 7 (last accessed 09 September 2021).
31 McNicholas Smith: *Lesbians on Television,* 2.
32 McNicholas Smith: *Lesbians on Television,* 4.
33 McNicholas Smith: *Lesbians on Television.*
34 McNicholas Smith: *Lesbians on Television,* 8.

Canadian media scholar Lisa Henderson describes the phenomenon of representations of homonormativity in the media, as follows: "comportment, family, and modes of acquisition are the class markers of queer worth, pulling characters and scenarios toward a normative middle, but not without deploying an array of other class meanings and values."[35] This illustrates the relevance of the representation of a "correct" and "good" queer identity, as this is inevitably linked to progress towards a perceived "equality," although limited to a certain group that adheres to these established markers of progress. At the same time, this kind of representation creates a new norm that is strengthened and externalized with the help of the affect of shame. One of the pioneers of queer theory, Eve Kosofsky Sedgwick, together with Adam Frank, explored this connection of shame and the theory of affect based on the work of psychologist and philosopher Silvan Tomkins.[36] They describe their approach to affect theory as a tool to gain a new access to queer theoretical research on issues of sexuality, sex, and desire by expanding it to include emotions and affects.[37] According to Sedgwick and Frank, the connection between sexuality and shame is not innate but rather socially created.[38] This affect of shame becomes a part of queer identity through external influences such as discrimination, resulting in an (unconscious) assimilation into the heterosexual norm and thus an assimilation into mainstream society. To sum up, heteronormative media representations support the emergence of a "right kind of gay." This will become evident in the following discussion on the step from the first lesbian representation on TV to a homonormative production structure of series narratives loaded with shame. By creating shame through the devaluation of alternative concepts and by devoting attention to heteronormative models, shame acts as a regulative for the discourse on "the right kind of gay."

3 Shame as a Regulative Tool

The L Word has now acquired a cult-like status and is still one of the few series with a predominantly female* queer cast. One of the most important recurring themes in this series, which features many different lesbian characters, is marriage and the creation of a family which is simultaneously linked to the shameful portrayal of a deviant lifestyle. This applies to the majority of all main characters, as they consider marriage the ultimate goal in their lives. One example is the planning of the wedding

---

35 Lisa Henderson: *Love and Money: Queers, Class, and Cultural Production.* New York, NY 2013, 34. https://doi.org/10.18574/nyu/9780814790571.003.0003.
36 Eve Kosofsky Sedgwick: *Touching Feeling: Affect, Pedagogy, Performativity.* Durham, NC 2003; Eve Kosofsky Sedgwick: *Shame and Its Sisters: A Silvan Tomkins Reader.* Durham, NC 1995.
37 Sedgwick: *Shame and Its Sisters.*
38 Sedgwick: *Shame and Its Sisters,* 4–7.

of Shane and her girlfriend Carmen. Shane has had "problems" with monogamous relationships since the beginning of the series, often having multiple sex partners simultaneously or cheating on her steady girlfriends. *The L Word* focuses on many different one-night stands and problems that arise as soon as she enters a monogamous relationship. After Shane cheated on Carmen at the beginning of their relationship, Carmen reads Shane the definition of monogamy from a dictionary:

> C: Monogamy is common among birds. It is the practice of having a single mate during a period of time. Does that mean anything to you?
>
> S: I am willing to try. Is that not enough? I am willing to try something that doesn't come naturally to me, that I don't understand but am willing to try!
>
> C: Birds, Shane. I am talking about a goddamn fucking bird. Asking you to be as civilized as a goddamn fucking bird.[39]

Carmen states that anything aside from monogamy is uncivilized and Shane's problems with monogamy are based on a lack of morals and loyalty, without confronting or unraveling as to why it might be difficult for Shane to live in a monogamous relationship. She does not even consider a non-monogamous lifestyle as an option and Shane remains in the role of the unhappy cheater who keeps hurting people around her, ultimately leaving Carmen at the altar during their wedding ceremony.

The Fosters, similarly, focuses on marriage and considers the right for same-sex-marriage as a given. There are a total of three marriage proposals and two weddings between Stef and Lena across five seasons. The second marriage in *The Fosters* also focuses on legal recognition and the associated achievement of normality and the acceptance that is in turn linked to it. Stef explicitly describes this thus:

> S: I like our marriage being recognized by the federal government. I know we don't need anybody's permission to love one another, but you know what, it feels good to have the same rights as every straight couple. To be included. To be protected under the law. God knows that right might be taken away from us, but, man, as long as we have it, I want it. You know I want to be equal. I want our love and family to be out and proud and if they try to take marriage away from us, then you're damn right I'm going to fight to keep it. Because you know, us getting married again, that piece of paper, that's about more than just us.[40]

This example demonstrates that the queer characters are aware that they have to adapt to the heteronormative ideal if they want to achieve equality and that this can only happen with the permission of dominant heterosexual society. They are also aware that this right can be taken away from them at any time. The desire for "normality" is oriented towards socially established ideals, such as same-sex marriage in this case, whereby the existing system is accepted and not questioned. The concern

---

39 The L Word: Lifesize. 2006. Season 03, episode 06. TC: 00:21:45.
40 The Fosters: The Letter. 2017. Season 04, episode 16. TC: 00:37:33.

that this right, which emulates a lifestyle model exemplified by heterosexuals under the guise of "equal" and signals belonging, could be taken without a right of co-determination unites the individuals seeking recognition. The fear that the dissolution of the marriage would put one's family members at a disadvantage, that they would no longer be "out and proud," thus becomes a struggle for the entire family, who would suffer from exclusion. In this process, the heterosexual members are equated with the queer individuals in their environment and put at a disadvantage. By creating shame, the identity of queer persons is to be classified as a flaw in this heterosexual system, thus becoming disruptive bodies that simultaneously also disadvantage heterosexual individuals.[41]

British-Australian queer theorist Sara Ahmed provides examples for the regulation of homosexual bodies by heterosexual ones. This is expressed, among other things, in that queer persons "may also be 'asked' not to make heterosexuals feel uncomfortable by avoiding the display of queer intimacy."[42] Ahmed argues that "[m]aintaining public comfort requires that certain bodies 'go along with it,' to agree to where you are placed."[43] This "public comfort" ensures a hegemonic heterosexuality, as the existence of any variations and their visibility is immediately effectively suppressed and marginalized.

The signaling of deviation as something shameful, which society stigmatizes and does not allow to exist, enables a justified exclusion, since acceptance and tolerance is possible within the previously set norms and thus a non-classification is linked to an intended exclusion of one's own person. Thus, an assignment of guilt automatically arises. Those who cannot adapt are themselves to blame for the lack of recognition in society. Tolerance and acceptance thereby become a generous gesture that allows queer people to belong and justify rejection if the standards are not met.

In the series *The Fosters*, the protagonists constantly operate in a predominantly heterosexual environment, Jenna, Stef and Lena's only lesbian friend, particularly sticks out. After her "failed marriage," she is portrayed as a pitiful single woman who unsuccessfully makes advances in Stef and Lena's circle of mostly straight friends. Stef and Lena express their dislike of Jenna's behavior and actively distance themselves from her. When Jenna flirts with another woman – Steph and Lena's neighbor Tess – in front of her husband, both even confront her and explicitly refer to marriage as an institution, towards which she has to behave respectfully.[44] Jenna is sent home and, after Tess agrees to a meeting, is monitored by Lena, who only agrees to the meeting under this pretext.[45]

---

41 David M. Halperin: *How to Be Gay*. Cambridge, MA 2012.

42 Sara Ahmed: *Cultural politics of emotion*. Edinburgh 2004, 148.

43 Sara Ahmed: Happy Objects. In: *The Affect Theory Reader*, ed. by Melissa Gregg / Gregory J. Seigworth. New York, NY 2010, 39. https://doi.org/10.1515/9780822393047-003.

44 The Fosters. *#IWasMadeInAmerica*. Season 05, episode 12.

45 The Fosters: *Line in the Sand*. 2018. Season 05, episode 13. (TC: 00:13:30).

Another aspect showcasing the limited visibility enabled by homonormativity is the reappraisal of the demand for the representation of lesbian individuals. Both series do not consider any butch characters. For instance, shame factors are utilized to mark Shane's departure from the presumed societal expectation of femininity. Dana, a closeted, professional tennis player, actively confronts her by stating that she looks too gay.[46] As butches endanger the male-female dichotomy, the existence of a woman presenting herself in a masculine way blurs the boundaries of the gender order and creates an in-between. Butches not only reveal the existence of gender norms by violating them, they also create a new space for identity outside the mainstream.[47] Halberstam discusses the butch under the rubric of "female masculinity" and describes this subject position as a way to question the binary system and dissolve the norm of femininity. He writes:

> Female masculinity within queer sexual discourse allows for the disruption of even flows between gender and anatomy, sexuality and identity, sexual practice and performativity. It reveals a variety of queer genders, such as stone butchness, that challenge once and for all the stability and accuracy of binary sex-gender systems.[48]

As a result, hardly any butch characters are shown and the feminine characters clearly distance themselves from these women so as not to endanger the norm. This also comes to the fore in *The L Word*. In the beginning, only Shane takes the position of a soft butch; however, she too is read as more androgynous and never refers to herself as butch. Due to the lack of confirmation of Shane's "butchness" as part of her identity, viewers are left to speculate. In the series itself, it long remains a taboo. When the series introduces the trans*man Max, who initially refers to himself as butch, the group reacts with incomprehension and rejection.[49] The friends emphasize that this term is outdated and uncool and therefore no longer fits into the lifestyle of the hip lesbian woman living in Los Angeles.[50] The series explicitly bans "butch" as a possible subject position by explicitly rejecting the term. Halberstam elucidates this as follows: "[w]hat *The L Word* must repudiate in order to represent *lesbian as successful* is the butch."[51]

Likewise in *The Fosters*, the term "butch" is used as something negative and insulting. In season three, Stef is diagnosed with breast cancer, which is why she decides to have a mastectomy. During this decision-making process, she discusses her fears and concerns about her love life, her physical well-being, as well as the recep-

---

46 The L Word: *Pilot*. 2004. Season 01, episode 01. (TC: 00:13:50).

47 Butches were often excluded from lesbian feminism in the 1970s and 1980s. See Jack Halberstam: *Female Masculinity*. New York, NY 2019. https://doi.org/10.1515/9781478002703.

48 Halberstam: *Female Masculinity*, 139.

49 The L Word: *Lobsters*. 2006. Season 03, episode 03.

50 McNichols Smith: *Lesbians on Television*, 53.

51 Halberstam: *The Queer Art of Failure*, 95.

tion of her changed appearance in the social environment with her wife, Lena. "A cop with a flat chest. I can hear the comments now. People already think I'm butch."[52] Based on this example, the negative social perceptions become apparent and are mirrored to the viewers. *The Fosters* picks up on this comment again in the same episode, after Stef has decided to get breast implants and cut her hair short. She reflects on her internalized homophobia and expresses her concern that without breasts, she will no longer be read as a woman. "Breasts and long hair do not make me a woman. And what the hell do I care if people think that I'm butch because they have an idea of what a woman is supposed to look like."[53] While the perception of one's own homophobia through social structures is evident, labels like "butch" and "dyke" are not invalidated as negative. Halberstam describes the problem the butch poses for gender order and exclusion in *The L Word as* "the butch [. . .] gets cast as anachronistic, as the failure of femininity, as an earlier, melancholic model of queerness that has now been updated and transformed into desirable womanhood, desirable, that is, in a hetero-visual model."[54]

Even though Stef frees herself from the offensive views of her environment by declaring that she will not be influenced by the opinions of others, she explicitly distances herself from this description. The attribution "butch" thus remains something negative and Stef continues to dwell in heteronormative structures or does not overcome them. Additionally, it becomes clear that Stef has a clear idea of what a butch should look like and that she does not want to be associated with it. Here, the affect of shame once again comes into play. Naming a subject that one does not want to resemble because it is socially disadvantaged reveals the form or default for tolerance that Sara Ahmed speaks of.[55]

The heteronormative structures and family models are thus not only linked to monogamous marriage, hardly any alternative life models are shown. Ahmed also picks up on this and refers to the social classification of the (cis-heterosexual) family as a "happy object" and ascribes the degradation to a "cause of unhappiness"[56] of all those who are not involved in procreation. "Some bodies are presumed to be the origin of bad feeling insofar as they disturb the promise of happiness, which I would re-describe as the social pressure to maintain the signs of 'getting along.'"[57] By fulfilling previously socially established ideas, the possibility of a happy life is promised. Any deviation from these is taken as a clear sign of an unhappy life.[58] Therefore, the main

---

52 The Fosters: *Rehearsal.* 2016. Season 03, episode 18, TC: 00:03:35.
53 The Fosters: *Rehearsal.* TC: 00:35:10.
54 Halberstam: *The Queer Art of Failure*, 95.
55 Ahmed: *Cultural Politics of Emotion*, 146.
56 Ahmed: *Happy Objects*, 30.
57 Ahmed: *Cultural politics of Emotion*, 39.
58 For further elaboration, see Laurens Berlant: *Cruel Optimism.* Durham 2011, whose important contribution to affect theory Kathleen Stewarts describes as a "a brilliant discussion of how objects and

task for Stef and Lena is to fulfill their role as mothers. This portrayal of a homonormative lifestyle is strategically designed to engage queer viewers and depict an idealized vision that demonstrates the potential for attaining a "normal" life. At the same time, stereotypes are reproduced by staging two women as caring mothers with little engagement outside of family structures. It is important to mention that both women classify their families as the center of their lives and do not express any needs outside of family life and the role of the mother.[59] In other words, Stef and Lena not only lead a homonormative life, they also present as desirable a homosexual life in a predominantly heterosexual society. In this way, they do not rebel against an unfair system but rather fit into it, or reclassify the "unhappy object" as a "happy object." The acceptance of these structures is consolidated by the affect of shame, which arises when one cannot fulfill the established norm and, as a consequence, experiences exclusion and discrimination. Sara Ahmed describes this as not fitting into a mold, as creating "discomfort," which results in the rejection of one's identity.[60]

4 Working Through Shame

Interestingly, the respective last season of both series take up the topic of shame and reconsider the reappraisal of the societal influence on the queer individual. In *The Fosters*, Stef begins therapy to deal with her father's rejection of her because of her sexuality, which has led to panic and anxiety attacks that negatively affect her relationship with her partner. Her therapist uses a similar definition to Eve Sedgwick's and defines Stef's shame as "unlike guilt, which is the feeling of doing something wrong, shame is the feeling of being something wrong. And this assault on the self, it can cause deep depression and severe anxiety."[61] Her father is explicitly marked as the trigger of shame and the influence of the heterosexual norm is identified. Given the lack of explicit engagement with homophobia and its resultant discrimination in previous discourse, this examination holds particular relevance. Additionally, in episode 18 of the fifth and final season, Stef confronts her deceased father and describes the desire to conform to the norm that had influenced her life for a long time. She explains that the search for her father's recognition has influenced her decisions at various stages of her life, such as her choice of career, marriage to a man, and so on. Her desire for normality is closely linked to the rejection she had previously experi-

scenes of desire matter not just because of their content but because they hold promise." (Kathleen Stewart: *Ordinary Affects*. New York, NY 2007, 1).

59 The Fosters: *Just say yes*. 2018. Season 05, episode 18. TC: 00:20:21.

60 Ahmed: *Cultural politics of Emotion*, 148.

61 The Fosters: *Mother's Day*. 2018. Season 05, episode 15. TC: 00:02:29.

enced from her father.[62] The affect of shame is thus additionally used in *The Fosters* to support the homonormative lifestyle. Stef's shame as a result of her father's intolerance is a problem for the relationship of the two women, thus the affect of shame is used to visualize a threat to homonormativity due to a lack of acceptance. This shame, which was and is triggered by the environment, endangers Stef and Lena's homonormative marriage, as it affects their mental health but also the expression of their own identity. Stef mentions her fear that her right to a relationship or to love could be taken away because of a deviation from the "normal."[63] This fear primarily refers to the legally defined norm and thus to the construct of marriage, which Lisa Duggan as well as Michael Warner defined as one of the main symbols of homonormativity. At the same time, Stef links her possibility to love to the recognition of an institution, here the state, as if it could not exist without legal consent. She explains,

> this shame that I carry around in me, that keeps me from being completely vulnerable with you, that sometimes, when we make love, makes me feel like what we're doing is not right, like I am not right. I love you and I am so proud of our family and yet I carry around this fear that it could be taken away from us, our right to love each other, because we're not normal.[64]

The Fosters thus exist exclusively within a homonormative framework with the goal of normality. Love outside of neoliberal values does not seem to exist for them. In addition, "normal" is never defined in the series and thus not questioned but tacitly refers to social majorities. The examination fails to address the fact that normativity is a construct primarily achieved through adaptation, as demonstrated by the desire to conform to societal expectations. Furthermore, by portraying the father as a source of shame and a symbol of a homophobic environment, the responsibility is assigned solely to overtly homophobic individuals and incidents, which many individuals may not identify with. However, it overlooks the presence of microaggressions and subliminal discriminations, such as inquiries about a spouse of the opposite sex or describing their relationship as alternative or intriguing, which initially remain unnoticed. Thereby, a reflection on heterosexual hegemony, on one's own actions, but also the questioning of the discriminating system of norms remains missing. Unlike in *The Fosters*, the many lesbian characters in *The L Word* form their own norm and move predominantly in lesbian and queer circles. Therefore, the shame factor is hardly addressed since it seemingly does not exist in the group constellation (with a few exceptions, e.g. gender expression of Shane and Max). Only when individual participants break away from the group are they subjected to discrimination. For example, Bette and Tina, when trying to adopt a second child, are first asked by the parents of the biological mother about their husbands and, when they identify themselves as lesbians, are asked to leave.[65] Or Dana

---

62 The Fosters: *Just say yes*. TC: 00:29:30.
63 The Fosters: *Just say yes*. 2018. TC: 00:33:19.
64 The Fosters: *Just say yes*. 2018. TC: 00:33:19.
65 The L Word: *Leaving Los Angeles*. 2009. Season 06, episode 04.

is rejected by her parents after coming out.[66] Through the character of Alice, *The L Word* draws attention to these problematic reactions and the behavior of the heterosexual environment. After she outed a basketball player who had previously made homophobic comments, she is offered a job on a talk show called "The Look." There, however, she encounters resistance due to her addressing of lesbian issues and her rather progressive views.

> Alice: Are you saying you don't want me to be out? [. . .]

> Producer: No, we definitely want gay. No! Gay is good. It brings ratings in daytime.

> Host 1: But you know, we just want the right kind of gay.

> Producer 1: Like fun gay not angry gay. Gay gossip, gay lifestyle. You know: Fun.[67]

The desire for a "right" kind of homosexuality illustrates the attempt to force queer persons into a normative model. In the process, Alice is threatened with the loss of her job if she does not comply with her employer's idea of the "fun gay" person.

Additionally, the neo-liberal economic structures and possibilities of queer become visible here. When it results in economic benefits, homosexuality is superficially accepted and even desired – however, only as long as it continues to take place within a framework that can be regulated at will. Consequently, there is a prevailing rejection of the self-determination of homosexual individuals. Drawing on Ahmed's theory to maintain public comfort discussed earlier, Alice and her actions are regulated and enforced by the structure of heteronormativity, by the guidelines placed upon her by the heterosexual environment. By abusing the existing power imbalances and employing tactics such as the threat of exclusion, exemplified through the termination of her contract, measures are taken to prevent the risk of her deviating from the norm. By addressing this reality, *The L Word* visualizes the pressure that a heteronormative society exerts on homosexual.

5 Conclusion

The increasing visibility of lesbian characters in popular media is impacted by a staging of a homonormative ideal, resulting in the prevention of a confrontation with divergences from heterosexual and heteronormative narratives. Showcasing and using compulsive heteronormative structures, such as the act of monogamous marriage and childrearing, supports the preservation of a hierarchical system that promises a "happy life"

---

66 The L Word: *Luck, Next Time*. 2004. Season 01, episode 09. TC: 00:31:26.
67 The L Word: *Lesbians Gone Wild*. 2008. Season 05, episode 07. TC: 00:12:59.

for its participants, which places heterosexual individuals at the top.[68] The measures taken to ensure the continuation of this hierarchy quite plainly also influence the representation of queer narratives in television formats. Through these normative structures, desirable models of life emerge which are supported by and disseminated through media representations. The supposedly positive changes in representation discussed in this contribution make it clear that social acceptance is particularly steered by the alignment with heterosexual ideals. The politics of representation that are negotiated here under the guise of progress and commitment to diversity are therefore inadequate and allow the cis-heterosexual majority society to regulate queer identity, which, in order to gain respect and tolerance and recognition of its own identity, must not move too far away from the heteronormative standard in order to avoid losing the acquired rights. As a result, there is no space to address the needs of people from one's own community who do not meet this standard and thus endanger one's own existence. Thus, exclusion takes place within one's own ranks, as is evident, for example, in the debates on "marriage for all" which is not "for all" or in the debates on rights for trans* people. This pattern of perpetuating exclusion for the sake of progress can be observed in a variety of past political movements and its visualization in the media is therefore especially important. The utilization of shame emerges prominently as a means to impede deviation, as it portrays any existence outside the established norms as abnormal and undesirable, deterring queer individuals from associating with it. Consequently, formulating an ideal, which Ahmed identifies as a "form of comfort,"[69] necessitating orientation towards it to attain recognition, acceptance, and tolerance.

As my discussion of these two successful but also rare series featuring lesbian protagonists reveals, the staging of the social ideal of the lesbian woman operates through the affect of shame and connects it to normative images of femininity. The politics of representation at work here create an ideal image of the young lesbian woman which viewers should aspire to embody. It becomes evident that even a supposedly positive development such as the inclusion of representations of lesbians in popular media must continue to be critically observed and that the strategies of representation continue to specifically exclude people who do not live up to the ideals of society.

Bibliography

Ahmed, Sara. *The Cultural Politics of Emotion*. New York, NY 2004.
Ahmed, Sara: Happy Objects. In: *The Affect Theory Reader*, ed. by Gregg, Melissa / Seigworth, Gregory J. New York, NY 2010, 29–51. https://doi.org/10.1515/9780822393047-003.

---

68 Ron Becker: *Gay TV and Straight America*. New Brunswick 2006, 4.
69 Ahmed: *Cultural Politics of Emotion*, 148.

Bassichis, Morgan / Spade, Dean: Queer Politics and Anti-Blackness. In: *Queer Necropolitics*, ed. by Haritaworn, Jinthana et al. London 2014, 191–206.

Becker, Ron: *Gay TV and Straight America*. New Brunswick, NJ 2006.

Berlant, Lauren: *Cruel Optimism*. Durham, NC 2011.

Duggan, Lisa: The New Homonormativity: The Sexual Politics of Neoliberalism. In: *Materializing Democracy: Toward a Revitalized Cultural Politics*, ed. by Castronovo, Russ / Nelson, Dana D. New York, NY 2002, 175–194.

Duggan, Lisa: *The Twilight of Equality? Neoliberalism, Cultural Politics, and the Attack on Democracy*. Boston, MA 2009.

Eng, David L.: *The Feeling of Kinship: Queer Liberalism and the Racialization of Intimacy*. Durham, NC 2010.

Ferguson, Roderick: *Aberrations in Black: Toward a Queer of Color Critique*. Minnesota, MN 2003.

Fisher, Deborah A et al.: "Gay, Lesbian, and Bisexual Content on Television: A Quantitative Analysis across Two Seasons." *Journal of Homosexuality* 52/3 (2007), 167–188. doi: 10.1300/J082v52n03_08.

Foucault, Michel: *The History of Sexuality. 1: An Introduction*, trans by. Robert Hurley. New York 1990.

Giffney, Noreen: *Queering the Non/human*. Aldershot 2008.

Giffney, Noreen / O'Rourke, Michael: *The Ashgate Research Companion to Queer Theory*. Farnham 2009.

GLAAD: *Where We Are on TV, 2010 – 2011*. https://www.glaad.org/sites/default/files/whereweareontv2010-2011.pdf, 7 (last accessed 09 September 2021).

Halberstam, Jack. *The Queer Art of Failure*. London 2011. https://dx.doi.org/10.1515/9780822394358.

Halberstam, Jack. *Female Masculinity*. New York, NY 2019. https://doi.org/10.1515/9781478002703.

Hall, Stuart: *Representation: Cultural Representation and Signifying Practices*. London 1997.

Halperin, David M. *How to Be Gay*. Cambridge, MA 2012.

Henderson, Lisa: *Love and Money: Queers, Class, and Cultural Production*. New York, NY 2013. https://doi.org/10.18574/nyu/9780814790571.003.0003.

Jagose, Annemarie. *Queer Theory: An Introduction*. New York, NY 1996.

Katz, Jonathan / Duggan, Lisa: *The Invention of Heterosexuality*. New York, NY 1995.

Laufenberg, Mike: Sexualität in der Krise. Heteronormativität im Neoliberalismus. In: *Gesellschaft. Feministische Krisendiagnosen*, ed. by Appelt, Erna / Aulenbacher, Brigitte / Wetterer, Angelika. 37 (2013), 227–245.

Lawrence v. Texas, 539 U.S. 558 (2003). https://supreme.justia.com/cases/federal/us/539/558/.

López, Quispe: Max Is Back: The L Word's Daniel Sea and Leo Sheng Discuss the Infamous Trans Character's Return. *Them* (09 December 2022). https://www.them.us/story/daniel-sea-leo-sheng-the-l-word-generation-q-interview-max-return (last accessed 18 June 2023).

McKinlay, Alan: *Foucault, Governmentality, and Organization*. London 2014.

McNicholas Smith, Kate: *Lesbians on Television – New Queer Visibility & The Lesbian Normal*. Bristol 2020.

Paternotte, David / Tremblay, Manon (eds.): *The Ashgate Research Companion to Lesbian and Gay Activism*. Farnham 2015.

Peele, Thomas. *Queer Popular Culture: Literature, Media, Film, and Television*. New York, NY 2011.

Sedgwick, Eve Kosofsky: *Tendencies*. New York, NY 1993.

Sedgwick, Eve Kosofsky: *Shame and Its Sisters: A Silvan Tomkins Reader*. Durham, NC 1995.

Sedgwick, Eve Kosofsky, et al. (ed.): *Touching Feeling: Affect, Pedagogy, Performativity*. New York, NY 2003. https://doi.org/10.1515/9780822384786.

Sedgwick, Eve Kosofsky: *Epistemology of the Closet*. Berkeley, CA 2008.

Stewart, Kathleen. *Ordinary Affects*. New York, NY 2007. https://dx.doi.org/10.1515/9780822390404.

Warner, Michael. *The Trouble with Normal: Sex, Politics, and the Ethics of Queer Life*. Cambridge, MA 2000.

Videography

The Fosters: Rehearsal. 2016. Season 03, episode 18.
The Fosters: The Letter. 2017. Season 04, episode 16.
The Fosters: Mother's Day. 2018. Season 05, episode 15.
The Fosters: Just say yes. 2018. Season 05, episode 18.
The L Word: Luck, Next Time. 2004. Season 01, episode 09.
The L Word: Lobsters. 2006. Season 03, episode 03.
The L Word: Lifesize. 2006. Season 03, episode 06.
The L Word: Lesbians Gone Wild. 2008. Season 05, episode 07.
The L Word: Leaving Los Angeles. 2009. Season 06, episode 04.

Creative Interlude

Kathrin Dreckmann

Artists Talk – A Conversation on Queer Pop

In the artist talk that follows, Berlin-based artist and producer Sue Lèwig, the author, musician, lecturer, DJ and radio host Thomas Meinecke, and scholar and artist Sookee engage in conversation on the topic of queer pop with Kathrin Dreckmann, assistant professor at the Institute for Media and Cultural Studies at Heinrich-Heine-University Dusseldorf.

Sue Lèwig's tripping techno composition such as epic downbeat breakbeat post-techno, slowly swells and breaks the tempo again and again, develops into a dramatic pressure machine on the dancefloor. She has releases on the record labels Kaos, Examine Archive and Seelen. Thomas Meinecke, a formative figure within what is referred to as German pop literature and, as a member of the band *Freiwillige Selbstkontrolle*, has also participated successfully and innovatively in pop music discourse since 1980. A particular interest in contemporary feminist theory permeates his work and informs the themes of his writing.

Through her music Sookee has been a sharp critique of a hip-hop scene that still largely serves and reproduces sexist, publicist, and racist prejudices. Her music can be understood not only as a counter-project to these tendencies, it also always represents an invitation to explore the content boundaries of hip-hop anew and to find strategies of empowerment for previously marginalized groups in music.

Kathrin Dreckmann: The idea of this artist talk is that after the extensive theoretical and academic examination of the topic of queer pop, we gain insights into the practical work that focuses on queer feminist themes and perspectives. I am very excited that we have three yet very different artists* visiting with us to lead the conversation: Sookee (musician), Sue Lèwig (musician), and Thomas Meinecke (author and writer).

I would like to open the discussion by taking up a question that Swiss media and culture theorist Astrid Deuber-Mankowsky raised in her book on the film BRIDGIT.[1] Astrid mentioned the swan. Especially in the animal world, the non-binary

---

1 BRIDGIT is a film shot on an iPhone by Charlotte Prodger for which she was awarded the Turner Prize in 2018 and deals with queer identity between nature and aesthetics through a cinematic gaze. Astrid Deuber-Mankowsky / Philipp Hanke (eds.): Queeres Kino / Queere Ästhetiken als Dokumentationen des Prekären. Vienna 2021.

Note: in Conversation with Sookee, Sue Lèwig, and Thomas Meinecke

becomes demonstrable as a concept. Sookee, how did you get the idea to write a song about *Queere Tiere* (queer animals).[2]

Sookee: Some people think that love is curable and controllable or selectable, which is not so. Desire and emotional attraction exist without them being influenceable or it being possible to decide who one falls in love with. The persons who deny this to others are also aware of this from their own experience, for example, if they have never loved or desired the same sex or if something has happened so far outside the realm of feasibility or intentionality. These people still believe that anything apart from heteronormativity could not work. Then they sometimes turn to theories on evolution and argue that same-sex desire will lead to the extinction of humanity because of liberalization. This view, of course, only works within a binary logic. This thinking, which I find absurd, led me to engage in this logic and pursue a thought experiment. Empirically, it is nonsense that there is no form of desire, cohabitation, relationship, collectivity, or sociality apart from heterosexuality. This also raises the question of why one draws on the animal kingdom at all and transfers human norms or phenomena to animals. What does this say about one's stability when a penguin is used to justify that someone can't handle same-sex love? That is absurd.

In my song *Queere Tiere* I set out to trace what this mindset is actually trying to accomplish. It took me half an afternoon to write the lyrics. If you google homosexuality and animals or intersex and animal world, there are countless results, because the relevant studies exist. Everything is journalistically processed and academically founded. I did not discover a secret science by chance. Every example and every concrete suffering mentioned in the song actually exists. Be it the two penguins from the New York Zoo or the giraffes from the study. Looking closely at the study, one can additionally also recognize how knowledge production works. This example from the song, "this is not a turf war, these are gay giraffes," refers to scientific research dating from the turn of the nineteenth to the twentieth century that show that two male giraffes perform certain practices with each other. The authors of these studies apparently could not handle the fact that there was some penetration after the scramble and instead explained this act as a turf war. In the research results this was omitted. Only in the additional material of the research did it become clear that the scientists questioned the meaning of this behavior. Scientific accuracy goes only this far.

I'm sorry if I'm being disrespectful. Yet, it's no secret in science that humans declare themselves to be the objective measure of the world. Of course, my comparison of humans with animals has also caused much criticism from an academic perspective. Nevertheless, we compare humans with animals more often. The idea is to lower the exaggerated position of humans a little bit. Although, this can end in fascism, as

---

2 The queer feminist song *Queere Tiere* by Sookee deals with queer behavior in the animal kingdom and toys with the parameters surrounding the arguments of homosexuality being against biology and not natural [Own translation, K.D.].

we all know. Therefore, *Queere Tiere* features satirical lyrics, while it was also my little entry into the more childlike musical world. The video turned out cute. I liked it a lot. Therefore, I then decided to continue in that direction. *Queere Tiere* marked the ending of her career as Sookee and the beginning of her new persona Sukini.

Kathrin Dreckmann: What Sue Lèwig and Sookee have in common is that they appropriate "male" sound spaces. Sue Lèwig realizes this appropriation by using technical devices that have masculine connotations, such as the synthesizer and the way she mixes and performs live, which didn't always go down well. As German media theorist Friedrich Kittler described in his text *Gramophone, Film, Typewriter,* the misuse of military devices such as the synthesizer and vocoder, which were important decoding systems during the 1940s were therefore used in spaces and career paths dominated by men. Do you still experience this while working with music technology? Do you still have to fight for a space in this male-dominated work?

Sue Lèwig: As a girl with blond, long hair, earrings and a summer dress, it was unimaginable and absurd that someone like that would know anything about sequencing, DAW, MIDI, VST instruments, was impossible that someone like that could have a say about big mixing consoles, be technically proficient, know how to program beats, and want to study sound engineering. It did not fit together. It did not fit the norm. This notion had been commonplace in the electronic music scene for a long time. You felt that strongly. I was interested in it from a young age, always found motherboards more appealing than playing with dolls, first playfully, then more and more adeptly. I knew the direction I wanted to go and that I wanted to intern at a recording studio. Today I am lucky and grateful that I always had mentors who supported me to learn to produce electronic music, who explained equipment, software, showed me things in the recording studio. Still, it was hard to gain knowledge in this male-dominated producer scene. Especially if you started very young and also like to be a woman or a girl and also sing, you often hear phrases like:
"Ah, you produce music, okay, so, you sing."
"Yes. And I write and produce the music."
"Ah, and who programs the beats, the music? Your boyfriend?"
"No, I do."
"Yes, but who produces it?"
"I do that too."
"Ah, I see."

It was definitely a challenge. Even if you have strong self-confidence, are tough, have a strong character, and have an irrepressible thirst for knowledge, it took incredible strength to make it in this industry.
It was a real struggle. Even though I have this tough side of being technically proficient. Sometimes there were moments when I wished I was a man or a boy so I could have it easier. This thought is nonsense, of course. Because I am happy and

proud of what I do and what I have achieved so far, and I am hungry for much more. Today it's already much more painless and I've had consistently positive experiences so far since I've been releasing tracks (2021) and performing LIVE (2018). The live engineers, promoters, producers trust me after a short time of getting to know each other. I also benefit from the current situation and I am happy about it. One example is the emancipation of the queer movement, where young queer artists find a place in the industry, go public with their stories and comfort their fans with their lyrics, fans who think and feel the same way as they do, so they realize that there are people who are like them. In such moments you start thinking about it for the first time, like it made me think about it myself. We don't have to bear everything silently, we can change things gently in a positive way and the first step is to realize it.

During the time I did a lot of internships in recording studios, I became addicted to creating music to a certain extent. At that time, I thought I only had a chance if I produced music with a man. That would have made it easier in the scene, but that's a mistake. To stay true to yourself and courageously find your very own way and persevere and dispel all doubts – that's important. And a symposium like this is important for creating acceptance. It's worth it because our world is diverse. Whether you identify as heterosexual, homosexual, bisexual, trans*, intersex, whether you identify as male or female, whether you feel like anything in between, or whether you have male, female, anything in between parts as a woman, it doesn't matter. It's perfectly fine, because nature has designed it that way.

Kathrin Dreckmann: Thomas called himself a feminist early on in the 80s. We were talking about pop feminism today because there are T-shirts at H&M and Urban Outfitters that say, "I'm a Feminist." My question, which is intentionally a little polemical, is, as a cis heterosexual male, do you look at queer pop differently these days, or has it always existed in that form?

Thomas Meinecke: I didn't call myself a feminist until the 90s. Although I had sympathized with the idea in the 80s. It's always such a story with sympathizing. When the Museum Ludwig in Cologne had an anniversary exhibition on queer art, *The Eighth Square*, they invited me to write a book about it. The book I wrote was called *Feldforschung* (*Field Research*), in which the Pet Shop Boys and Mae West played a role, and that opened up the whole pop context, which for me goes back to the nineteenth century.

For me, it just goes on. The roots for house in Chicago's South Side and ballroom in Spanish Harlem were underground in the 80s. I was out with an African-American social worker on the South Side and wanted him to show me all the spots, but he said he had no idea. It was "a gay thing." He could show me the rap scene, which isn't that wild in Chicago now, but he couldn't show me the house scene. You had to know people who would introduce you. What's also fascinating is that techno, unlike hip-hop, basically has no street. It has a pronounced invisibility. You couldn't really get to it. It was the same with house or ballroom. When Willi Ninja died, perhaps the most prominent voguing dancer, I was in New York. There was a memorial at the Cielo Club on the Westside in Manhattan with Mom and Pop. Willi Ninja's family and all the other famous voguing dancers were there, but it was also open to the public. I could buy a ticket there as a "fag hag" and go to the Cielo Club and see all these people, also in action. They moved me to tears. I have a hunch that this arrives via Baudelaire, vaudeville, and Mae West and whatnot, where I think that's the whole idea. Yes, not least, a central chapter in Judith Butler's book *Gender Trouble*, the film by Jenny Livingston about the ballroom community in Harlem, about recognizing what we do, not being men and women, but performing as men and women.

This community is vital and beautiful. And it is its beauty that touches and captures me. I stood there in tears, because before that, I never trusted myself to go and ask about these places, to stand there and watch, because I thought it was a world of its own, a total sophistication. And then I read up on it. Just this concept of realness, everyone talks about realness. I also talk about realness, because I think it's one of the most interesting, also philosophically interesting concepts from the community, which is also so great in terms of worldview; because this reality of being able to perform is not granted to this group of marginalized people. Thus, they manufactured a highly sophisticated cultural technique.

1979 was the year of the Disco Sucks movement. Sylvester was one of the very great disco artists. Everyone probably knows his hit *You Make Me Feel Mighty Real*. I think it's so great that you take it for granted: That's real. We've discussed the term "authenticity" over the last two days. I want to take it up now. Who is allowed to do that? Are we? And if so, who is this "we" actually? I would say I'm the total fan. I'm devoted. Yet, I still don't allow myself to go right in because I think it's so beautiful that we get this as a kind of art form in the highest sophistication. It's very elaborate, and many acts of imitation or emulation are so crude, uncouth, and strident. I actually feel it's very soulful and deep, and that's why I think this term, the ballroom category "realness" is fantastic. It's such a highly evolved art form that I say, "Yeah, I can just adore that and be moved by that." Architecture can do that too sometimes, just think of the ongoing bass drum in the club as ancient columns. So in that sense: a funny answer to your question.

It has always been difficult. Maybe since minstrelsy or even vaudeville. I love that Mae West says she learned her act from female impersonators in the 1910s, over 100 years ago. A derivation – the original comes after the copy. We can see that also in Mae West. Later Elvis Presley walked all over the screens and had heavy eye makeup on. But nobody talked about it. No one said that man wears heavy eye makeup, which is very interesting. But then he moved his hips. That was a big scandal because he moved his hips. And, supposedly, he was wearing a toilet roll in his pants. So he was also a drag king because of the loo roll in his pants. Others say it was a chrome bar, a chrome pole. I don't know. But it's interesting that with Elvis, male impersonation was already there in a cross-female direction. I think this "everything has always been there" sounds so limp. It's not. It's highly explosive.

Kathrin Dreckmann: One must also then approach the matter in a nuanced way. The argument here has been that there is an increased presence of topics that we can locate in the field of queerness in its broadest sense. Here we have very different perspectives.

Based on this panel, one could consider whether the question of positioning the drag or ballroom scene in relation to posing or voguing needs to be addressed again more pronouncedly in academic research. So that not only the gendering of poses and gestures in music videos and on stage are open to negotiation. What becomes clear in this interview, as well as with a view to the history of queer pop, is that posing and voguing refer to systems that are constantly renegotiated. Pop performances in particular can uncover layers of different encodings and allow encodings to float anew, re-negotiating the subject matter and, if necessary, ironizing it. Susan Sontag's essay *Notes on Camp* is the earliest evidence of such mechanisms. However, reflecting on pop cultural masterpieces is only possible if their historicity allows for negotiating exclusion and inclusion, as it were. Artist such as The Carters and Janelle Monáe gain their particular advantage precisely because of this. They empower posing and cast it anew. They equally question binary constructions between male, female, white and black in the music industry. Exactly this questioning already appears in Sontag's question of exaggeration. It also comes to the fore in PARIS IS BURNING and is the core of Butler's gender theory. So there is only one thing left to say: Pop is beautiful.

Bibliography

Deuber-Mankowsky, Astrid / Hanke, Philipp (eds.): *Queeres Kino / Queere Ästhetiken als Dokumentationen des Prekären.* Vienna 2021.

Part III: **Queer Affect**

Joanna Staśkiewicz

Killing the Pain with Pleasure: On the Queering Effect of the Neo-Burlesque

Abstract: Drawing on research into performance studies, queer affect studies, and queer historiography, this paper argues that neo-burlesque functions as a queer emotional theater, which, similar to the concept of *Theater of Cruelty* by the French writer and dramatist Antonin Artaud, emotionally jolts both the performers and the audience and thus can contribute to a playful, sometimes punkish-furious rewriting of both personal history and political-social realities. Using the example of neo-burlesque performances from New Orleans and Warsaw, I will examine whether and, if so, how neo-burlesque can solve a temporary affirmative detachment from one's own personal history but also from the *chrononormativity* of everyday life as per US-American queer scholars Elizabeth Freeman and Jack Halberstam regarding the system of stimulation into maximal productivity, capital accumulation, and towards heteronormative life strategies. Thereby I will discuss whether new-burlesque can be seen as a playful-pleasurable or sometimes even an enraged way of resisting this chrononormativity and the weight and gravity of the wounds of daily life.

Keywords: Burlesque, queer, performance, emotion, affect, erotic, humor, masquerade, New Orleans, Warsaw

> Emotions tell us a lot about time; emotions are the very 'flesh' of time.[1]

Since the mid-1990s, the popularity of the erotic performance art of neo-burlesque has seen worldwide growth. From Dubai to Shanghai, New York to Buenos Aires, neo-burlesque is taking urban centers by storm, both in queer bars and in other, more established venues. The prefix *neo* refers to the revival of burlesque art, which was established in London in the 1860s and whose first performer was Lydia Thompson. Starting her theatrical career with pantomimes and extravaganzas of Victorian burlesque – parodies of a higher, "classical" art of plays, Greek myths, and literary works – Thompson, along with other female performers, took on male roles, appeared in men's clothing or skin-colored tights, engaging in a then shocking form of cross-dressing that lent the burlesque an erotic significance. Thompson and her tour brought burlesque to the United States, made it popular there, and ensured that burlesque would emerge as a theatrical game of seduction without explicit nudity, taking its place alongside vaudeville and circus as an important form of entertainment art, particularly for the working classes. The US burlesque reached its peak in the 1930s and found its way into the established thea-

---

1 Sara Ahmed: *The Cultural Politics of Emotion*. New York, NY 2014, 202.

ters but moved underground after the Catholic mayor of New York, Fiorello La Guardia, closed burlesque theaters out of concern for moral decay. Burlesque did not disappear, however, but was increasingly replaced by more explicit striptease and go-go dances. It was not until the 1990s, particularly in the US, that a revival of the art form as *neo-burlesque* took place; practiced by performers of all genders, it stands in contrast to the earlier wave of burlesque that lasted until the 1960s and was more of a female performance art.

It is not possible to speak of *the* neo-burlesque, however, given the complexity of the genre – which can be described, in short, as "a multi-disciplinary performance art that, throughout history, has built on different theatrical traditions including playing, singing, dancing, clowning, and, since the late 19th century, stripping."[2] Attending a neo-burlesque show for the first time in 2016 in New Orleans, I experienced what can best be described as confusion. It was a nerdlesque show: a kind of neo-burlesque that takes its cues from pop culture scripts such as Hollywood blockbusters, popular series, Japanese anime, or comic books. On this occasion, it was a tribute to STAR WARS and PULP FICTION.[3] Performers created a utopian world on stage and crossed boundaries – not only of gender binaries but also of the human and non-human, as well as of temporalities. A glittering world of erotic play was created where the erotic did not, in fact, play the central role but was accompanied by the humorous and the parodic. The performers embodied both human beings and, through their costume play, futuristic non-human beings of a world of fantasy, in a kind of *posthumanist drag* that recalls the concept of the cyborg by the US-American science studies scholar Donna Haraway, who, as a non-human and genderless figure, eludes any categories and thus has an emancipative and queer potential.[4] Using their bodies, the performers enacted their own interpretations of figures which differed from the "original" pop-cultural scripts. They mixed the visible queer "non-normative"[5] practices of camp, drag, and cross-dressing with the less-visible queering impact of, for example, tease, which seemed to correspond to normative heterosexual practices of desire. Hence the confusion – these different bodily forms of presentation were perplexing at first sight, but they also revealed the complexity of neo-burlesque performances, which cannot be accounted for through seduction and the visibility of queerness alone. As Canadian gender studies scholar Laura Brightwell notes, "queer anti-normativity" can overplay

---

2 Marie-Cécile Cervellon / Stephen Brown: All the Fun of the Fan: Consuming Burlesque in an Era of Retromania. *NA – Advances in Consumer Research* 42 (2014), 271.

3 For more about *nerdlesque*, see for example, Stevi Costa: Accio Burlesque! Performing Potter Fandom Through "Nerdlesque." In: *Playing Harry Potter. Essays and Interviews on Fandom and Performance*, ed. by Lisa S Brenner. Jefferson, NC 2015, 108–113; Joanna Staśkiewicz: The New Burlesque as an Example of Double-Simulacrum. *Forum Socjologiczne* (2017), 111–122.

4 Donna J. Haraway: *Simians, Cyborgs, and Women. The Reinvention of Nature*. London 1991, 163. See also Paul Mountfort / Adam Geczy / Anne Peirson-Smith: *Planet Cosplay. Costume Play, Identity and Global Fandom*. Bristol 2019.

5 Annamarie Jagose: *Queer Theory. An introduction*. New York, NY 1997, 71.

visible differences on the bodily surface, leading to the danger of exclusion of non-visible or normative-coded queer appearances from the queer community.[6] This paper therefore concerns itself less with the physical surface of bodies[7] but focuses on emotions and stories and examines the effect of emotional exposure in neo-burlesque. I will examine whether neo-burlesque, through the liberation of affects, forms a queer, carnivalesque space in which emotions and humor offer a temporary liberation from everyday wounds. My thesis is that emotions and their embodiment in the performance of neo-burlesque offer a queer theatrical purgation, a temporary relief from everyday structures, and playful rewriting of these structures, both for performers and the audience.

In the first part of my paper, I will explore neo-burlesque as an emotional theater in the sense of Antonin Artaud, using approaches of performance and storytelling theories, queer affect research, and queer historiography. Then, using two performances from New Orleans as examples, I will analyze the political impact of emotions in neo-burlesque in more detail based on the concept of punkish-pleasurable strategy of irritation and emotional take-off. In the next part, the concept of *erotohistoriography*, as a sensual rewriting of history, will be presented in order to explore neo-burlesque as an act of processing past personal traumas as well as questioning the national Catholic politics of one's own country, using two performances from Warsaw as examples.

1 Transforming Emotions into Erotic Performances

An actor is like a physical athlete, with this astonishing corollary; his affective organism is similar to the athlete's, being parallel to it like a double, although they do not act on the same level. The actor is a heart athlete.[8]

In his book *The Theatre and Its Double*, the French writer and dramatist Antonin Artaud calls for an emotional upheaval on stage: The theater, he argues, should not be

---

6 Laura Brightwell: The Exclusionary Effects of Queer Anti-Normativity on Feminine-Identified Queers. *Feral Feminisms* 7 (2018). https://feralfeminisms.com/wp-content/uploads/2019/04/2-Laura-Brightwell.pdf (last accessed 23 August 2022).

7 In previous essays, I have focused on a "corporeal surface" analysis of, for example, elements of drag, masquerade, and the so-called transgressive "bawdiness" of bodies, describing neo-burlesque as a kind of humorous, glittering, magic "queer circus," and showing how humor and a carnivalesque upside-down have a queering effect in which gender norms, ideals of beauty, and current social debates are grotesquely revealed: Joanna Staśkiewicz: Queering in der (neo-) Burlesque. *Navigationen: Zeitschrift für Medien- und Kulturwissenschaften* 18 (2018), 119–132; Joanna Staśkiewicz: The Queering Relief of the Humor in the New Burlesque. *Whatever. A Transdisciplinary Journal of Queer Theories and Studies* 4 (2021), 187–218, and Joanna Staśkiewicz: Gelsomina Transgressed: A Subversion of Fellini's World in the Clownish Neo-Burlesque. *Journal of Italian Cinema & Media Studies* 9 (2021), 63–81.

8 Antonin Artaud: *The Theatre and Its Double* [1938], trans. by Victor Corti. London 1993, 88.

simply pretty or entertaining but emotionally exhausting, cruel, or even painful. The performer should become an "athlete of the heart" who takes the audience out of their comfort zone with a physical performance that is more visual than textual. Gestures, atmosphere, the breaking of the fourth wall, and the reduction of the stage set to what is necessary are intended to provide a stirring mess of emotions for performers and audience alike. The US-American writer and essayist Susan Sontag describes Artaud's concept as a principle of "art as ordeal"[9] and a connection of body and mind, a connection that Artaud desperately strove for in his personal life. As Sontag puts it, "Artaud imagines the theatre as the place where the body would be reborn in thought and thought would be reborn in the body."[10]

Although neo-burlesque may not adhere to Artaud's theater concept in every way, particularly given the roots of burlesque in the supposedly "low" arts of humor and entertainment, and that the costumes and props frowned upon by Artaud are central components of neo-burlesque, I would nevertheless like to argue that neo-burlesque can certainly embody an emotional churn. Here, I am following the circus researcher Helene Stoddard, who sees in the circus a place for a non-textual *Theatre of Cruelty*, where physical representations aspire to and are capable of triggering emotions. As Stoddard writes: "In the notion of the body as hieroglyphic [Artaud] offers us the suggestion that the performing body, stripped of verbal language, may harbour meanings for an audience and which may indeed exist as an element of their immediate effect rather than despite it."[11] Neo-burlesque performance is, like the circus act, generally non-verbal: It involves an "act of undressing"[12] in which, rather than relying on the language of the performer, facial expressions, gestures, movement, costumes and props are set in motion to tell a story. As the British design theorist Barbara Brownie notes, burlesque performers fulfil the role of "storytellers": "The striptease performance can be considered as an 'altered image,' in which the image – the costumed body of the performer – is altered by a series of similar actions, and thus steadily progresses toward a resolution."[13] Ranging from the biographical "ego entanglement"[14] of the performers to the ostensibly apolitical act of "undressing" and the explicitly political manifesto, what connects these different forms of stories told with the body are emotions. If, indeed, as the British-Australian writer and queer, postcolonial, and critical race studies scholar Sara Ahmed has it, "[e]motions tell us a lot about time; emotions are the very 'flesh' of time," then the body of the burlesque performer might equally be described as "the very flesh of time" – a kind of barome-

---

9 Susan Sontag: Introduction. In: Antonin Artaud: *Antonin Artaud. Selected Writings*, ed. by Susan Sontag, trans. by Helen Weaver. Berkeley 1988, xxxii.

10 Sontag: Introduction, xxxvi.

11 Helen Stoddart: *Rings of Desire. Circus History and Representation*. Manchester 2000, 83.

12 Barbara Brownie: *Acts of Undressing. Politics, Eroticism, and Discarded Clothing*. London 2017, 3.

13 Brownie: *Acts of Undressing*, 30.

14 Nina Tecklenburg: *Performing Stories. Erzählen in Theater und Performance*. Bielefeld 2014, 185.

ter of the current sociopolitical situation visualized through the body of the performer. Herein lies another similarity to Artaud's Theatre of Cruelty, which supposedly possesses what Artaud refers to as a "mysterious aspect," where ancient myths are transferred through physical representation and "incarnated in moves, expressions and gestures, before gushing out in words."[15]

The cathartic effect of emotion in neo-burlesque, however, is not limited to the performers since acts of individual liberation through physical performance are also acts of social unification and solidarity. As Ahmed describes it, emotions "involve different orientations to others"[16] and thus create a space of "sociality."[17] In this sense, storytelling in neo-burlesque is itself performative and is not restricted to the visual representation of bodies. Here, I follow the German theater scholar Nina Tecklenburg, who sees storytelling as a cultural practice of performance, where realities are produced dynamically and through process: Alongside the formation of the narrator, the theater stage becomes a playful, experimental field of contingencies. In an earlier essay, I described this field within the burlesque as a "queer safe space" and, following the US-American sociologist Angela Jones, a *queer heterotopia*. Jones, building on Michel Foucault's concept of heterotopia, sees in the notion of a queer heterotopia the possibility of an everyday withdrawal from restrictions and humiliations: "These are spaces with no ordered categories that qualify and rank bodies. This will require the radical transformation of bodies, subversive performances, and transforming our minds, our souls, and our thoughts."[18] Such queer heterotopias are not bound to any particular forms or practices; their main characteristic is the subversion of hegemonic power relations, especially with regard to sex, gender, and sexuality. In a later text, Jones broadens her understanding of queerness, seeing it as not limited to sexual orientation or gender subversion, and emphasizing its status both as process and as a rebellion against narrow, essentialist social norms and binaries. For Jones, "[q]ueerness is always being made, remade, being done, being redone, and being undone. It is a quotidian refusal to play by the rules, if those rules stifle the spirit of queers who, like caged birds, cannot sing."[19]

Such a process-based understanding of queerness, together with its refusal to operate within the heteronormative matrix, is also developed by the US-American queer studies scholar Jack Halberstam in *In a Queer Time and Place*. Halberstam forwards a concept of a queer time that is distinct from the hegemonic, heteronormative, social-economic-productive social time of reproduction and family life, describing queerness

---

15 Artaud: *The Theatre and Its Double*, 82.

16 Ahmed: *The Cultural Politics of Emotion*, 202.

17 Ahmed: *The Cultural Politics of Emotion*, 8.

18 Angela Jones: Queer Heterotopias. Homonormativity and the Future of Queerness. *Interalia: A Journal of Queer Studies* (2009), 15.

19 Angela Jones: Introduction. Queer Utopias, Queer Futurity, and Potentiality in Quotidian Practice. In: *A Critical Inquiry into Queer Utopias*, ed. by. Angela Jones. New York, NY 2013, 14.

as "an outcome of strange temporalities, imaginative life schedules, and eccentric economic practices."[20] A similar approach is taken by the US-American literature and queer studies scholar Elizabeth Freeman with her concept of chrononormativity, the time in which people are stimulated into maximal productivity and capital accumulation, and towards heteronormative life strategies.[21] As an escape from chrononormativity, Freeman proposes a strategy of erotohistoriography: "a politics of unpredictable, deeply embodied pleasures that counters the logic of development."[22] According to Freeman, erotohistoriography is a pleasurable means of forgetting both the narrowness and even traumata of everyday life and the heteronormative hegemony of chrononormativity: "Against pain and loss, erotohistoriography posits the value of surprise, of pleasurable interruptions and momentary fulfilments from elsewhere, other times."[23]

Particularly in times of political backlash, queer utopian spaces appear as spaces of longing, where an "everyday life of queer trauma"[24] and a desolate "here and now"[25] can be momentarily forgotten and "filled with affirmative meaning that makes life liveable and society meaningful."[26] These spaces honor's conceptualization of carnival by the Russian philosopher and literary critic Mikhail Bakhtin, as a temporal suspension of official norms and hierarchies, a popular culture of laughter, and an affirmation of "silliness" in the form of the grotesque and parody. Carnival, for Bahktin, was a "feast of becoming, change and renewal. It was hostile to all that was immortalised and complete."[27] It is precisely this hostility to the "immortalised and complete" as well as its suspension of hierarchies that make carnival a queering practice, recalling what the German queer studies scholar Antke Engel described as the "queer strategy of equivocation or undisambiguation as a means of disrupting heteronormativity in particular and regimes of normalcy in general."[28] In the following section, I will use selected neo-burlesque performances in New Orleans and Warsaw to discuss the extent to which emotions can, in this type of performance, be queered and queering, and where narratives emerge in the process.

---

20 Jack Halberstam: *In a Queer Time and Place. Transgender Bodies, Subcultural Lives.* New York, NY / London 2005, 1.

21 Elizabeth Freeman: *Time Binds. Queer Temporalities, Queer Histories.* Durham, NC 2010, 3.

22 Freeman: *Time Binds*, 59.

23 Freeman: *Time Binds*, 59.

24 Ann Cvetkovich: *An Archive of Feelings. Trauma, Sexuality, and Lesbian Public Cultures.* Durham, NC 2003, 15.

25 José Esteban Muñoz: *Cruising Utopia. The Then and There of Queer Futurity.* New York, NY 2009, 1.

26 Alice Koubová et al.: *Play and Democracy. Philosophical Perspectives.* London 2021, 46.

27 Mikhail Bakhtin: *Rabelais and His World* [1965], trans. by Hélène Iswolsky. Cambridge 1968, 109.

28 Antke Engel: Queer Reading as Power Play. Methodological Considerations for Discourse Analysis of Visual Material. *Qualitative Inquiry* 25 (2018), 10.

2 From Pleasurable Punkish "Piss-Take" to Manifesto-Undressing in the Neo-Burlesque: Two Examples from New Orleans

In her analysis of contemporary feminist performances, Jacki Willson, the British performance and gender studies scholar, discusses the tongue-in-cheek humor of the female burlesque performance as a "piss-take" in which carnivalesque laughter subverts norms and makes both "nonsense of the normal" and the "normal appear ridiculous."[29] Achieving a political impact through its use of juxtaposition and the grotesque, such humor reveals the absurdity and ridiculousness of norms in a manner that recalls the anarchistic and destabilizing role of the clown: "Playing the fool destabilizes clichés by juxtaposing the *'deviant'* or the *'spoiled'* in relation to the *'ideal'* or the *'norm'*, thus exposing the way in which particular cultures and [their] people impose foolish rules."[30] A similar strategy is "bawdy unruliness," a concept used by Willson to describe a kinky "porn-panto" protest of sex-workers and activists in London 2014;[31] here, the bawdy is understood as political, capable of disrupting notorious heterosexual binaries such as whore and virgin, or dirtiness and purity. Subversive bawdiness has also been theorized extensively by the British media and communications scholar Gemma Commane, who describes how the so-called "dirty bodies" of performers challenge the patriarchal heterosexual matrix in relation to female sexuality. The terms "Bad Women" and "Dirty Bodies" are used by Commane to indicate "direct links to dangerous forms of femininity, such as the slut, the woman who is far too kinky, the bisexual and the woman who expresses her self-identity in disapproving ways (i.e. too honest, too confrontational, too gay, etc.)"[32] – a "too-muchness" that is denigrated as "bad" since it does not conform to the scripts of current beauty ideals or mainstream sexuality.

These conceptualizations of humorous and sexually pleasurable feminist performance are reminiscent of the "negative strategy"[33] and "embodied jouissance"[34] of queer-feminist punk rock theorized by the Austrian queer and American studies scholar Maria Katharina Wiedlack. Following Elizabeth Povinelli, Tavia Nyong'o, and José Muñoz, anti-social queering becomes, for Wiedlack, a pleasurable strategy of an

---

29 Jacki Willson: "Piss-Takes," Tongue-in-Cheek Humor and Contemporary Feminist Performance Art. Ursula Martinez, Oriana Fox and Sarah Maple. *n.paradoxa: international feminist art journal* 36 (2015), 5.
30 Willson: "Piss-Takes," 10.
31 Jacki Willson: Porn, pantomime and protest. The politics of bawdiness as feminine style. *Porn Studies* 5 (2018), 426–439.
32 Gemma Commane: *Bad Girls, Dirty Bodies. Sex, performance and safe femininity*. Bloomsbury 2020, 4.
33 Maria Katharina Wiedlack: *Queer-Feminist Punk. An anti-social history*. Vienna 2015, 145.
34 Wiedlack: *Queer-Feminist Punk*, 92.

"irritation of normativity."[35] Expressing anger and resistance against hegemony, it is a "pleasurable embrace of negativity, aimed to entertain and possibly educate as an additional benefit,"[36] a strategy, moreover, that leads to solidarity and transforms anger into a "liveable activism."[37] It was precisely such an "embodied jouissance" and joyful resistance against normativity that I recognized in the burlesque-punk performance I witnessed in June 2018 in New Orleans as part of the event Stripped Into Submission: Where Burlesque Meets BDSM, organized by the burlesque group Society of Sin. The show, described by its organizers as being comprised of sex-positive, "fetish-influenced burlesque and variety acts,"[38] took place in the alternative queer-friendly bar Hi-Ho Lounge in the Marigny district, away from the touristy French Quarter. Visitors to the bar are mostly young and local, although the events are increasingly attended by tourists. Like the AllWays Lounge and Siberia Lounge next door, the bar offers to the local burlesque-, cabaret-, clown-, and sideshow scene, as well as the queer community, a stage and a kind of "safe space."

One of the performers of Stripped Into Submission was Dick Jones Burly, who has been shaping the New Orleans scene with her burlesque work for several years, offering, for example, burlesque evenings parodying the "Emokids," a US-American emotive, punkish youth culture of the 1990s and 2000s. Dick Jones, who describes herself as "[t]he hick with the balls to call herself Dick,"[39] began her performance in an outfit that seemed like a promise of a representation of a vamp, femme-fatale femininity, her dark pageboy wig and leather jacket bringing an element of rebelliousness to her look. At first, with its performer moving sensually-seductively to the sounds of The Stripper by David Rose, the show appeared calm, serene, and enjoyable. Later, however, as she transformed into a punk rebel on stage, the atmosphere changed and the performance become more emotional. To the sounds of Joy Division's *She's Lost Control*, Dick Jones removed her wig to reveal her short shaved hair, beginning a frantic stage performance that culminated in a hilarious scene of rolling around on the floor in a celebration of rebellious "femininity." As in Commane's concept of the "Bad Girl." binaries were challenged: good and bad girl, seductive diva and rebellious punk. Such a joyful and dynamic performance of rolling around on stage blended joy and punk rebellion, recalling Sara Ahmed's understanding of the effect of pleasure, which allows bodies to take on more space.[40]

As the negativity of a heteronormative submission to the seductive script of a *femme fatale* faded into the background, the performance of joy in one's own physi-

---

35 Wiedlack: *Queer-Feminist Punk*, 145.

36 Wiedlack: *Queer-Feminist Punk*, 123.

37 Wiedlack: *Queer-Feminist Punk*, 4.

38 See: The Society of Sin, *Webpage.* https://www.thesocietyofsin.com (last accessed 30 April 2022).

39 See: The Society of Sin, *Webpage.* https://www.thesocietyofsin.com/society-members (last accessed 30 April 2022).

40 Ahmed: *The Cultural Politics of Emotion*, 164.

cality came to the fore. Rolling around with pleasure on the floor in a display of "loss of control," Dick Jones was, by the end of the show, performing her liberation from the control of the script of seduction. Her performance recalls the distinction made by Jack Halberstam between different interpretations of the song She's Lost Control, first in the original by Joy Division, and then in a cover version by Grace Jones.[41] While in the original, vocalist Ian Curtis sings in a form of reported speech about a woman who tells him that she has lost control, in her version, Grace Jones tells us in the first person that she herself has lost control. This, for Halberstam, represents a queering of the context, since the Grace Jones cover ends with screams, reminiscent of female hysteria but no longer at the service of the "spastic masculinity"[42] of the male punk singer. Like a "laugh of Medusa" in the manner of the French feminist writer Hélène Cixous, who in her manifesto calls women to *écriture féminine*,[43] a hysterical expression, in the sense of a liberating and creative one, Dick Jones' burlesque act also became "hysterical" – with a laugh that was rushing, physical, erotic, and liberating.

While Dick Jones' punkishly emotional depiction of "losing control" represents an act of liberation, the act of undressing in burlesque can also have a politically oppressive effect, as I will show using the following performance by burlesque performer, art model, and studied theater professional Lefty Lucy, who has been living in New Orleans since 2015. This particular burlesque show took place in September 2018 at the AllWays Lounge in New Orleans at the weekly Bingo Burlesque. At that time, hearings were being held for the conservative judge Brett Kavanaugh – who had been accused of sexual harassment – as nominee for the Supreme Court. Lefty Lucy presented an impromptu show that evening, prepared spontaneously following her words introducing the show. She began her performance by arriving on stage in a white dress similar to that of Marilyn Monroe in the film THE SEVEN YEAR ITCH, white high-heels, and a blonde, Marilyn-esque wig. The first part of her performance brought to mind a "revivalist burlesque," which Gemma Commane describes as a tease "used to cheekily suggest sexual naughtiness in a coquettishly assertive manner."[44] The seductiveness of Lefty's clothing, however, soon began to recede, and the act of undressing no longer appeared playful; indeed, as each layer of clothes was removed, a sense of vulnerability, almost of shame began to appear. After removing her dress and blonde wig, her white underwear was revealed, her panties smeared with blood-like red paint. Lefty ended the show with her breasts completely uncovered – without the nipple pasties that are customary in the burlesque. This combination of a white, innocent-looking dress, the imitation blood on her panties, and her nakedness at the end evoked a feeling of helplessness and objectification; it was a powerful manifesto that could be felt in the silence of the touched audi-

---

41 I refer here to the lecture *Trans*Feminism and Performance* given by Halberstam on 9 December 2019 in Berlin at Sophiensäle.

42 Halberstam: *Trans*Feminism.*

43 Hélène Cixous: The Laugh of the Medusa. *Signs*, 1/4 (1976), 875–893.

44 Commane: *Bad Girls, Dirty Bodies*, 166.

ence that lasted a few seconds before applause broke out. As Barbara Brownie points out, "[u]ndressing is a gesture – an active and purposeful event – whereas nakedness is a passive state of being. As an active gesture undressing can involve more agency than nakedness."[45] Lefty Lucy, however, was able to bring both together: a passive "nakedness" and an "act of undressing"; it was, then, perhaps this connection of vulnerability and revelation that made her act such a strong protest. Hers was a silenced rage represented by an almost naked body – yet her nakedness was not silent, it was an act of "expressing the unspoken."[46]

3 Burlesque as a "Battlefield" and Erotohistoriographic Strategy

As has been outlined above, the neo-burlesque can be aligned with Artaud's Theatre of Cruelty, particularly in the sense that its performers incorporate their emotions into the show, and that neo-burlesque is essentially a visual and non-verbal art form. Neo-burlesque is not silent, however, for it uses different forms of linguistic communication, whether by means of a song whose lyrics describe the story of the performance, or through the use of lip synchronization by performers to emphasize their identification with the lyrics. Indeed, performers can even speak directly, whereupon their oral statements become a form of activism. Burlesque performance thus operates on several levels, and, as Maria Katharina Wiedlack explains in reference to the activism and queer, feminist-punkish "production of meanings and knowledge," this production must take place in textual, oral, performative, and emotional realms.[47]

In Poland in particular, I have witnessed several shows where performers have addressed the audience directly, one of which took place in February 2018 at the Warsaw club Madame Q. At that time, demonstrations against the tightening of the abortion law were taking place across the country. In early January 2018, the Polish parliament rejected a proposal to liberalize abortion put forward by the Ratuj Kobiety 2017 (Save Women 2017) civic committee but approved a bid by Stop Aborcji (Stop Abortion) to further tighten regulations and eliminate the possibility of legal termination of pregnancy due to severe defects in the fetus. This situation triggered protests by women's organizations and demonstrations.[48] Disputes over the abortion law in Poland, which is considered one of the most restrictive in Europe, have been going on

---

45 Brownie: *Acts of Undressing*, 3.

46 Joanna Townsend-Robinson: Expressing the Unspoken. Hysterical Performance as Radical Theatre. *Women's Studies* 32 (2003), 533.

47 Wiedlack: *Queer-Feminist Punk*, 24.

48 See, for example: Michael Zok: "To Maintain the Biological Substance of the Polish Nation": Reproductive Rights as an Area of Conflict in Poland. *Hungarian Historical Review* 10/2 (2021), 357–381 and

for several years; since 2020, abortion has been prohibited even in the case of genetic defects. Particularly large protests in 2016 became known as the Black March of Polish Women.

The performer Lola Noir directly referred to these protests during her act in February 2018 at Madame Q, using the unofficial anthem of the protest Pole Walki (Battlefield) as musical background to a performance in which she sang about bodily self-determination. A well-known patriotic Polish saying used during the Partitions of Poland, *"Nic o mnie beze mnie"* ("Nothing about me without me") is repeated several times during the chorus. Lola Noir began her performance by dancing to the song in accordance with its folk rhythms. Her clothing was also reminiscent of Polish regional costumes, consisting of a white shirt, red corsage, and a long red skirt. The link to the red and white national colors of Poland was even more evident in the white and red flowers that decorated her hair. Over the course of the performance, Lola Noir stripped off layers of clothing until she was left only with black panties and nipples covered crosswise with black tape, together with the red and white flowers in her hair. As with Lefty Lucy, the conclusion of this performance was not sexualized; rather, in a pose reminiscent of a protest, Lola Noir was left standing with her body partially exposed, a black inscription on her chest and belly spelling out the aforementioned quote: "Nothing about me without me." She shouted these same words out at the end of the performance, her clenched fist raised in the air, and her gaze expressing a rage directed at the audience, self-determined and loud.

Although reminiscent of Dick Jones' punkishness, this was a performance stripped of any element of joy. Her "act of undressing" seemed like a statement rather than an erotic display (as was the case in the performance by Lefty Lucy) – a statement of partial nudity heightened by an angry facial expression that equated partial nakedness with the "letting-be-seen"[49] of the Italian philosopher Giorgio Agamben, where it was not the nakedness that made the display powerful but the face itself. Moreover, the scream at the end of the performance recalled the scream of Artaud in the Theatre of Cruelty, which, in Jay Murphy's reading,[50] represents an ecstatic practice of suspension that allows for a rupture of the limitations of body, temporality, and space, providing a space for new meaning, or perhaps only a suspension of anger. Lola Noir's scream cannot, however, be separated from her body, for on it is inscribed the same quote; thus, in "embodying the female voice," it inverts the famous plea by the US-American art historian and film theorist Kaja Silverman for a "disembodying [of] the female voice."[51] While Silverman's disembodiment of the female voice was intended as an act of libera-

---

Julia Hussein / Jane Cottingham / Wanda Nowicka / Eszter Kismodi: Abortion in Poland. Politics, Progression and Regression. *Reproductive Health Matters* 26 (2018), 11–14.

49 Giorgio Agamben: *Nudities* [2009], trans. by David Kishik / Stefan Pedatella. Stanford 2011, 89.

50 Jay Murphy: Artaud's Scream. *Deleuze Studies* 10/2 (2016), 140–161.

51 Kaja Silverman: *The Acoustic Mirror. The Female Voice in Psychoanalysis and Cinema.* Bloomington 1988, 141.

tion from the confinement of corporeality, Lola Noir's embodiment of the voice is a manifesto for a corporeal self-determination and a reappropriation of the body over which politics dares to dispose. This explicitly written and expressed rage concerning bodily heteronomy and the question of reproductive rights renders the performance of Lola Noir a manifestly political act, where subversive joy becomes eclipsed by subversive rage.

Finally, focusing on a performance entitled Celibacy by Warsaw burlesque performer and LGBTQ activist Gąsiu, I would like to show how burlesque can become an act of joyful-campy resistance against rigid religious laws. Gąsiu, who describes himself as a "queer rebel," has spoken in several interviews of his Catholic upbringing in a Catholic lyceum, repeatedly drawing on Catholic and national myths in his performances and appropriating national poems in a queer performance.[52] In Celibacy he burlesques the question of forbidden desire within the Catholic Church, first appearing on stage in a golden costume with transparent fabric parts, together with an elongated black lace veil over his face. Appearing genderless, his well-defined body is both male- and female-connoted, with long platinum-blond hair and high heels, and without any typical mask-like drag makeup. Gąsiu describes his variety of drag as a "genderfuck" that defies categorization and acts as a "satire of female impersonation through expressive makeup or heeled shoes."[53] His art brings to mind the notion of masquerade proposed by British fashion scholar Efrat Tseëlon as a pleasurable, carnivalesque caricature that challenges categorizations and questions dualisms: "Masquerade unsettles and disrupts the fantasy of coherent, unitary, stable, mutually exclusive divisions. It replaces clarity with ambiguity, certainty with reflexivity, and phantasmic constructions of containment and closure with constructions that in reality are more messy, diverse, impure and imperfect."[54] Tseëlon's definition, similar to Judith Butler's concept of performativity,[55] underlines the queer effect of the masquerade, which destabilizes gender boundaries per se and thus differs, for example, from the classical approach of femininity as masquerade by British psychoanalyst Joan Rivière,[56] which is based on the categories of femininity and masculinity. However, it might also be argued, following German theater scholar Lea-Sophie Schiel, that Gąsiu's performance style is not caricature as parody but rather a pastiche of

---

52 In one of his burlesque drag performances, for example, he appropriated the Polish national epic *Dziady* by Adam Mickiewicz in his own new iteration, campily distancing himself from the religious-national weight of its original meaning. See: Staśkiewicz: *The Queering Relief of the Humor in the New Burlesque.*

53 Ewa Paluszkiewicz: *Rebel Queer,* 202. https://www.yumpu.com/xx/document/read/65731217/rebelqu eer-zine/10 (last accessed 30 April 2022).

54 Efrat Tseëlon: Introduction. Masquerade and Identities. In: *Masquerade and Identities. Essays on Gender, Sexuality and Marginality,* ed. by Efrat Tseëlon. London 2001, 3.

55 Judith Butler: *Gender Trouble. Feminism and the Subversion of Identity.* New York, NY 1990.

56 Joan Rivière: Womanliness as a Masquerade. *International Journal of Psychoanalysis* 10 (1929), 303–313.

gender roles, an imitation that is without an original.[57] Following remarks by the US-American queer studies scholar Judith Butler on gender parody and parody in general as "parody [. . .] *of* the very notion of an original,"[58] Schiel emphasizes that although pastiche is also an imitation, it is above all the "comic" without requiring an original, it is only a parody: "The pastiche is a norm-less, empty, sheer parody."[59] If parodic exaggeration is no longer possible in the absence of any original, then perhaps pastiche is a better term to describe the indefinability of Gąsiu's drag.

Celibacy is partly a spoken show: Gąsiu begins his performance by slowly moving towards the center of the stage, declaiming the prayer Ave Maria Gratia Plena through a megaphone in the style of a priest leading a Catholic procession. After a few lines of prayer, the performance changes – Gąsiu puts the megaphone aside and begins to vogue to the musical sounds of Madonna's song Erotica. The queering effect of Gąsiu's drag pastiche is heightened in his performance through this vogueing, which is a type of dance movement that the German dance scholar Jutta Krauß describes as having the potential to stage gender, to explore gender boundaries, and to demonstrate a "pleasure in the body."[60] Moreover, vogueing represents an "embodied gender knowledge,"[61] a practice that transcends fluid gender constructions.[62]

At the end of his performance, Gąsiu stands on stage with gold-colored panties and black lace stockings, with a veil still over his face. His final poses are reminiscent of the figure of Jesus, particularly the image of the Merciful Jesus painted after a vision experienced by the Polish nun Faustyna Kowalska emphasizing divine mercy. In the image, Jesus holds his hand over his heart and two bright rays of light can be seen emanating from within it. Adopting a similar pose, Gąsiu holds one hand over his heart with the other extended in a gesture of blessing. One of his hands is bound in a sort of handcuff with straps; on the other, a black latex glove, holding the megaphone. The resemblance to Jesus is further strengthened by a black crown that Gąsiu places on his head at the end of the show, reminiscent of Jesus' crown of thorns. In 2019, Gąsiu described his performance as an act "which is the result of one sexual encoun-

---

57 Lea-Sophie Schiel: *Sex als Performance. Theaterwissenschaftliche Perspektiven auf die Inszenierung des Obszönen.* Bielefeld 2020, 143–147.

58 Butler: *Gender Trouble*, 138.

59 Schiel: *Sex als Performance*, 144.

60 The origins of the dance art of vogue can be found in the homosexual and transsexual Latino and African-American Ballroom scene of the 1960s in New York's Harlem district. Since the 1990s, vogue has enjoyed increasing popularity, especially within the LGBTQ community; having become mainstream, it is now popular as a campy dance style among a young urban population. See: Constantine Chatzipapatheodoridis: Strike a Pose, Forever. The Legacy of Vogue and Its Re-Contextualization in Contemporary Camp Performances. *European Journal of American Studies 11* (2017), and Jutta Krauß: *Voguing on Stage – Kulturelle Übersetzungen, vestimentäre Performances und Gender-Inszenierungen in Theater und Tanz.* Bielefeld 2020.

61 Krauß: *Voguing on Stage*, 193.

62 Krauß: *Voguing on Stage*, 236.

ter that resulted in a string of thoughts on the difference (or lack thereof) between religious fanaticism and unbridled desire."[63] His performance, however, does not come across as an expression of anger but rather as a pleasurable performance in which cultural or religious scripts are rewritten with relish and "the unspoken" can be expressed through the body. Themes such as the play of sexual desire, inner turmoil, and simultaneous self-punishment are expressed through the gesticulating play of the hands, with the one hand in a pointed handcuff performing together with the other in rubber latex a kind of danced dialectical disagreement. By the end, Gąsiu stands on stage like a queer Jesus, full of self-doubt, distributing his blessings with one hand and taking them back with the other. He leaves the stage declaiming the prayer Ave Maria Gratia Plena through the megaphone, as he did at the beginning.

Gąsiu's performance writes itself into the strategy of the group Glitter Confusion, a trashy-campy artist collective of which he is a member that strives for a kind of queer heterotopia. As Gąsiu describes it, the activities of the collective are designed to playfully undermine the dominance of heteronormative norms: "Our actions are about building another space-time continuum worth getting lost in."[64] Like the aforementioned erotohistoriography, emotions and a distancing from chrononormativity are deployed by the group in a pleasurably sexualized manner. As Freemann points out, "erotohistoriography posits the value of surprise, of pleasurable interruptions and momentary fulfilments from elsewhere, other times."[65] However, this concept or resolution does not lead to a wholesale forgetting of pain or anger, or a rewriting as pleasurable performance, it becomes rather a way of "shaking" the anger. This pleasurable-liberating act discharge offers a kind of playful resistance, reminiscent of the "sexualising affect" that Marie-Luise Angerer describes as "a symptom, as a node that resists something at the same time as allowing it to be enjoyed."[66] It should, however, not be forgotten that the effect of the "sexualised affect" in the neo-burlesque – the Bakhtinian carnival par excellence – signifies only a temporary liberation. For such queer heterotopic exceptions unhinge the heteronormative hegemony only momentarily; after leaving these queer spheres, "the supremacy of the official playing space" is entered into once again.[67]

---

63 Gąsiu: *Już dziś we Wrocławiu!* Facebook, November 30, 2019: www.facebook.com/gasiu.official/pho tos/ju%C5%BC-dzi%C5%9B-we-wroc%C5%82awiu-mighty-real-dragshow-30112019-hah-wroc%C5% 82aw-x-twoja-stara-w/3191377307604182/ (last accessed 30 April 2022).
64 Paluszkiewicz: *Rebel Queer*, 28.
65 Freeman: *Time Binds*, 59.
66 Marie-Luise Angerer: *Vom Begehren nach dem Affekt*. Zurich 2007, 108.
67 Hayley Malouin: Queer Hatchings. Carnival Time and the Grotesque in Circus Amok. *Performance Matters* 4/1–2 (2018), 173.

4 Conclusion

At the beginning of this essay, I mentioned the confusion I felt on my first visit to a burlesque event, whereupon it became clear to me that a complex art of representation was on display, one that cannot be reduced to a fusion of eroticism and comedy nor to seduction or the question of empowerment through physical representation. The effect of burlesque is comparable to what Jack Halberstam has argued regarding the "silly archives"[68] – that a banal pop-cultural text can say more about social structures than a serious scientific text. Moreover, as Maria Katharina Wiedlack has pointed out in relation to queer-punk performance, it is "a negative strategy insofar as it refuses fixation. This political strategy aims at the irritation of normativity. Irritation is also what makes jouissance political."[69] My own initial "irritation" therefore represented nothing more than a recognition of the queer and political effect of neo-burlesque that had not been obvious at the very beginning. It was also the effect that Artaud had demanded of the theater, where simple gestures have a deep intellectual effect, namely that it "aims to exalt, to benumb, to bewitch, to arrest our sensibility."[70] As I have demonstrated, neo-burlesque performance acts like a "re-examination,"[71] not only of the motives of the external world but also of the internal world of performers and audiences alike. This queers both personal stories but also national or religious narratives. Neo-burlesque is therefore far more than an erotic performance, it is a queer political practice that can shake things up. Hence, perhaps we can talk not only about neo-burlesque as erotohistoriography but rephrasing the latter term as *emotiohistoriography*: Neo-burlesque offers not only a temporary theatrical liberation from the social, political, and local conditions, but also enables the liberating transformation of the old emotions of both the performers and the spectators through a queer emotional spectacle wrapped in sparkling glitter.

Bibliography

Agamben, Giorgio: *Nudities* [2009], trans. by David Kishik / Stefan Pedatella. Stanford, CA 2011.

Ahmed, Sara: *The Cultural Politics of Emotion*. New York, NY 2014.

Angerer, Marie-Luise: *Vom Begehren nach dem Affekt*. Zurich 2007.

Artaud, Antonin: *The Theatre and Its Double* [1938], trans. by Victor Corti. London 1993.

Bakhtin, Mikhail: *Rabelais and His World* [1965], trans. by Hélène Iswolsky. Cambridge 1968.

Brightwell, Laura: The Exclusionary Effects of Queer Anti-Normativity on Feminine-Identified Queers. *Feral Feminisms* 7 (2018). https://feralfeminisms.com/wp-content/uploads/2019/04/2-Laura-Brightwell.pdf (last accessed 23 August 2022).

---

68 Jack Halberstam: *The Queer Art of Failure*. Durham 2011, 20.

69 Wiedlack: *Queer-Feminist Punk*, 149.

70 Artaud: *The Theatre and Its Double*, 70.

71 Artaud: *The Theatre and Its Double*, 71.

Brownie, Barbara: *Acts of Undressing. Politics, Eroticism, and Discarded Clothing*. London 2017.

Butler, Judith: *Gender Trouble. Feminism and the Subversion of Identity*. New York, NY 1990.

Cervellon, Marie-Cécile / Brown, Stephen: All the Fun of the Fan. Consuming Burlesque in an Era of Retromania. *NA- Advances in Consumer Research* 42 (2014), 271–275.

Chatzipapatheodoridis, Constantine: Strike a Pose, Forever. The Legacy of Vogue and its Re-contextualization in Contemporary Camp Performances. *European Journal of American Studies* 11/3 (2017).

Cixous, Hélène: The Laugh of the Medusa. *Signs* 1/4 (1976), 875–893.

Commane, Gemma: *Bad Girls, Dirty Bodies. Sex, Performance and Safe Femininity*. Bloomsbury 2020.

Costa, Stevi: Accio Burlesque! Performing Potter Fandom Through "Nerdlesque." In: *Playing Harry Potter. Essays and Interviews on Fandom and Performance*, ed. by Brenner, Lisa S. Jefferson, NC 2015, 108–132.

Cvetkovich, Ann: *An Archive of Feelings. Trauma, Sexuality, and Lesbian Public Cultures*. Durham, NC 2003.

Engel, Antke: Queer Reading as Power Play. Methodological Considerations for Discourse Analysis of Visual Material. *Qualitative Inquiry* 25/4 (2018), 1–12.

Foucault, Michel: Of Other Spaces. *Diacritics* 16/1 (1986), 22–27.

Freeman, Elizabeth: *Time Binds. Queer Temporalities, Queer Histories*. Durham, NC 2010.

Gąsiu: *Już dziś we Wrocławiu!* Facebook, November 30, 2019: www.facebook.com/gasiu.official/photos/ju% C5%BC-dzi%C5%9B-we-wroc%C5%82awiu-mighty-real-dragshow-30112019-hah-wroc%C5%82aw-x-twoja-stara-w/3191377307604182/ (last accessed 30 April 2022).

Halberstam, Jack: *In a Queer Time and Place. Transgender Bodies, Subcultural lives*. New York / London 2005.

Halberstam, Jack: *The Queer Art of Failure*. Durham, NC 2011.

Haraway, Donna J.: *Simians, Cyborgs, and Women. The Reinvention of Nature*. London 1991.

Hussein, Julia et al.: Abortion in Poland. Politics, progression and regression. *Reproductive Health Matters* 26/52 (2018), 11–14.

Jagose, Annamarie: *Queer Theory. An Introduction*. New York, NY 1997.

Jones, Angela: Queer Heterotopias. Homonormativity and the Future of Queerness. *Interalia: A Journal of Queer Studies* 4 (2009), 1–20.

Jones, Angela: Introduction. Queer Utopias, Queer Futurity, and Potentiality in Quotidian Practice. In: *A critical inquiry into queer utopias*, ed. by Jones / Angela. New York, NY 2013, 1–17.

Koubová, Alice et al.: *Play and Democracy. Philosophical Perspectives*. London 2021.

Krauß, Jutta: *Voguing on Stage – Kulturelle Übersetzungen, vestimentäre Performances und Gender-Inszenierungen in Theater und Tanz*. Bielefeld 2020.

Malouin, Hayley: Queer Hatchings. Carnival Time and the Grotesque in Circus Amok. *Performance Matters* 4/1–2 (2018), 163–99.

Mountfort, Paul / Geczy, Adam / Peirson-Smith, Anne: *Planet cosplay. Costume play, identity and global fandom*. Bristol / Chicago 2019.

Muñoz, José Esteban: *Cruising Utopia. The Then and There of Queer Futurity*. New York, NY 2009.

Murphy, Jay: Artaud's Scream. *Deleuze Studies* 10/2 (2016), 140–161.

Paluszkiewicz, Ewa: *Rebel Queer*. 2021. https://www.yumpu.com/xx/document/read/65731217/rebelqueer-zine (last accessed 30 April 2022).

Rivière, Joan: Womanliness as a Masquerade. *International Journal of Psychoanalysis* 10 (1929), 303–313.

Schiel, Lea-Sophie: *Sex als Performance. Theaterwissenschaftliche Perspektiven auf die Inszenierung des Obszönen*. Bielefeld 2020.

Silverman, Kaja: *The Acoustic Mirror. The Female Voice in Psychoanalysis and Cinema*. Bloomington, IN 1988.

Sontag, Susan: Introduction. In: Antonin Artaud: *Antonin Artaud. Selected Writings*, ed. by Sontag, Susan, trans. by Helen Weaver. Berkeley, CA 1988, xvii–lix.

Staśkiewicz, Joanna: The New Burlesque as an Example of Double-Simulacrum. *Forum Socjologiczne* 8 (2017), 111–122.

Staśkiewicz, Joanna: Queering in der (neo-)Burlesque. *Navigationen: Zeitschrift für Medien- und Kulturwissenschaften* 18/1 (2018), 119–132.

Staśkiewicz, Joanna: Gelsomina Transgressed. A Subversion of Fellini's World in the Clownish Neo-Burlesque. *Journal of Italian Cinema & Media Studies* 9/1 (2021), 63–81.

Staśkiewicz, Joanna: The Queering Relief of the Humor in the New Burlesque. *Whatever. A Transdisciplinary Journal of Queer Theories and Studies* 4 (2021), 187–218.

Stoddart, Helen: *Rings of Desire. Circus History and Representation.* Manchester 2000.

Tecklenburg, Nina: *Performing Stories. Erzählen in Theater und Performance*, Bielefeld 2014.

Townsend-Robinson, Joanna: Expressing the Unspoken. Hysterical Performance as Radical Theatre. *Women's Studies* 32/5 (2003), 533–557.

Tseëlon, Efrat: Introduction. Masquerade and Identities. In: *Masquerade and Identities: Essays on Gender, Sexuality and Marginality*, ed. by Tseëlon, Efrat. London 2001, 1–17.

Wiedlack, Maria Katharina: *Queer-Feminist Punk. An Anti-social History.* Vienna 2015.

Willson, Jacki: "Piss-Takes" Tongue-in-Cheek Humor and Contemporary Feminist Performance Art. Ursula Martinez, Oriana Fox and Sarah Maple. *n.paradoxa: international feminist art journal* 36 (2015), 5–12.

Willson, Jacki: Porn, Pantomime and Protest. The Politics of Bawdiness as Feminine Style. *Porn Studies* 5/4 (2018), 426–439.

Zok, Michael: "To Maintain the Biological Substance of the Polish Nation": Reproductive Rights as an Area of Conflict in Poland. *Hungarian Historical Review* 10/2 (2021), 357–381.

Peter Rehberg
Affective Sexualities

Abstract: The fanzine *Butt* stages a different style of desire that does not reduce sexuality to the mere fulfillment of fantasies, but offers, beyond a psychoanalytical understanding of sexual encounters, new forms of contact. One way to understand this stylistic shift within post-pornography would be to say that in *Butt*, sexuality is transcended by affects. Through a critical engagement with theories of affect, a concept of *affective sexualities* emerges as a mixed phenomenon. For a strict distinction between sexuality and affects is not easily tenable. However, in order to counteract the desexualization of a queer analysis in the field of affect theory, the discussion about the critical potential of affects must be tied back to the topic of sexuality. To this end, we can read moments of affect in Foucault, which are addressed through the barely elaborated concept of *pleasure*, and which, in turn, maintain a proximity to Deleuze's concept of *desire*. In the context of *Butt*, however, what is at stake is not the processing and shifting of institutionalized forms of power as in the case of Foucault's example of S/M, but rather a different conception of *love*, as Lauren Berlant suggests, that can no longer be categorically distinguished from desire.

Keywords: Affect, Sedgwick, Freud, Berlant, Desire, Pleasure, Queer Love

> Indeed, erotics [sic] is, among other things very much about presence: dwelling in the other's nearness; feelings of unity and being together; glimmering eyes; sharing a bottle of wine; walking along the Elbe; [. . .] sentimentality is part of it, and so is heart-throbbing.[1]

> Once the sexual is staged as the losing sight of self rather than its assertion or consolidation or indeed triumph, the obsession with sex becomes an obsession with a certain kind of love.[2]

1 Post-Phallic Masculinity

The attention to the male body, its surfaces, zones, and details do not work unrestrictedly toward an idea of masculinity. The gay gaze registers a becoming of the body's forms that aims to leave the category of gender behind. In *Butt*,[3] gender is aestheti-

---

1 Henning Bech: *When Men Meet: Homosexuality and Modernity.* Chicago, IL 1997, 69.

2 Leo Bersani / Adam Phillips: *Intimacies.* Chicago, IL 2008, 96–97.

3 *Butt* is a gay fanzine with photos and interviews, published from 2001 onwards in Amsterdam and later in New York. Since 2011, *Butt* has only been published online, including a digital archive and a social network (buttmagazine.com), yet in 2022 there was a relaunch of *Butt* in its print form. In 2006, a *Butt* book with a best of selection of interviews and photos from the first five years was published by Taschen (see Jop Van Bennekom / Gert Jonkers [eds.]: *Butt Book: The Best of the First 5 Years of*

cally transcended: instead of a Butlerian gender performance that destabilizes masculinity through parody, or a celebration of the destruction of the masculine ego-ideal, which Bersani foregrounds, we find a non-essentialist transformation of the materiality of the male body. With Deleuze, we can say that the photographs in *Butt* document a *male becoming*. It is not the male body confirmed in its coded masculinity that is at the center of *Butt*'s post-pornographic interest, but a maleness that oscillates back and forth between denaturalization and re-naturalization and in this rhythmic movement shifts the concepts of maleness and masculinity: *Butt* does not present a phallically organized scheme of masculinity/maleness, but a male body that reorganizes itself in the exhibition of different zones of the body.

In the context of the aesthetics of every day, a conception of the body is offered that moves away from the optimized porn image. The body parts which are presented do not fit into a fetish catalog or a checklist of sexual preferences which can be matched to specific erotic interests. In *Butt*, the reworking of the meaning of the male body takes place under the condition of a gay gaze and desire that cannot, however, unhesitatingly be considered sexual. *Butt* not only proposes an alternative body politics, rather it also brings a different conception of desire into play, one that leaves pornographic instrumentality behind. The mutability of the male body corresponds to a form of sexuality that is not only to be understood as a purely libidinous program.

Its pornographic content is hardly authoritarian in the sense of confirming the laws of genre. Rather, *Butt* creates alliances that renegotiate the representation of sex. In this way, an alternative idea of male sexuality is sketched out, as Paul Smith, for example, has also envisaged: "perhaps it would be useful to see what might happen if some more substantialist notion of male sexuality were pulled – heuristically and provisionally –away from the phallus."[4] In order to conceptualize the post-phallic understanding not only of maleness and masculinity, but of sexuality and sex, in this

---

Butt– *Adventures in 21st Century Gay Subculture*. Cologne 2006), and in December 2014, an expanded new edition of the *Butt* book was published under the title *Forever Butt*. Even beyond the magazine and its spin-offs, in the 2000s, *Butt* inspired a new gay indie aesthetic that has become a global phenomenon, focusing on an aesthetic, sexual lifestyle that brings together pornography and art. In the wake of *Butt*, a range of queer fanzines have emerged: *Kink, Kaiserin, Basso, They Shoot Homos Don't They?* With their young, bearded, imperfect men, they are visually close to *Butt* & Co. and its comparatively puritanical approach of only printing interviews and portraits of mostly naked young men. *Butt*'s photos, printed in documentary style and on pale pink paper, can be situated in the context of the post-porn movement. Post-porn involves a renegotiation of the genre of pornography: *Butt* opens up the pornographic image to new aesthetic and narrative possibilities and proposes other conceptions of gender and sexuality.

4 Paul Smith: Vas. In: *Feminisms: An Anthology of Literary Theory and Criticism*, ed. by Robyn R. Warhol / Diane Price Herndl. New Brunswick, NJ 1991, 1022. The fact that a non-phallic sexuality is not only euphorically celebrated on the queer side, but is also filled with fear has been described by Jonathan Kemp in his reading of Schreber: "Between the disciplinary command to have a body and the actual sensations of the body lies a space which, for men at least, is the cause of great anxiety." Jonathan Kemp: *The Penetrated Male*. New York, NY 2013, 31.

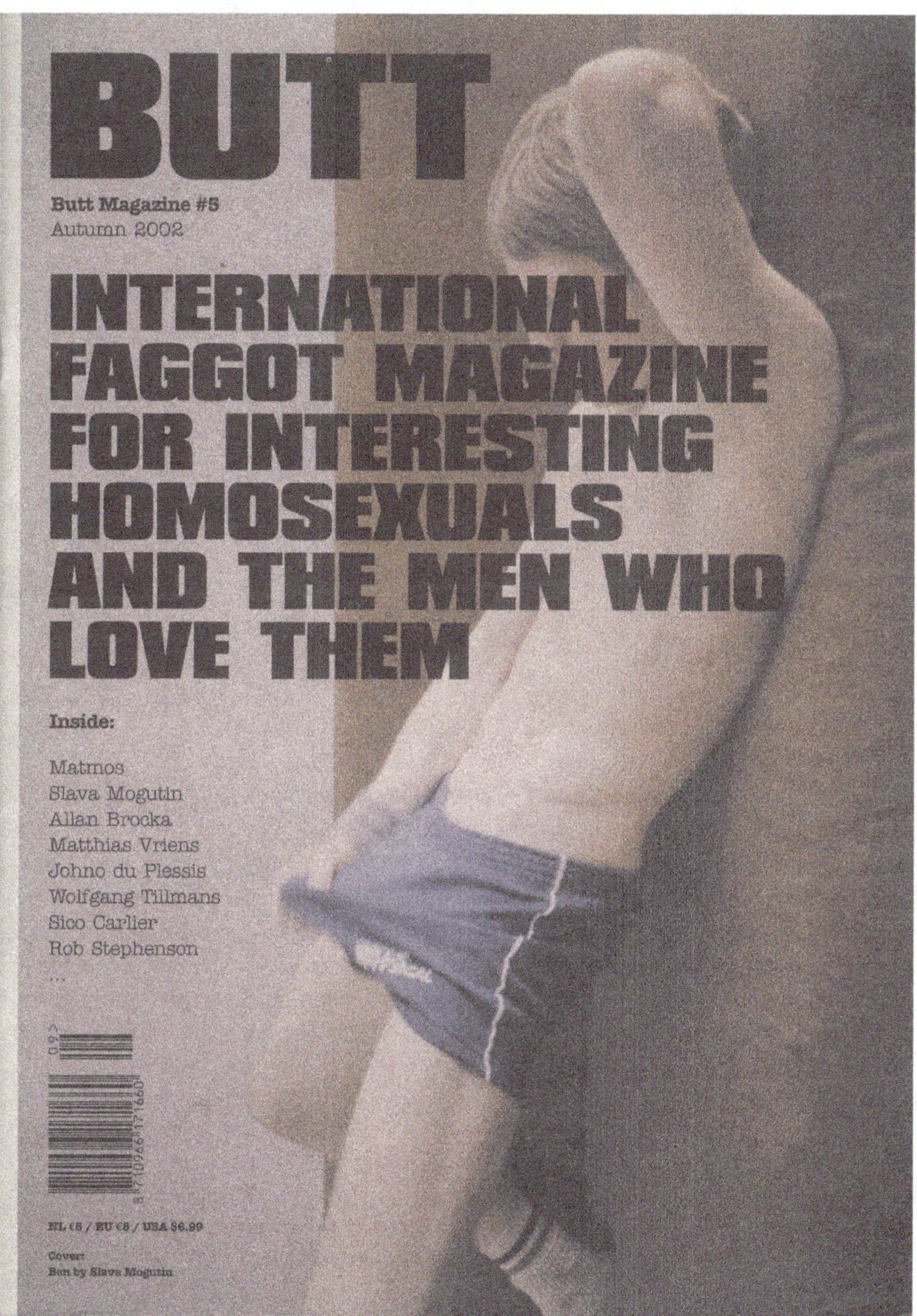

Fig. 1: Ben photographed by Slava Mogutin. In: Van Bennekom, Jop and Gert Jonkers (ed.) Butt # 5, Autumn 2002, Cover.

chapter, I open a discussion between theories of sexuality on the one hand and affect theory on the other.

While affect theory owes its categories and epistemologies to psychology, psychoanalysis, and Deleuzian philosophy, in order to develop connections between an affective and a sexual paradigm, I am focusing here on Michel Foucault's remarks concerning "bodies and pleasures" (in contrast to the dispositive of sexuality and truth), and on Laurent Berlant's concept of a "queer love." A conceptual pairing that is traditionally conceived of as dialectic if not antagonistic – the difference between pleasure/desire on the one hand and love on the other – must be deconstructed, I will argue, in order to establish a theoretical language that matches what's at stake with the representation of sexuality in *Butt*. To get there, I will start by outlining the importance of affect for the genre of pornography, before I excavate a specific queer line of thought that helps to grasp the meaning of *Butt*'s post-pornographic photos that owe their beauty as much to affect as to sex. I will conceive of *Butt*'s visual culture as a documentation of *affective sexualities*, that is to say as a mixed phenomenon in which the sexual and the affective dimensions of the ways in which gay men connect to each other continuously return in new constellations.

2 Porn and Affect

No discipline is more sentimental than the one that represses sentiments.[5]

DIY-porn challenges familiar patterns of commercial pornography, such as the elimination of anything that does not serve to increase sexual arousal. In this respect, it would, for example, be wrong to judge online pornography as a quasi-paralyzing form of sexual representation, within which the conventionality of pornographic imagery is always confirmed again. Instead, pornography should also be seen as a creative practice.[6] Indeed, porn can be queer insofar as it presents "unresolved visions of desiring."[7] What I am suggesting is that one way to distinguish between pornography and post-pornography is to understand the contextualization that post-pornography undertakes, using an everyday aesthetic as a means to open the genre toward emotions and affects.[8]

---

5 Guy Hocquenghem: *The Screwball Asses*. Los Angeles, CA 2010, 38.

6 Shaka McGlotten: *Virtual Intimacies: Media, Affect, and Queer Sociality*. Albany, NY 2013, 14.

7 Nick Davis: *The Desiring-Image: Gilles Deleuze and Contemporary Queer Cinema*. Oxford / New York, NY 2013, 7.

8 The terminology in the context of affect theory is often ambiguous and contradictory. Depending on the theoretical genealogy and methodology, there is talk of affects, affections, emotions, or feelings. Moreover, the multifaceted use of the English term "affect," and the question of how best to translate it, often confuses this situation. While my position, which I will further elaborate, takes up Sedgwick's impulse to use affects to critique the paradigm of sexuality, in doing so, I do not follow Sedgwick's

As Steven Marcus categorically noted 50 years ago, affects or emotions usually have no place in pornography: "Pornography is not interested in persons but in organs. Emotions are an embarrassment to it, and motives are distractions. [. . .] Sex in pornography is sex without the emotions."[9] In the pornographic representation of sex, emotions and affects are not part of the concept of sexuality. Sexuality is reduced to sex as an act. Marcus' observations here refer to a personalized and codified form of affects in the sense of emotions. To the extent that pornography does not focus on individuals but on sexual types, subjective expressions of emotion are left out. Starting from this antagonism, which is crucial for pornographic narratives, the question arises as to what it would mean to shift the rules of pornography as a genre, and to see emotionality – especially if we understand it not only as the inner richness of individual personalities, but in a non-psychological context of affect – in the representation of naked bodies.

In her analysis of digital pornography, Susanna Paasonen reminds us of the importance of affect in the presentation of sexual acts: "Affect is an important analytical tool in studies of online pornography due to the visceral nature of both the imageries and the reactions they give rise to."[10] Affect here refers to a dimension beyond pornographic representation, as Zabet Patterson also explains:

> The pornographic image can be a particularly dense semantic site, but it is one which functions only in and through a direct visceral appeal of the body. The appeal of the pornographic image is importantly corporeal, and images become effective as porn to the extent that they elicit certain bodily sensations, almost involuntarily.[11]

So, what if we do not limit the "visceral nature" of both the pornographic act and its reception to an understanding of sexuality as desire and the fantasies that guide it but rather consider the bodies, body parts, objects, and environments that interact here beyond the paradigms of sexuality in terms of affect as a material and non-psychological dimension of connecting?

Tomkins reception, which understands affects as discrete, legible units of subjectivation. Rather, I understand affects first of all in terms of Massumi's Deleuze reception, where affects are understood as a prelinguistic, precognitive, trans-subjective force. While this notion of affects is helpful in the context of a critique of sexuality, it also proves problematic in the light of Deleuze's texts on affects. For on the one hand, Deleuze reserves the concept of affects for aesthetic processes; in relation to non-aesthetic processes, on the other hand, he speaks of affections. I am following the direction of his terminology here and therefore propose, for what is usually called "affect" in affect theory, either the more open concept of the affective, or, if it concerns concrete processes, that of affection. Without discussing these terms in detail, Claudia Breger also suggests translating the English "affect" with the affective and not with "affect." Claudia Breger: *Nach dem Sex? Sexualwissenschaft und Affect Studies.* Göttingen 2014, 16.

9 Steven Marcus: Pornotopia. In: *Sexual Revolution,* ed. by Jeffrey Esscoffier. New York, NY 2003, 394.

10 Susanna Paasonen: *Carnal Resonance: Affect and Online Pornography.* Cambridge, MN / London 2011, Loc 676/3979.

11 Zabet Patterson: Going On-Line: Consuming Pornography in the Digital Era. In: *Porn Studies,* ed. by Linda William. Durham, NC / London 2004, 106.

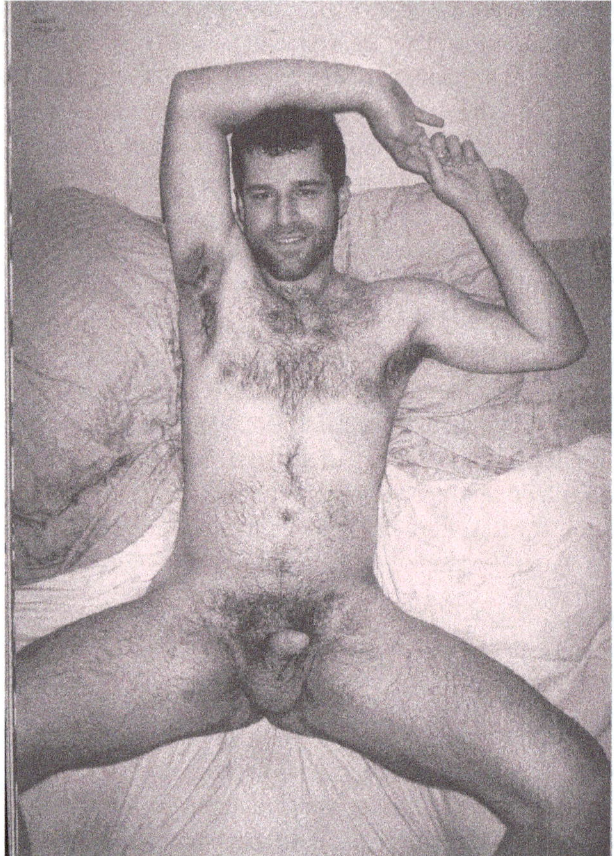

Fig. 2: Jason Whipple photographed by Miguel Villalobos. In: Van Bennekom, Jop and Gert Jonkers (ed.) Butt # 18, Winter 2006–07, 18.

Affect has two main functions in this context: first, to name a realm of bodily experience beyond historically familiar forms of desire and sexuality. This critical perspective has a tradition: Gilad Padva, for example, confirms what Richard Dyer contends in his argument (which is in turn indebted to Foucault) that what is at stake in critical studies on sexuality is not a liberation *of* sexuality, but rather a liberation *from* sexuality.[12] Second, by turning to affect, it is assumed that this post-sexual realm is not

---

12 Richard Dyer: Coming to Terms: Gay Pornography. *Only Entertainment*. New York, NY / London 1992, 121–134; Gilad Padva: Male Bodies, Fantasies and Identifications in the Naked Issue of Attitude Magazine. *International Journal of Sexuality and Gender Studies* 7/4 (2002), 284. Or, to put it another way, the problem of sex is not only, or not necessarily, to be solved by having more or better sex, but rather by what that sex encompasses. Cf. Nick Davis' discussion of Linda Williams Davis: *The Desiring-Image*, 99.

fully translatable into identifiable forms. Affective dynamics do not follow a habit and they do not take place within a secure and demarcated territory. In an interview with Gregg and Seigworth, Lawrence Grossberg says about affect: "basically, it's become everything that is non-representational or non-semantic – that's what we now call affect."[13]

In this chapter, I am interested in affect in relation to sex and sexuality as part of the post-pornographic culture. The point is to find a theoretical language that can do justice to the occurrence of desire and sexuality, as presented in *Butt*. Can affect be understood as a way of transgressing normative representations of sexuality in pornography? Can *affect* be furthermore understood as a transgression of forms of existing sexual "transgressions" that are all too well-rehearsed and have thus already lost their transgressive force? What remains of a critical perspective that takes sexuality as its starting point, if we use affect theory as a critique of the paradigm of sex and sexuality? Does affect replace sexuality?[14]

If we go on to understand affect theory as part of a feminist perspective, this brings us back to a familiar debate regarding the place of sex and sexuality within a queer project that aims, among other things, to bring together feminist and gay perspectives that are not always reconcilable.[15] Eve Sedgwick, on whose later texts many basic assumptions about affect in the context of queer theory can be traced, already admitted nearly 20 years ago that: "The sexual interest of the essays, as I've mentioned, seems to decrease".[16] In a review of Lauren Berlant and Lee Edelman's *Sex, Or the Unbearable*, Tim Dean recently responded to this problem again, raising a polemic concerning the manner in which he primarily understands the affective turn to be a desexualization of queer studies, a movement which can similarly be seen in the history of the institutionalization of queer studies in the United States.[17] In the same

---

13 Melissa Gregg / Gregory Seigworth (eds.): *The Affect Theory Reader*. Durham, NC / London 2010, Loc. 4271/5490.

14 According to Marie-Luise Angerer's diagnosis, the affective dispositif has meanwhile replaced the sexual one Marie-Luise Angerer: *Desire After Affect*. Lanham, MD 2014. See also Breger: *Nach dem Sex? Sexualwissenschaften und Affect Studies*.

15 Bersani is skeptical here and speaks of a "puritanical feminism" Leo Bersani: *Homos*. Cambridge and London 1995, 55. In summary, for him, this means: "The relation of gay men to feminism is bound to be more problematic than anyone wants to admit" Bersani: *Homos*, 63. Twenty-five years after Bersani's "Is the Rectum a Grave?" Lynne Huffer's outline of queer ethics *Are The Lips a Grave? A Queer Feminist on the Ethics of Sex* and a recourse to Luce Irigaray, seeks to reactivate a tradition of queer feminism Lynne Huffer: *Are the Lips a Grave? A Queer Feminist on the Ethics of Sex*. New York 2013. In *Orgasmology*, Annamarie Jagose also thwarts this threatening opposition between queer and feminist in a clear way. Annamarie Jagose: *Orgasmology*. Durham, NC / London 2013.

16 Eve Kososfsky Sedgwick: *Touching Feeling: Affect, Pedagogy, Performativity*. Durham, NC / London 2003, 21.

17 Tim Dean: No Sex Please, We're American. *American Literary History*. 27/3 (2015), 614–624.

issue of *American Literary History*, Berlant and Edelman counter that Dean's concept of sexuality – in its restriction to sex as a sexual act – is too limited.[18] Is it possible to talk about sexuality in a different way through the use of affect theory, or do we, in turning to affect, depart from the realm of the sexual altogether?

The much-discussed post-pornographic film SHORTBUS,[19] for example, succeeds in offering a counter-program to the commodification of mainstream sexuality through emotions, but in so doing, the film reverts to narrative patterns of selfhood and identity, as German critic Diedrich Diederichsen elaborates:[20]

> These images, however, also have in common with the rest of indie porn the idea that they, like a film like *Shortbus*, always want to read sexual experiences and pornographic experiences only as extensions and conquests of a self-actualizing self whose goal is closure and identity. The irreducibly fetishistic structure of desire must thus always be translated into tolerable morals, ethics or self-images, with the success that then [. . .] porn becomes stuffy and reactionary.[21]

Do the *Butt* boys with their images and stories chart another path that lies between a sentimentally tamed desire on the one hand and sexual rigor on the other?[22] The premise of my investigation is centered on the notion that the sexuality in *Butt* differs from the representation of sex in mainstream porn. The aesthetic of the imperfect and mutating male body corresponds to an idea of sexuality that, in contrast to the aggressive sexual narcissism of mainstream porn, contains an "aesthetics of sexual awkwardness," as Lauren Berlant puts it.[23] Post-pornography would thus be understood as a sexual-affective field that does not propose a sexual representation reducible to fantasies, and which thus has a less ideological politics of attachment to offer, without slipping into the sentimentality of canonized emotions. *Butt*'s post-pornographic aesthetic is about renewing a promise that Lauren Berlant and Lee Edelman have formulated as follows: "Sex [. . .] holds out the prospect of discovering new ways of being and of being in the

---

18 Lauren Berlant / Lee Edelman: Reading, Sex, and the Unbearable: A Response to Tim Dean. *American Literary History* 27/3 (2015), 79–90.

19 Nick Davis recalls the exuberant reception *Shortbus* received. The film was credited with correcting the direction queer cinema had taken 15 years after the proclamation of "New Queer Cinema." Davis: *The Desiring-Image*, 96–105.

20 For a fuller discussion of SHORTBUS, see Jagose: *Orgasmogology*, 93–105; Davis: *The Desiring-Image*, 96–105.

21 Diedrich Diederichsen: *Kritik des Auges: Texte zur Kunst.* Hamburg 2008, 271, [Own translation, P.R.].

22 Hocquenghem writes, regarding this perspective on gay subculture early on in the 1970s: "[. . .] homosexual desire is mechanically recited rather than invented. It is because this desire functions exclusively around sex, and not on the totality of the body." Hocquenghem: *The Screwball Asses*, 23.

23 Lauren Berlant: Starved. In: *After Sex? On Writing since Queer Theory*, ed. by Janet Halley / Andrew Parker. Durham, NC / London 2012, 79.

world."[24] At issue is the status of these sexual-affective representations; at stake, after the loss of conventional pornographic fantasies, are new and creative ways of living in a sexual/affective space that is not yet controlled by biopolitics.

Within a psychoanalytic framework, *jouissance* as a decentering experience is seen to be the primary force by which ideological formations are interrupted. While authors such as Foucault primarily strive to define these sexual potentials as being beyond genital sexuality, Bersani understands gay anal intercourse as being a scene of *jouissance*. The dissolution of the subject, as Annamarie Jagose describes it, occurs at the moment of orgasm.[25] In this regard, David Halperin writes:

> Only something so very bad for the integrated person that the normalized modern individual has become can perform the crucial work of rupture, of social and psychological disintegration, that may be necessary in order to permit new forms of life to come into being.[26]

Lauren Berlant's version of affect theory, which becomes the focus of attention toward the end of this chapter, is about finding the unbinding power of *jouissance* in affect beyond sex. The project of "living with negativity" – an experimental way of living that is not anchored in conventional fantasies – is thus not meant to be limited to sexual experience in general, and gay sexual experience in particular.[27] Such a perspective represents a critique of the narrowness of the concept of sexuality insofar as this concept has nevertheless been formative for queer theory, as Tom Roach explains: "The primary subcategories through which we understand sexuality – principally homo- and heterosexuality – have provided an all too efficient framework for classifying and evaluating human affection."[28] By shifting the concept of sexuality from coded sexual acts and positions toward affect, the juxtaposition of sexual identity, on the one hand, and *jouissance,* on the other, is destabilized.

I am suggesting that *Butt*'s aesthetics offers a path that leads away from sexuality as a coded system toward an "aesthetics of existence."[29]

With *Butt*, it is not a matter of overcoming sex and sexuality, but of opening them up and reorienting them by making room for affect. This results in a double movement: on the one hand, the concept of affect serves to relativize Foucauldian notions of sexuality and sex and to emphasize their ontological dimension; on the other hand, turning to Foucault, is a movement that is directed against the tendency toward desexualization within affect theory. What would it mean to think of the sexual as

---

24 Berlant / Edelman: *Reading, Sex, and the Unbearable*, 625–629.

25 Jagose: *Orgasmogology*, 11–15.

26 David Halperin: *Saint Foucault: Towards a Gay Hagiography*. New York, NY / Oxford 1995, 107.

27 Berlant / Edelman: *Sex, or the Unbearable*, 63–118.

28 Tom Roach: *Friendship as a Way of Life: Foucault, Aids, and the Politics of Shared Estrangement.* Albany, NY 2012, 12.

29 Halperin: *Saint Foucault: Towards a Gay Hagiography*, 72–79; Roach: *Friendship as a Way of Life,* 77–78.

affect? Berlant's notion of "queer love," which undermines the psychoanalytical de-marcation of desire and love, will further help to define the repertoire of styles, attachments, and situations in the sexual-affective world of the *Butt* boys.

3 Affect as Pleasure, Pleasure as Affect: Foucault

> The ultimate horizons of the ethical project of the self are not so much its original trauma (as Freud would have it) and its inevitable death (as Heidegger urged) as its aesthetic becoming and cultural generativity. But, for Foucault, this was not an aestheticist becoming, or at least it was not only an aestheticist becoming, in a cultivated development of the self [. . .] It is also situated in (and in theory it might be thought and lived as) a series of unmotivated, even unformed, deflections and devolutions in the social relations of sensuous erogenous human being – in effect a counterbecoming or what might best be called an unbecoming.[30]

In the context of affect theory, Foucault has yet to be treated as an important author. This is not surprising to the extent that within queer theory, he has been primarily read as an author of the history of sexuality. First and foremost, Foucault addresses sexuality within the space of discursive formations and thus as a question of institutions and power.[31] This perspective has, above all, been popularized by Judith Butler's texts, when she, for example, writes in relation to the possibilities and limits of alternative formations of sexuality and gender:

> Here it seems wise to reinvoke Foucault who, in claiming that sexuality and power are always coextensive, implicitly refutes the postulation of a subversive or emancipatory sexuality which could free of the law.[32]

Without question, this reading of Foucault is more than legitimate. Above all, Foucault's critique of the "repression hypothesis" is a contribution that focuses on sexuality as a question of discourse. However, Foucault also makes some proposals that seek to think through sexuality beyond the paradigm of power and knowledge. At the end of *The History of Sexuality Volume 1*, there is the much-cited allusion to a world of "bodies and pleasures,"[33] which seems to escape the paradigm of sexuality as *scientia sexualis*,

---

30 Withney Davis: *Queer Beauty: Sexuality and Aesthetics from Winckelmann to Freud and Beyond.* New York, NY 2010, 251.

31 This perspective is also noticeable in Foucault's engagement with Freud. Foucault treats psychoanalysis primarily as a question of social institutions and hardly engages with the concepts of psychoanalysis.

32 Judith Butler: *Gender Trouble: Feminism and the Subversion of Identity.* New York, NY / London 1990, 29.

33 Michel Foucault: *The History of Sexuality: An Introduction.* Volume I. New York, NY 1978, 159.

which Foucault still sees at work in psychoanalysis.[34] In later texts, such as the preface to the writings of Herculine Barbine, or in his meditations on friendship, or occasionally in interviews, Foucault repeated and commented on this formulation.[35] Here, as Lynne Huffer writes "this other Foucault" appears.[36] These alternative ideas of a sexuality beyond sexuality, however, are hardly elaborated from a theoretical perspective. Bersani comments, for example, that Foucault's "move from desire to pleasure remains schematic, unexplained."[37] According to Sedgwick, Foucault failed in the project of developing an alternative conceptual apparatus for the analysis of a sexuality that exists beyond dominant power formations.[38] Indeed, her own project of a queer theory of affect can, in contrast to her early work, be understood as a continuation of this project.[39] In doing so, however, Sedgwick shifts the emphasis from the Foucault of sexuality to the realm of non-sexual affects. On the other hand, for Bersani, the unresolved status of "bodies and pleasures" is an opportunity to read Foucault against Foucault and to place him in proximity to a psychoanalytical ontology of the drives:

> The ambition of performing sex as only power is a salvational project, one designed to preserve us from a nightmare of ontological obscenity, from the prospect of a breakdown of the human itself in sexual intensities, from a kind of selfless communication with 'lower' orders of being.[40]

Bersani's project is one in which the overall aim is to think Freud and Foucault together, i.e., to put an ontology of sex alongside the discursive understanding of sexuality.[41] In these moments, "beyond discourse" in Foucault, Butler recognizes the point in which the sexual, in its ontological dimension, appears as a regression of Foucault's otherwise systematic critique of power. Bersani is not alone in his interest in further developing the potentials of the beyond of sexuality that appears in Foucault's texts, both Tom Roach and Elizabeth Grosz emphatically share this somewhat vague project. Last but not least, it is precisely this inarticulateness that – somewhat surprisingly –

---

34 For an overview of the most important reactions from Jagose, Halperin, Warner et al. to this passage in Foucault, see Huffer: *Are the Lips a Grave? A Queer Feminist on the Ethics of Sex*, 73–74.

35 Jagose: *Orgasmogology*, 185–189.

36 Huffer: *Are the Lips a Grave? A Queer Feminist on the Ethics of Sex*, 82.

37 Leo Bersani: *Is the Rectum a Grave? And Other Essays*. Chicago 2010, 182. See Bersani's remarks on forms of eroticism as desexualized pleasure in Foucault. Bersani: *Homos*, 80.

38 Halley and Parker summarize: "Sedgwick argues that Foucault himself failed to elaborate any of his utopian hunches, and that queer theory–which she sees almost completely dedicated to reproducing this failure–entrenches and solidifies (better said perhaps symptomatizes) the repressive hypothesis in every purported denunciation of it." Janet Halley / Andrew Parker: *After Sex? On Writing since Queer Theory*. London 2011, 10.

39 This point is also made by Claudia Breger when she writes: "To my knowledge, no one has yet traced in detail how the conceptualizations of affect that occasionally appear in these later works of Foucault in the context of the techniques of the self-anticipate motifs of contemporary studies of affect [. . .]." Breger: *Nach dem Sex? Sexualwissenschaft und Affect Studies*, 18.

40 Bersani: *Is the Rectum a Grave? And Other Essays*, 29.

41 This is also possible insofar as Foucault ignores rather than engages with psychoanalysis.

brings Foucault closer to psychoanalysis, where, as Elizabeth Grosz shows, these questions are just as poorly articulated. "The reorganization of this libidinal structure – which Foucault nowhere discusses – is precisely what I believe that psychoanalysis has not been able to adequately address."[42]

An understanding of affect theory that does not marginalize sex and sexuality but includes them in the discussion of the dynamics of affect, thus has the potential to become the common denominator between Freud and Foucault, even if this remains essentially unarticulated in both Freud or Foucault. It is through the reference to affect theory that this territory can be revealed, and a bridge to affect theory can certainly be built via Foucault's remarks on pleasure.[43]

Beyond the discussion of affect, the question of an extended understanding of sexuality has been pursued through the use of the keyword "erotic"[44] or within queer theory as a question of "sensuality." An example of this can be found in Bersani, who understands "sensuality" as a non-psychological category beyond sexuality: "sensuality, depsychologized, is prevented from mutating into the sexual."[45] A similar idea can be found in Roach's definition of "sensuality" as a surface phenomenon.[46] If affect is the name for the non-identificatory, deconstructive and productive potentials of a sexuality beyond its psychoanalytic understanding as a drive, it shares this zone of indeterminacy, which is not yet conditioned by historical and institutionalized forms of power, with Foucault's "bodies and pleasures," and with "sensuality" as articulated by Bersani and Roach. What I am proposing here is to understand affect in relation to Foucault's "bodies and pleasures," thus emphasizing the vicinity of affect, sex, and sexuality.

The phenomenon of pleasure appears interesting to Foucault insofar as it takes place on the surface of the body without being understood as the response to an already encoded desire, a lack or the fulfillment of a fantasy. That is to say that pleasure occurs without any prior knowledge of its possibility: pleasure is not the object of knowledge. José Muñoz highlighted the importance of this moment for the project of queer theory: "it also seems important to dwell upon modes of being in the world that might be less knowable than sex."[47] Pleasures take place at the border of a registerable desire and of coherent sexual identities. They are not in the possession of the subject:

---

42 Elizabeth Grosz: Experimental Desire: Rethinking Queer Subjectivity. In: *The Routledge Queer Studies Reader*, ed. by Donald E. Hall / Annamaire Jagose / Andrea Bebell / Susan Potter. New York, NY / London 2013, 202.

43 Roach: *Friendship as a Way of Life*, 21, 129; Frida Beckman: *Between Desire and Pleasure: A Deleuzian Theory of Sexuality*. Edinburgh 2013, 38.

44 Zygmunt Baumann: On Postmodern Uses of Sex. *Theory, Culture & Society* 15/3–4 (1998), 19–33; 20–21. Elizabeth Freeman: *Time Binds: Queer Temporalities, Queer Histories*. Durham, NC / London 2010, 13.

45 Leo Bersani: *Thoughts and Things*. London / Chicago, IL 2015, 12.

46 Roach: *Friendship as a Way of Life*, 5.

47 José Esteban Muñoz: The Sense of Watching Tony Sleep. In: *After Sex? On Writing since Queer Theory*, ed. by Janet Halley / Andrew Parker. Durham, NC / London 2011, 142.

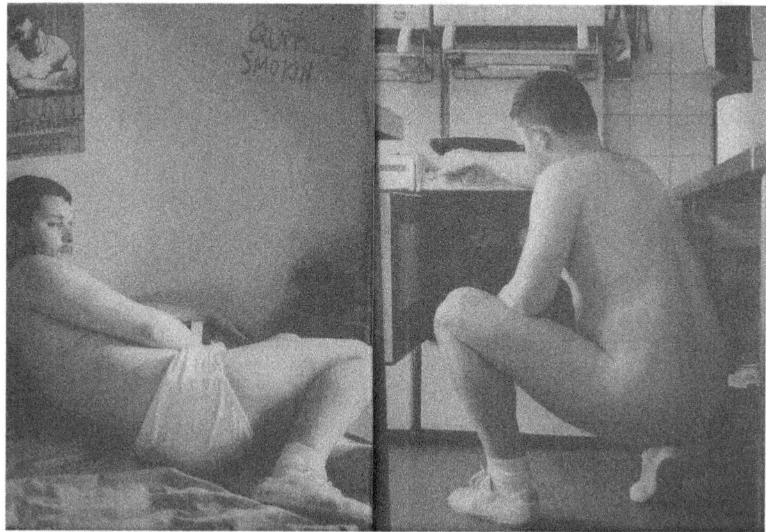

Fig. 3: Julian photographed by Wolfgang Tillmans. In: Van Bennekom, Jop and Gert Jonkers (ed.) Butt # 16, Summer 2006, 11–12.

> It is an event "outside the subject", or at the limit of the subject, taking place in that something which is neither of the body nor of the soul, which is neither inside nor outside – in short, a notion neither assigned nor assignable.[48]

Non-codified pleasures can be considered to be a queer event.[49] The sexual is never completely regulated by the regime of sexuality and sex thus remains bound to the unknowable. In the register of affect, Foucault's pleasure would be a way of naming the site of a non-historical, non-psychoanalytic sexuality.[50]

The question arises as to the manner in which the destabilizing modality of an affective sexuality can make itself felt, and as to how it is realized. While a psychoanalytically understood sexuality as *jouissance* is said to have the quality of a momentary interruption that is supposed to gain transformative value for the process of subjection, e.g., as ego-shattering, and which can be allegorized by the orgasm but does not have to be limited to it, affects are about processual transformations over a longer period of time. What place could affective sexuality take here, and what rhythm

---

48 Foucault quoted in Halperin: *Saint Foucault: Towards a Gay Hagiography*, 94.
49 The difficulty of naming a "queer event" has been pointed out by Lee Edelman, among others. Cf. Chapter 3 Edelman: Unbecoming: Pornography and the Queer Event. In: *Post/Porn/Politics*, ed. by Tim Stüttgen. Berlin 2010.
50 Frida Beckmann comes to a similar conclusion when she writes: "I would argue that as those multiple surfaces rub against each other, a pleasure must be possible that is not about culmination, or 'erectilinear' pleasure, as Marjoire Worthington would have it, see Worthington 2004, 393, but about sexual and deeply pleasurable resonances." Beckman: *Deleuze and Sex*, 13.

would it follow? While for Foucault S/M held the promise of a reorganization of pleasure, Lauren Berlant's project is to question the difference between desire and love. In following these trajectories, we approach the images and histories of *Butt*'s affective and sexual intimacies evoking *Butt*'s aesthetic program that we should understand as a new rhythm of pleasures and affects.

4 S/M

such a program may necessarily involve some radical, perhaps even dangerous, experimentation with modes of what used to be called making love.[51]

Like affect in Sedgwick, pleasure in Foucault gains the function of making porous the boundaries of sexual subjectivities. Bodily encounters take place in a situation that remains open to the occurrence of new pleasures. They become the occasion for a continuous process of self-transformation. "The relationship I think we need to have with ourselves when we have sex is an ethics of pleasure, of intensification of pleasure."[52] Pleasures are tied to an ethical project,[53] and therefore cannot simply mean "orgasm" as the endpoint of a rehearsed sexual script.[54] One of Foucault's best-known examples for reorganizing pleasures is S/M.[55] S/M should be understood as an experimental context in which the exploration of pleasure leads to a redefinition of sexuality.[56] In this, Foucault follows Freud, who in the *Three Essays* had already pointed out the difficulties of making sexual experiences accessible via a binary logic of pleasure and pain, or forepleasure and end-pleasure. In *Beyond the Pleasure Principle*, Freud pursued this problem with the introduction of the death drive. After Foucault, such an interpretation of sexual experiences which lie beyond the subject has found expression, above all, in the investigations of Bersani, Dean, and Edelman. Here, sexual experiences are always a matter of transgressing concepts of identity and desire, which are habitually regulated by biopolitics, through a dissolution of bodily boundaries.

For the aforementioned authors, these forms of dissolution are always located in the space of sexual subcultures, their practices and rites. Foucault's sexuality is transgressed by an excessiveness of sexual stimuli. Even if this experience itself can no lon-

---

51 Bersani: *Homos*, 81.

52 Michel Foucault: An Ethics of Pleasure. In: *Foucault Live: Collected Interviews, 1961–1984*. New-York, NY 1989, 377. For an account of Foucault's ethical project vis-à-vis institutionalized forms of sexual morality, see, for example: Jeffrey Weeks: *Invented Moralities: Sexual Values in an Age of Uncertainty*. New York, NY 1995.

53 Roach: *Friendship as a Way of Life*, 33.

54 Jagose: *Orgasmogology*, 3.

55 Or fisting. For a reading of fisting, see, for example: Huffer: *Are the Lips a Grave? A Queer Feminist on the Ethics of Sex*, 73–90.

56 Bersani: *Homos*, 81–83.

ger necessarily be understood as sexuality in the narrower, genital, sense, access to it in the archives of Bersani, Dean, or Edelman is given exclusively through gay sexual encounters: S/M, fisting or barebacking. This brings us back to the problem that in queer studies, transgression is thought of exclusively as an option for (gay, male) sexuality. Accordingly, Annamarie Jagose characterizes Halperin's and Bersani's projects as follows: "for both critics the erotic practices associated with male-male sexual subcultures continue to offer the most recognizable models for political engagement through sexual practices."[57] While Sedgwick's approach to affect theory, for example, risks leaving sexuality behind altogether, a reconnection to sexuality via Foucault's notion of pleasure entails the return of this problem. To this end, Lynne Huffer asks: "Can women, like men, forge a queer praxis and a new way of life? Which body parts are required to get the job done? Can women do it too?"[58]

Butt offers a different archive of gay sexualities than Foucault's S/M subculture. The question is therefore not only whether women can do it too, but also whether men can do it differently. I would like to end this contribution by following Lauren Berlant's suggestion that sexuality and affect, or in her terminology, desire and love, can conceptually be brought together. While the critique of authors such as Heather Love and Jack Halberstam sets itself up in opposition to the material choices of Foucault, Bersani, Dean, and Edelman, Berlant's project is to question the boundaries between sexual experiences on the one hand, and affective experiences on the other, as opposed to merely affirming the notion of affect against sexuality. Indeed, Berlant's perspective coincides with the one developed here: to understand the intimate scenes in *Butt* as both affective and sexual. Or, as Guy Hocquenghem wrote: "The gays in my dream, my lovers, my friends, my enemies and myself, we can no longer distinguish desire from what is called love."[59]

5 A New Love

As for us, we must rid it [love] of that sentimental glue that socialist as well as capitalist culture has enjoined to smother raw emotion, anesthetize the sensory.[60]

A Lover's Discourse is an attempt to get rid of 'love'– its roles, its attitudes – in order to find the luster that remains when the stereotypes have been sent packing.[61]

57 Jagose: *Orgasmogology*, 202.
58 Huffer: *Are the Lips a Grave?*, 78.
59 Hocquenghem: *The Screwball Asses*, 42–43.
60 Hocquenghem: *The Screwball Asses*, 40.
61 Wayne Koestenbaum: *My 1980s and Other Essays*. New York, NY 2013, 52.

A queer gaze that would question the psychic separation of love and desire, as well as the social forms that follow from it, is hard to be found in psychoanalysis.[62] What might a critique of sexuality in the name of love that is not nostalgically installing a romantic program as a defense against a sexuality supposedly permeated by the logic of capitalism look like? How might the relationship between love and desire be rethought, beyond the duality of love as possession and selfish desire as its counterpoint: "What do we need to know and do in order not to repeat the usual denunciations and utopianisms?"[63] In the past 20 years, this question has played a crucial role in the history of queer sexual politics,[64] and has more recently been discussed under the label of "polyamory."[65]

Berlant argues for an instability of love which is comparable to the instability that desire brings.[66] Like Marcuse and his concept of Eros, she is structurally interested in a dissolution of the difference between love and sexuality, but without Marcuse's conciliatory utopianism, "sentimentality, say, might be a much bigger threat to someone's defenses than any sexual event is."[67] The risk of being together,[68] from her

---

62 Adams Phillips / Barbara Taylor: *On Kindness*. London / New York, NY / Toronto 2009, 90.

63 Berlant: Love (A Queer Feeling). In: *Psychoanalysis and Homosexuality*, ed. by Tim Dean / Christopher Lane. Chicago, IL 2000, 437.

64 Cf. Mike Laufenberg: An Army of Lovers Cannot Lose. In: *I is for Impasse: Affektive Queerverbindungen in Theorie_Aktivismus_Kunst*, ed. by Käthe von Bose / Ulrike Klöppel / Katrin Köppert / Karin Michalski / Pat Treusch. Berlin 2015, 61–72. Where he states that, among other things: "The escape from the molar categories of the sexuality dispositif that we now associate with queer was in fact driven by a desire and a lust to be different with each other: to feel differently, to love differently, to desire differently." Laufenberg: *An Army of Lovers Cannot Lose*, 69.

65 In the advice book genre, Dossie Easton and Janet W. Hardy have addressed the issue of polyamorousness. Dossie Easton / Jannet Hardy: *The Ethical Slut: A Practical Guide to Polyamory, Open Relationships and Other Adventures*. Berkeley 1997. Overall, however, their successful book is more of an account of sexual promiscuity, which they also address under the name of "love," and in this respect offers little guidance for the question of the promiscuity of affects. Some critical questions posed in Hipster Porn, such as the sovereignty of the subject or the negativity of sex, have no place in this practical guide. In this respect, it is a sex-positive, sexual reconciliation project, as one might say with regards to Bersani. For a critical discussion of the polyamorous subculture in neoliberalism, see Volker Woltersdorff: "I Want To Be A Macho Man": Schwule Diskurse über die Aneignung von Männlichkeit in der Fetisch- und SM-Szene. In: *Unbeschreiblich Männlich: Heteronormativitätskritische Perspektiven*, ed. by Robin Bauer / Josch Hoenes / Volker Woltersdorff. Hamburg 2007, 107–120.

66 Berlant: Love (A Queer Feeling), 433.

67 Berlant: *Cruel Optimism*. Durham, NC / London 2011 Loc. 1989/4461.

68 Mike Laufenberg also formulates the goal of a reorganization of love: "In order to grant affection through love a constituting capacity, it is necessary to overcome the appropriation of love through sentimentality, romanticization or identity politics. The two predominant corrupted forms of love, the identitarian love between equals (for example, familialism, nationalism, racism) and the fusing love (love as an ideology of becoming one in couple relationships or as a religious love of God; cf. Michael Hardt / Antonio Negri: *Empire*. Cambridge and London 2000, 192ff.), should be opposed by alternatives that do not personalize or essentialize love." Laufenberg: *An Army of Lovers Cannot Lose*, 70.

point of view, is a form of self-expansion as boundary violation, a movement which Berlant calls queer insofar as it does not necessarily have to be enshrined in the form of the couple.[69]

> The ways of describing self-extension – the desire to become more than oneself, to become exchangeable, to become oriented towards a publicness that corresponds to an expanding interiority suggests the appropriateness of naming love a queer affect.[70]

Love as affective expansion would have the potential to put barriers between inside and outside, ego and environment, private and public at risk and, as such, to operate similarly as regards sexuality, sex, or desire. Thus, Berlant writes: "Foucauldian categories of pathogenic sexuality could then be seen as the detritus of normal love's failures to organize the subject."[71] Analogous to Foucault's pleasures, affects would be experiences that have not yet been codified, that have not yet found their form, that are without a defined place within the constitution of subjects and relations. A symbolic definition has not yet taken place.

If we pursue such a design of affective mobility as an alternative to the psychoanalytic program of love, a crucial question at this point is whether we can think love beyond the category of "personhood." In a conversation with filmmaker Werner Schröter, Foucault describes this problem by distinguishing between love and passion:

> It's a distinction between two kinds of individuation: one, love, through persons, and the other through intensity, as though passion dissolved persons not into something undifferentiated but into a field of various persisting and mutually interdependent intensities [. . .]. Love's a state of, and a relation between, persons, subjects. But passion is a subpersonal event that may last as long as a lifetime [. . .], a field of intensities that individuates independently of any subject.[72]

In contrast, Berlant's reformulation of a queer love is no longer about the interiority of persons, but about a non-psychological affective expansion beyond individuals.[73] This possibility of love beyond the psychological or psychoanalytic subject is also considered by Bersani and Philipps:

> Love is perhaps always – as both Plato and Freud suggest – a phenomenon of memory,[74] but what is remembered in the expansive narcissism of an impersonal intimacy is not some truth

---

69 In addition to self-emptying as part of the structure of the feeling love, its instability, according to Berlant, is also conditioned by a series of contradictions such as conventionality/uniqueness, knowledge/non-knowledge, form/mysteriousness. Berlant: *Love (A Queer Feeling)*.

70 Berlant: Love (A Queer Feeling), 443.

71 Berlant: Love (A Queer Feeling), 440.

72 Kenneth Surin: Existing Not as a Subject but as a Work of Art: The Task of Ethics or Aesthetics? In: *Deleuze* and *Ethics*, ed. by Nathan Jun / Daniel W. Smith. Edinburgh 2011, 149.

73 Anu Koivunen: Yes We Can? The Promises of Affect for Queer Scholarship. *Lambda Nordica* 15/3–4 (2010), 55.

74 Surin: Existing Not as a Subject but as a Work of Art, 162.

about the self, but rather, as Philipps says, "a process of becoming", or, in other terms, evolving affinities of being.[75]

6 Incoherent Love

The desired result is a systematic openness: an open system.[76]

indiscernibility, imperceptibility, and impersonality remain the end points of becoming.[77]

A love that does not find its form is a love that does not fit into the world of domesticity, monogamy, privacy, and permanence. It is a love that does not take emotion or affect as reconciliation in the face of desire's restlessness. It is a love that cannot keep its promise, that does not conform to the script of the happy ending but is more likely to lead to betrayal.[78] For Berlant, love is interesting as a phenomenon insofar as it must fail: "love as an exercise in failure."[79]

Beyond its fantasy as a protective zone in which subjects are assured a comfortable home, love would be a risky form of self-expression, "in love, the human subject is exceptionally open to otherness."[80] Love is uneconomic insofar as it exposes the subject to the danger of not being able to carry the prize home again as a calculable gain. As "wrong" or "disappointed," love cannot be thought of as a profitable investment in life planning. Love that can be described in such a way – as an endless form of uncertainty – is not culturally admitted or expressed. Rather, love is either captured by the "marriage plot," or is accepted only as a dramatic delay on the way to a given goal. Stylized in the genre of the *amour fou* and dressed as an intensity of experience, uncertain love is granted an unruly life of its own that is permitted, if not required, within the eventfulness of youth.

Berlant's dissecting gaze, however, aims to allow love to stand beyond these cultural classifications as a capacity for unpredictable and unreliable experiences and attachments. Without its conventional, narrative framework, love as an affective self-expression, becomes an experience in which the subject neatly cannot settle into the context of reliable genres. Such a love risks cultural unintelligibility that cannot be sublimated in the gesture of "love as blindness" or "love as stupidity" and to this end, Berlant speaks of "love's sheer incoherence."[81] Here the critical interest of affect the-

---

75 Bersani / Phillips: *Intimacies*, 124.

76 Brian Massumi: *Parables for the Virtual: Movement, Affect, Sensation.* Durham / London 2002, 18.

77 Elizabeth Grosz: *Volatile Bodies: Toward a Corporeal Feminism.* Bloomington / Indianapolis 1994, 179.

78 Compare, for example, Bersani's reading of betrayal in Genet as a gay mode of anti-relationality in Bersani: *Homos.*

79 Lauren Berlant: *Desire/Love.* New York, NY 2012, 21.

80　Bersani / Phillips: *Intimacies*, 74.

81　Berlant: Love (A Queer Feeling), 441.

ory is to subvert the binding forces of conventional emotions and the genres in which they have been historically organized, given that Berlant's project relies on revealing love's incoherence as an existential condition:

> To my mind, love is queered not when we discover it to be resistant to or more than all its known forms, but when we see that there is no world that admits how it actually works as a principle of living. This designation refracts as negativity the state of affect I have been calling incoherence.[82]

Incoherence occurs as an impulse to question and abandon existing genres: Historically generated organizing structures of social life that can be exposed as forms of institutionalized power. Without its ideology cast as a fantasy of fusion, the idea of love no longer conjures a violent defense against its own destabilizing moments. In Berlant's work, however, this movement does not occur in the name of better, future-oriented genres (or "better stories" as Grossberg writes). Following Foucault, for Berlant, the project of affect theory cannot be about a program, but is rather about a practice of affective distraction. Unlike Love,[83] Berlant is concerned with making room for incoherence as a condition by which our existence is ontologically defined. Here again, there is a structural similarity to Bersani's self-shattering sexuality. Both Bersani and Berlant understand negativity as an ontological condition of subjectivity where Berlant's contribution is to contest sex and sexuality's monopoly on the subject of negativity, not thematically via negative affect or emotions like shame, but through the unstable structure of affect itself.

What, in the archive of queer theory, is primarily related to the experience of gay sex, Berlant claims to be able to say about the experience of love as a queer feeling. Love, not only as experimental sexuality but also as an expenditure unbound by any genre, becomes a practice of becoming/unbecoming, in which incalculable affective constellations undo subjective and social stabilities.[84] With the disclosure of the affective incoherence of love, the juxtaposition of a sexuality that leads to unknown pleasures on the one hand, and love as a fantasy of fusion on the other, becomes unstable. Both love and sexuality (or desire, pleasure) appear here as experiences of negativity. What distinguishes them if no familiar genres organize their division of labor anymore? How does a sexuality as pleasure articulate itself if not through identity, and how does a love that does not bind itself to persons show itself? If we assume, following Berlant, a structural similarity between love and desire, by what criterion can they be distinguished? To what extent does it still make sense here to speak of sexuality *or* love? Is there a temporal or spatial difference, is there a rhythm that carries us from one scene to the next, or do the two ways of connecting with the world, affectively or sexually, collapse in a space they now share? In contrast to the notion of the

---

82 Berlant: Love (A Queer Feeling), 443.
83 Heather Love: *Feeling Backward: Loss and the Politics of Queer History.* Cambridge / London 2007, 4.
84 Davis: *Queer Beauty.*

erotic or to sensuality, which aims to summarize these two libidinous/affective modalities, I here suggest the notion of *affective sexualities*, which reminds us that we are speaking of a mixed phenomenon when we place the disintegrating power of sexuality in relation to that of love, even if our aim is to envisage a field beyond the rehearsed oppositions of love and desire.

Bibliography

Angerer, Marie-Luise: *Desire After Affect*. Lanham 2014.

Baumann, Zygmunt: On Postmodern Uses of Sex. *Theory, Culture & Society* 15/3–4 (1998), 19–33.

Bech, Henning: *When Men Meet: Homosexuality and Modernity*. Chicago, IL 1997.

Beckman, Frida (ed.): *Deleuze and Sex*. Edinburgh 2011.

Berlant, Lauren. Love (A Queer Feeling). In: *Psychoanalysis and Homosexuality*, ed. by Dean, Tim / Lane, Christopher. Chicago, IL 2000, 432–451.

Berlant, Lauren: *Cruel Optimism*. Durham, NC / London 2011.

Berlant, Lauren. *Desire/Love*. New York, NY 2012.

Berlant, Lauren / Lee Edelman: Reading, Sex, and the Unbearable: A Response to Tim Dean. *American Literary History* 27/3 (2015), 625–629.

Bersani, Leo: *Homos*. Cambridge, MN / London 1995.

Bersani, Leo: *Is the Rectum a Grave? And Other Essays*. Chicago, IL 2010.

Bersani, Leo: *Thoughts and Things*. London / Chicago, IL 2015.

Butler, Judith: *Gender Trouble: Feminism and the Subversion of Identity*. New York, NY / London 1990.

Davis, Whitney: *Queer Beauty: Sexuality and Aesthetics from Winckelmann to Freud and Beyond*. New York, NY 2010.

Davis, Nick: *The Desiring-Image: Gilles Deleuze and Contemporary Queer Cinema*. Oxford / New York, NY 2013.

Dean, Tim: The Biopolitics of Pleasure. *The South Atlantic Quarterly* 111/3. Issue: Future Foucault: Afterlives of Bodies and Pleasures. Durham, NC 2012, 477–498.

Dean, Tim. No Sex Please, We're American. *American Literary History* 27/3(2015), 614–624.

Diederichsen, Diedrich: *Kritik des Auges: Texte zur Kunst*. Hamburg 2008.

Dyer, Richard: Coming to Terms: Gay Pornography. In: *Only Entertainment*. New York, NY / London 1992, 121–134.

Edelman, Lee: Unbecoming: Pornography and the Queer Event. In: *Post/Porn/Politics*, ed. by Stüttgen, Tim. Berlin 2010, 194–211.

Foucault, Michel: *The History of Sexuality: An Introduction*. Volume I. New York, NY 1978.

Foucault, Michel: An Ethics of Pleasure. In: *Foucault Live: Collected Interviews, 1961–1984*. New York, NY 1989, 371–380.

Freeman, Elizabeth: *Time Binds: Queer Temporalities, Queer Histories*. Durham, NC / London 2010.

Gregg, Melissa / Seigworth, Gregory J. (eds.): *The Affect Theory Reader*. Durham, NC / London 2010.

Grossberg, Lawrence: *Cultural Studies in the Future Tense*. Durham, NC / London 2010.

Grosz, Elizabeth: *Volatile Bodies: Toward a Corporeal Feminism*. Bloomington / Indianapolis, IN 1994.

Grosz, Elizabeth: Experimental Desire: Rethinking Queer Subjectivity. In: *The Routledge Queer Studies Reader*, ed. by Hall, Donald E. / Jagose, Annamaire / Bebell, Andrea / Potter, Susan. New York, NY / London 2013, 194–211.

Halberstam, Jack: *The Queer Art of Failure*. Durham, NC / London 2011.

Halley, Janet / Parker, Andrew (eds.): *After Sex? On Writing since Queer Theory*. Durham, NC / London 2011.

Halperin, David M.: *Saint Foucault: Towards a Gay Hagiography*. New York, NY / Oxford 1995.

Hardt, Michael / Negri, Antonio: *Empire*. Cambridge, MA / London 2000.

Hocquenghem, Guy: *The Screwball Asses*. Los Angeles, CA 2010.

Huffer, Lynne: *Are the Lips a Grave? A Queer Feminist on the Ethics of Sex*. New York, NY 2013.

Jagose, Annamarie: *Orgasmology*. Durham, NC / London 2013.

Koestenbaum, Wayne: *My 1980s and Other Essays*. New York, NY 2013.

Koivunen, Anu: Yes We Can? The Promises of Affect for Queer Scholarship. *Lambda Nordica* 3/4 (2010), 40–62.

Laufenberg, Mike: An Army of Lovers Cannot Lose. In: *I is for Impasse: Affektive Queerverbindungen in Theorie_Aktivismus_Kunst*, ed. by von Bose, Käthe / Klöppel, Ulrike / Köppert, Katrin / Michalski, Karin / Treusch Pat. Berlin 2015, 61–72.

Love, Heather: *Feeling Backward: Loss and the Politics of Queer History*. Cambridge, MA / London 2007.

Marcus, Steven: Pornotopia. In: *Sexual Revolution*, ed. by Escoffier, Jeffrey. New York, NY 2003, 380–398.

Massumi, Brian: Translator's Foreword. In: Deleuze, Gilles / Guattari, Félix: *A Thousand Plateaus: Capitalism and Schizophrenia*. Minneapolis, MN/ London 1987, IX–XV.

Massumi, Brian: *Parables for the Virtual: Movement, Affect, Sensation*. Durham, NC / London 2002.

McGlotten, Shaka: *Virtual Intimacies: Media, Affect, and Queer Sociality*. Albany, NY 2013.

Muñoz, José Esteban: The Sense of Watching Tony Sleep. In: *After Sex? On Writing since Queer Theory*, ed. by Halley, Janet / Parker, Andrew. Durham, NC / London 2011, 142–150.

Paasonen, Susanna: *Carnal Resonance: Affect and Online Pornography*. Cambridge, MA / London 2011.

Padva, Gilad: Heavenly Monsters: The Politics of the Male Body in the Naked Issue of Attitude Magazine. *International Journal of Sexuality and Gender Studies* 7/4 (2002), 281–292.

Patterson, Zabet: Going On-Line: Consuming Pornography in the Digital Era. In: *Porn Studies*, ed. by Linda Williams. Durham, NC / London 2004, 104–123.

Phillips, Adams / Barbara Taylor: *On Kindness*. London / New York, NY / Toronto 2009.

Roach, Tom: *Friendship as a Way of Life: Foucault, Aids, and the Politics of Shared Estrangement*. Albany 2012.

Sedgwick, Eve: Melanie Klein and the Difference Affect Makes. In: *After Sex? On Writing since Queer Theory*, ed. by Halley, Janet / Parker, Andrew. Durham, NC / London 2011, 283–301.

Sedgwick, Eve Kososfsky: *Touching Feeling: Affect, Pedagogy, Performativity*. Durham, NC / London 2003.

Smith, Paul: Vas. In: *Feminismus: An Anthology of Literary Theory and Criticism*, ed. by Warhol, Robyn R. / Herndl, Diane Price. New Brunswick, NJ 1991, 1011–1029.

Surin, Kenneth: Existing Not as a Subject but as a Work of Art: The Task of Ethics or Aesthetics? In: *Deleuze and Ethics*, ed. by Jun, Nathan / Smith, Daniel W. Edinburgh 2011, 142–153.

Van Bennekom, Jop / Jonkers, Gert (eds.). *Butt Book: The Best of the First 5 Years of* Butt– Adventures in 21st Century Gay Subculture. Cologne 2006.

Weeks, Jeffrey: *Invented Moralities: Sexual Values in an Age of Uncertainty*. New York, NY 1995.

Winnubst, Shannon: The Queer Thing about Neoliberal Pleasure: A Foucauldian Warning. *Foucault Studies* (14 September 2012), 79–97.

Woltersdorff, Volker: 'I Want To Be A Macho Man': Schwule Diskurse über die Aneignung von Männlichkeit in der Fetisch- und SM-Szene. In: *Unbeschreiblich Männlich: Heteronormativitätskritische Perspektiven*, ed. by Bauer, Robin / Hoenes, Josch / Woltersdorff, Volker. Hamburg 2007, 107–120.

Worthington, Marjorie: 'The Territory Named Women's Body': The Public and Pirate Spaces of Kathy Acker. *Literature, Interpretation, Theory* 15 (2004), 389–408.

Part IV: **Queer Futures**

Vera Mader

Is She the Girl from the Anti-Video? On FKA twigs' Chronopolitics

Abstract: This contribution discusses three audiovisual works by British pop artist FKA twigs (*Papi Pacify*, 2013; *Video Girl*, 2014; *CAPRISONGS*, 2022), forwarding the notion of a Black feminist chronopolitics specific to them. Drawing on Black Atlantic Futurism, Black feminist and media theory, I not only ask how twigs adopts an asynchronous temporal orientation in order to disrupt the linear timeline of Eurocentric modernity but also intervene into naturalized distributions of power therein. These works allow us to glimpse at a utopia that speaks as much of the pleasurable, generative possibilities of a Now as of a decolonial future that gazes back upon the histories and embodied experiences of gendered, racialized and sexualized oppression.

Keywords: FKA twigs, Chronopolitics, Black Feminism, Black Atlantic Futurism, Time Axis Manipulation, Video Girl, Pop, Queer Futurity, Astrology, Black Technology

In Ethiopian-American R&B singer Kelela's 2015 video for *Rewind*,[1] we see the artist, her eyes set on the camera, approaching and distancing herself from the viewer amid flickering strobe lights. She tells a story of mundane heartbreak that happened to a friend: Being in a club, connecting with someone, leaving without expressing their interest in an overt way – trying to reconnect later, yet without luck.[2] This going backwards – spatially, as performed in the video, and temporally, as expressed in the song lyric's figurative use of the verb "to rewind" – implies that the chain of events could be altered, after all – maybe even to a different outcome of her friend's night out. Yet, the song indulges in this moment of in-betweenness and suspended possibility.

Going forward, I want to trace moments of restructuring time in the audiovisual works of another artist, London-based musician FKA twigs. I engage British cultural critic Kodwo Eshun's concept of an Afrofuturist chronopolitics as a sort of speculative media materialism, where rewinding a video or music tape provides an instructive point of departure. Through such speculation, I analyze how twigs' Black feminist sensibilities subvert the hegemonic orders usually layered in media time. Further, I draw on US-American cinema and media studies scholar Kara Keeling's work critiquing the cinematic, particularly her notion of imposing different "spatiotemporal coordinates"[3]

---

1 Kelela: "Rewind" (Official Video). Directed by Eric K Yue. 19 September 2015. Music video, 04:00. *YouTube*. Available online: https://www.youtube.com/watch?v=py6PgXq0yDM (last accessed 17 April 2022).
2 Ruth Saxelby: Kelela Decodes Every Track from her Hallucinogen EP. *The Fader* (15 October 2015). http://www.thefader.com/2015/10/09/kelela-hallucinogen-track-by-track (last accessed 17 April 2022).
3 Kara Keeling: *The Witch's Flight. The Cinematic, the Black Femme, and the Image of Common Sense*. Durham, NC 2007, 34.

which structure our perception of a social reality. I look at how twigs adopts practices of editing audiovisual material as they are common sense in popular culture to forward an artistic vision that in many ways disrupts the common sensicality of what we see when we watch a music video. What I propose, then, is not to regard practices of "time axis manipulation"[4] as counter-hegemonic per se, given that the commercial(ized) art of music video production widely draws on such aesthetic practices. Instead, I explore twigs' interventions as asynchronous to naturalized normative distributions of power, distorting the linear timeline of Eurocentric modernity as they allow us to glimpse at a utopia that speaks as much of the pleasurable, generative possibilities of a Now as of a decolonial future that gazes back upon the histories and embodied experiences of gendered, racialized and sexualized oppression. In line with Black critiques of time, this claim to structure and inhabit one's own temporality constitutes a claim to agency.[5]

My contribution thus approaches the discussed materials through a lens of uncomfortable citational politics situated between a media materialist discourse (arguably hegemonic and Western) and queer and decolonial theory. I follow this question as it has been invoked in 1971 by Black US-American poet and critic Amiri Baraka, who at a time of national nuclear armament asked his fellow Black creators: If machines are extensions of their inventor-creators (a thought he attributes to cyberneticist Norbert Wiener), then what could a creation powered by a Black ethos accomplish?[6]

Ultimately, I aim to consider how twigs' work complicates binary constructions between colonial/decolonial, hegemonic/subversive technology and regressive/progressive time that I circumscribe over the course of my argument. In light of this, I situate asynchrony as a temporal orientation in the audiovisual works of FKA twigs which takes into account both the inevitability of being situated *by* existing power relations in late racial capitalism[7] as well as what resistance to them or negation of them might look like. In the last portion of this essay, I look at how twigs' insistent orientation toward the future by adopting the popular culture and "technology" of astrology provides a means for building affective community, in which the *feeling* of a

---

4 Friedrich A. Kittler: *Gramophone, Film, Typewriter,* transl. by Geoffrey Winthrop-Young / Michael Wutz. Stanford, CA 1999, 34.

5 See for example, Rasheedah Philips: Organize Your Own Temporality. In: *Organize Your Own:The Politics and Poetics of Self-Determination Movements.* Chicago, IL 2016, 48–54.

6 Imamu Amiri Baraka: Ethos & Technology. In: *Raise, Race, Rays, Raze. Essays since 1965.* New York, NY 1971, 155–157.

7 The term "racial capitalism" denominates the mutual imbrication of racism and capitalism. It was introduced in 1983 by American Black studies scholar Cedric J. Robinson, who in his seminal book *Black Marxism. The Making of the Black Radical Tradition* traces the development of the modern world economic order as it constitutively draws on the forced labor and enslavement of "racially othered" populations. Cedric J. Robinson: *Black Marxism. The Making of the Black Radical Tradition.* Chapel Hill, NC / London 2000, 42–62.

time yet to come comprises dissent to the violently structured present and a notion of asynchrony to this very present as reparative strategy.[8]

1 A Speculative Media Materialism?

Taking his cue from British cultural studies scholar Paul Gilroy's *Black Atlantic* theory of transculturation, Kodwo Eshun theorizes a Black musical tradition he calls *Black Atlantic Futurism*. In his seminal 1998 book *More Brilliant than the Sun*, Eshun's theorization departs from the materiality at work in music production, as his stance seems decidedly media materialist: Terms such as Skratchadelia,[9] the turntablization of Black music, the cuts and breaks in hip-hop – all refer to the manipulation of physical media allowing for a given temporal order to be reversed, interrupted, restructured, and rearranged.[10] Here, Kelela's *Rewind* serves as a useful point of departure. Eshun recasts this going back and forth on the axis of recorded time as a notion of time travel, facilitating the creation of Afrocentric historical discontinuums.[11] While for German media theorist Friedrich Kittler, the breakthrough of recording technology marks the end of all history, superseded by the onset of a "media age,"[12] Eshun locates the creation of history and the rerouting of a digital diaspora precisely in the possibility of a revision and manipulation of time brought about by recording devices. For instance, as sampling appropriates the means of technological reproduction, it holds potential to subvert existing power structures: "Technology changes the form of power, the nature of identity, the essence of the enemy."[13] In light of this, Eshun's "Machine Music" methodologically comes from "freaking with the formula," messing with time axes and rule books,[14] altering time on the level of its material manifesta-

---

8 I would like to thank the editors for their comments and generous support, as well as Philipp Hohmann and Audrey Black for giving me notes and writing advice.

9 Kodwo Eshun: *More Brilliant than the Sun. Adventures in sonic fiction.* London 1998, -004.

10 In the German media theorist Friedrich Kittler's 1986 book *Gramophone, Film, Typewriter*, Kittler concedes audio recording technologies the ability to manifest the Lacanian Real materially, speaking of a spatialization of temporal phenomena in writing systems. See Kittler: *Gramophone, Film, Typewriter*, 15.

11 Eshun: *More Brilliant than the Sun*, 184.

12 Kittler: *Gramophone, Film, Typewriter*, 18; Drawing an analogy between the phonograph and the human brain, Kittler dismisses memory as a uniquely human capacity: "If the focusing of blurred mental images by way of attention amounts to nothing more or less than changing the time axis of acoustic events by increasing playback speed or indulging in time axis manipulation (TAM), then there is no reason to celebrate attention or memory as miraculous abilities." Kittler: *Gramophone, Film, Typewriter*, 34.

13 Eshun: *More Brilliant than the Sun*, 122.

14 Eshun: *More Brilliant than the Sun*, 020.

tion. By rendering temporality intrinsically malleable, the materiality of media provides a means of speculation.

Technology in Eshun's analysis of African diaspora musical traditions is then not tied to a media determinist *a priori* condition of time-space or era; rather, he shifts perspective onto its use as a force enabling artistic as well as social agency. Consequently, Eshun views media technology not as restricted to the oppressive use of the "master's tools"[15] but as simultaneously rewrought to form a liberatory force by way of musical expression. In the following, I argue that the work of FKA twigs continues to be situated in this double bind: While the disseminative structures of media and technology intrinsically bear potential for violence and exposure as becomes evident in the disproportionate surveillance and policing of Black and marginalized communities, twigs makes use of its emancipatory potential in rearranging not only acoustic but also audiovisual events.

In Eshun's theory of a chronopolitics, as in twigs' art, adjusting temporal orders according to one's own sense of time constitutes a claim to agency. Manifestations of Afrofuturism, as Eshun elaborates, constitute a retrospective as well as proleptic reorientation of the reparative practice of counter memory associated with Gilroy's Black Atlantic tradition as response to the histories of slavery and racial violence.[16] In this sense, such a chronopolitics does not pursue a revisionist project. Rather, as per Gilroy, chronopolitical interventions "infiltrate a Now,"[17] intervene in the hegemonic notion of linear temporality and open up temporal orientations to a range of competing possibilities, future projects, and utopias.

Now, expanding on the idea of manipulated time based on materiality of media, I turn to the audiovisual exploits of FKA twigs, who uses the music video as a form to address structures of violence, while at the same time tapping its reparative potential. Thus, I ask how this work mobilizes asynchrony as a Black feminist chronopolitics which points to different modes of relating to present (temporal) orders and allows us to discuss the disruptive potential that being out of sync bears.

2 Performance as Black Female Labor: Diverting the Extractive Gaze in Video Girl, 2014

From the beginning of her career, being a dancer for various artists' music videos as well as in her independent work has informed FKA twigs' identity as an artist. In her

---

15 Audre Lorde: The Master's Tools Will Never Dismantle the Master's House. In: *Sister Outsider. Essays and Speeches*, Berkeley, CA 2007, 110–113.

16 Kodwo Eshun: Further Considerations on Afrofuturism. *CR: The New Centennial Review* 3/2 (2003), 287–302, here 289.

17 Eshun: *Further Considerations on Afrofuturism*, 297.

2014 *Video Girl*,[18] twigs explores her position in the music industry in relation to questions of the surveillance and confinement of Black life, playing on tropes of "threatening" Blackness and a feminized notion of passivity.

As twigs' ethereal hums at the beginning of the track slowly give way to a rattling beat, the video's visuals conflate her lyrical account of being gazed at with a scene of a *white* man being executed by injection.

During the entire video twigs is positioned in front of a window, looking into the execution ward, watching calmly, sometimes averting her eyes. Yet her role beyond being a spectator, and even her relationship to the convict, both remain undiscernible. By the time her vocals enter, she appears under the scene's surveillance, dancing provocatively in a confined space while the convict remains tied to his deathbed. Juxtaposing this performance of hypersexualized femininity with the scene's CCTV coverage, the images are crosscut with twigs erupting in broad, aggressive dance movements so as to perform her version of "thuggish" Black masculinity, dressed in a coat of chain mail and bejeweled from headdress down to arms and fingers.

The song lyrics repeat the prying questions of people who approach twigs after recognizing her from one of the music videos she's been in: "Is she the girl that's from the video?" and her subsequent refusal to be identified as one of the dancers, while being visibly on top of her craft as both singer and dancer. If, as performance scholar Judith Hamera writes, "Dancing is work: a job, the product of labor,"[19] then twigs' working body is a performing body and so is her performing body a working body. Her disidentification thus concerns not the profession and artistic expression of dancing as such but the music industry's structural default by which the labor of Black women becomes objectifiable and at the same time invisibilized.[20] The history of popular music throughout the twentieth and twenty-first centuries shows that the presence and celebration of Black artists and performers has not been inconsistent with the continued disenfranchisement of Black people as a direct continuation of the modern economic order, for which the exploitation of Black labor serves as a holdover from the plantation system to late (industrial) capitalism.

In the video, it seems that this refusal is reflected in the characteristics of twigs' dancing, her moving in and claiming of a space which is crucially a space of confinement (the execution ward) as well as a space confining her to the role of being a

---

18 FKA twigs (2014): "Video Girl." Directed by Kahlil Joseph. 29 October 2014. Music video, 04:35. *YouTube*. Available online: https://www.youtube.com/watch?v=2jhTiLuGezI (last accessed 17 April 2022).
19 Judith Hamera: The Labors of Michael Jackson. Virtuosity, Deindustrialization, and Dancing Work. *PMLA* 127/4 (2012), 751–765, 752.
20 This observation calls to mind the 2019 video for *Cellophane*, in which twigs virtuously pole dances on a vast theater stage, thus colliding "high" and "low" art forms by elevating the "slum art" of stripping to the aristocratic scene of ballet. FKA twigs (2019): "Cellophane." Directed by Andrew Thomas Huang. 24 April 2019. Music video, 04:21. *YouTube*. Available online: https://www.youtube.com/watch?v=YkLjqFpBh84 (last accessed 22 February 2023).

dancer (the music video). The flow of her dancing is repeatedly interrupted, almost as if she is forced and struggles to persist, yet takes visible pleasure in the performance, in watching and in being watched. twigs' abrupt movements are chopped by flickering lights to the effect that they resemble the asynchronous, poor representation of low-resolution video. The constant suspension of action extends to the media technology at use, namely the recording of her performance on video as it manifests itself intradiegetically through the presence of the surveillance camera.[21] In a sense, twigs' bodily performance of temporal interruption and suspended movement, while imitating the performance of technical media, evades a surveillance logic demanding complete transparency and legibility. Therefore, twigs adopts asynchrony as a dissident temporal orientation that actively destabilizes racial capitalism's hegemonic order by marking a difference linked to technical (dys)functionality[22] from within the economic rationale of surveilling and policing Black life. Thus, FKA twigs' appropriation of media time diverts and re-directs gazes, including her own, and complicates the split between active/passive roles with regard to the extractive relations in the writing of recorded time, as well as Black (female) cultural production at large.

Toward the end of the video, the song stops to a change of scene: In slow motion, a Black man almost completely submerged in the dark background smiles to reveal his grills, or set of dental inserts derived from precious metals and stones, with blood dripping from his lips to the sound of a heartbeat. In this showing off of riches, time is both arrested and intensified. His grin seems to convey: *"My mouth isn't your gold mine. It's MINE,"* offering an inversion of the extraction economies profiting from Black life and art which twigs' lyrics address in relation to the development of her own career. In *Video Girl*, twigs addresses her role as a dancer standing in as "one" of the exceptional video girls sustained by an entertainment industry which capitalizes on the work of Black female performers, as the chorus goes: "Is she the girl that's from the video?" Here, I turn to Kara Keeling's work on Blackness and the cinematic, which picks up Frantz Fanon's assertion that colonial violence is a problem of time, as the constant re-instantiation of past trauma upholds the dominant order which continuously forecloses an equitable future beyond the Black/*white* binary. If Blackness is confined by its historicity, the cinematic apparatus facilitating the appearance of the past in the present actively reifies this colonial temporal relation, therefore proving "relevant to an understanding of how cinematic processes work to secure and maintain hegemonic political economies." In Fanon's writing as Keeling understands it, a Black person's becoming is

---

21 Simone Browne notes that surveillance cannot be studied without taking into account its racializing effects. By reifying boundaries along racial lines, practices of surveillance were historically constitutive of Blackness. Simone Browne: *Dark Matters. On the Surveillance of Blackness.* Durham, NC 2015, 8.

22 A similar relation between the (rhythmic) submission to music and servitude/bondage has for example been drawn in Grace Jones' *Slave to the Rhythm*, produced by Trevor Horn. Manhattan Island Records 1985.

overdetermined by and caught in the circulation of pre-given (cinematic) images and negative stereotypes. Fanon's Black experience is refused an ontological "own" and figures as a state of waiting, which, in his book *Black Skin, White Masks,* he compares to waiting for himself to appear on a movie theater's screen. Keeling writes:

> In Fanon's case [Blackness] is to exist in an interval wherein the terms of waiting have been pre-ordained. What ends the wait is what has been anticipated, even when it is the black's explosion, and so the cycle continues and the interval endures. [. . .] The hellish cycle wherein the past constricts the present so that the present is simply the (re)appearance of the past, felt as affect, restricts by anticipating in advance the range of the black's (re)actions to his present experience.[23]

Keeling's reading of Fanon discusses a Black person's self-recognition and simultaneously their disidentification with the images they are presented with as the temporal relation of the interval, proposing that this colonial mode of representation relies on a "closed cycle of anticipation and explosion."[24] These "excesses" of Black particularity disrupt a colonial order only to await its violent re-instantiation. Despite its immediate sanctioning, what Fanon calls an "explosion" contains the impossible possibility of decolonization by breaking this cycle of anticipation and violence.

In this sense, the last line in *Video Girl* – "I can't recognize me" – not only points to an inherent asynchronous disjunction in the cycle of mediated representation and artistic, economic, and self- recognition, it also denies twigs' Black feminist particularity access to such recognition within the hegemonic temporal orders. Due to this problem of the confinement of Blackness in the confrontation with the cinematic apparatus, Keeling departs from discussing the cinematic vis-à-vis a politics of representation, borrowing from French philosopher Gilles Deleuze's notion of the cinematic to complicate the quest for Black representation in light of its impossibility. Cinematic images, in Deleuze's understanding, do not merely represent, they form a material-affective layer in the construction of social reality.[25] Expanding on this notion of the cinematic, Keeling insists on the twofold affective (technological) constitution of Blackness *in the interval*: as a state of being stuck in this violent cycle of repetition and as the impossible possibility of an opening for an affective surplus, generated precisely within the sensory-material relations of cinematic images as they exploit and extend into social reality. Such a dynamic between a liberatory use of audiovisuality and the reinstitution of oppression is further explored in the generative gaps in twigs' earlier video for *Papi Pacify*.

---

23 Keeling: *The Witch's Flight,* 36.
24 Keeling: *The Witch's Flight,* 35.
25 Keeling: *The Witch's Flight,* 31.

3 Papi Pacify, 2013: The Interval as the Expanded Now in Which Past and Future Collapse

In twigs' 2013 video for *Papi Pacify*,[26] the artist is alternately held, caressed, smothered, choked, and released by a Black man whose muscular, tattooed upper body takes up most of the screen. The scene presents an at once violent and sensual meditation on anxious attachment, with twigs' singing voice asking her partner repeatedly to "pacify her love"; this request is answered by fingering her mouth as if calming a baby with a pacifier. The black and white film images are stopped and rewound, progressing reluctantly, caught in rhythmic repetition. This inconclusive playing back and forth of the recordings initiates a redistribution of agency in which relations of power and desire are being negotiated.

If, in Fanon's formulation, Blackness is attributed a belatedness with regard to a hegemonic temporal and social order, I want to suggest the notion of asynchrony in the chronopolitics I'm discussing here as a way to relate to the twofold existence "in the interval," as Keeling puts it. States of "too late" or "too soon" weave around and in-between imposed temporal orders; they go along, but ultimately evade the imposition of a timeline dictated by the dominant regime of Eurocentric modernity. Keeling identifies the interval as the temporal structure of coloniality, foreclosing decolonial possibility in moments of waiting and suspended action, while at the same time providing an opening for new images and (counter-)memories challenging the very coloniality the interval has been instituted by.[27]

Similarly, film theoretician Trinh T. Minh-ha casts the interval as a generative opening in (re-)arranging sound and images at the heart of cinematic practice: The interval "allows words to set in motion dormant energies and to offer, with the impasse, a passage from one space (visual, musical, verbal, mental, physical) to another."[28] As Trinh's intervals "designate a temporal hiatus, an intermission, a distance, a pause, a lapse, or gap between different states"[29] or modes of expression, they constitute a means of thinking/enacting relationality on the basis of their materialization.

Allowing for this kind of speculation in the interval, the relationship between domination and subordination that is mapped onto the gender difference in *Papi Pacify* is far from being obvious. twigs' head remains center of screen as she stirs the audience and her screen partner, exerting some sort of precarious control over the scene. To further sustain this uncomfortable balance, the video makes use of the dis-

---

26 FKA twigs (2019): "Papi Pacify." Directed by FKA twigs and Tom Beard. 13 October 2019. Music video, 05:02. *YouTube*. Available online: https://www.youtube.com/watch?v=OydK91JjFOw (last accessed 17 April 2022).

27 Keeling: *The Witch's Flight*, 40.

28 Trinh T. Minh-ha: *Cinema Interval*. New York, NY 1999, xi.

29 Trinh: *Cinema Interval*, xiii.

orienting effects of time axis manipulation. Adding to the affective structure of being in the interval, *Papi Pacify* generates the Afrofuturist temporality of an expanded Now in which past and future collapse, à la Eshun, and pleasure is derived from the supposed "threat" emanating from the Black male body. The reluctantly progressing back and forth between images produces temporal gaps and instigates "ways of being and connecting"[30] across the constrictions of time and space (as in Kelela's Rewind, mentioned in the beginning) that exceed off-screen sociality by, for instance, complicating the binary between victim and perpetrator.

Despite the ostensibly heterosexual desire the viewer is presented with in the video, it might prove useful to point to queer critiques of time as they have adopted asynchrony, or states of being out of time or out of space, as a means of building affective communities. To American literary scholar Elizabeth Freeman, who writes her introduction to *GLQ. A Journal of Gay and Lesbian Studies'* special issue on Queer Temporalities, this sensation qualifies as a queer phenomenon: "something felt on, with, or as a body, something experienced as a mode of erotic difference or even as a means to express or enact ways of being and connecting that have not yet arrived or never will."[31] Freeman's suggestion resonates with José Esteban Muñoz's concept of queer futurity, a concept which Muñoz, drawing on German philosopher Ernst Bloch's notion of a "not yet," uses to allocate future possibility to present moments of pleasure. In his 2009 *Cruising Utopia*, queer interruptions to normative time refuse recognition by hegemonic meaning-making systems and narratives of identity while providing alternative arrangements and relationalities of bodies in time and space – anticipating a "mode of being and feeling that was then not quite there but nonetheless provides an opening."[32]

twigs' chronopolitics as I have so far described them rework technical media into challenging hegemonic constructions of a social reality (that is just as much an *audiovisual* reality) along with the common sensical distribution of power and agency therein, in order to create an open-ended possibility of a "radical Elsewhere."[33] In accordance with the queer critiques cited above, twigs evokes a notion of futurity beyond the teleological concept of a future. Rather, as I explore by turning to the mixtape *CAPRISONGS*, in which FKA twigs and her collaborators envision such an Elsewhere as it is being enacted in modes of affective kinship.

---

30 Elizabeth Freeman: Introduction. Queer Temporalities. *GLQ. A Journal of Gay and Lesbian studies* 13/2–3 (2007).

31 Freeman: *Introduction. Queer Temporalities*, 159.

32 José Esteban Muñoz: *Cruising Utopia. The Then and There of Queer Futurity*. Durham, NC 2009, 9.

33 Keeling: *The Witch's Flight*, 1.

4 Future as Felt Potentiality in the Present: Astrology as a Spiritually- and Future-Oriented Social Technology in *CAPRISONGS*, 2022

Concluding this essay, I want to consider such a mode of anticipating a future as *felt potentiality* in the present that might as well provide a reparative approach. On 06 January 2022, FKA twigs shared the following on her Instagram to announce the release of her mixtape:

> hey i made you a mixtape, because when i feel you, i feel me and when i feel me, it feels good
>
> . . .
>
> CAPRISONGS is my journey back to myself through my amazing collaborators and friends.
> CAPRISONGS . . . it's bronzer in the sink, alco pop on the side, a cherry lolly, apple juice when ur thirsty, friends in the park, your favorite person, that one sentence somebody said to you that changed everything, a club pre-game, your bestie who is always late but brings the most to the party, meeting a friend at the airport, just togetherness
> my world
> london
> hackney
> la
> new york
> Jamaica
> It's my stubborn caprisun ass telling me to work thru my pain by delivering at work, don't think just go studio and create my saggi moon being the enigmatic temptress craving the club, to dance and to be social and my pisce venus hot mess disastrous heart falling in love all over again but this time with music and with myself[34]

Quoting the first line of mixtape opener *ride the dragon*, FKA twigs introduces *CAPRISONGS* as a "journey back to [her]self" for which she is indebted to her many collaborators and friends. She narrates herself through astrology, deploying a pop cultural reference system that anticipates the future in order to make legible a present feeling (herself) as part of an affective community spanning her diasporic, multi-local situatedness. As a cultural phenomenon, astrology has long been viewed – along with other categories of social "deviancy"[35] – as a feminized and racialized superstition and supplementary belief system "discordant with the now universal state of enlighten-

---

34 FKA twigs: *Instagram* (06 January 2022). https://www.instagram.com/p/CYZeAVotLsp/?igshid=MDJmNzVkMjY= (last accessed 19 April 2022).

35 In 1976, sociologist Robert Wuthnow contended that astrology is not a merely "countercultural phenomenon" in the San Francisco Bay Area but is most popular among "more traditionally marginal members of society" such as "the more poorly educated, the unemployed, the non-whites, females, the unmarried, the overweight, the ill, and the lonely." See: Astrology and Marginality, *Journal for the Scientific Study of Religion* 15/2 (1976), 157–168, here 167.

ment."[36] I am thus not trying to debunk astrology for its reliance on "pseudo-rationality,"[37] or even arguing that claiming the occult might challenge enlightenment common sense, for example by returning to an essentialized version of a "feminine" mode of being. Instead, I ask how embracing astrology and fortune-telling in FKA twigs' *CAPRISONGS* generates modes of affective knowledge and community – a reparative feeling of togetherness – in the wake of (historical) trauma as it has been theorized by Black studies scholars.[38]

CAPRISONGS being twigs' record with the most featured collaborators so far, it mixes recordings of conversations between friends concerning everyday issues from relationships to self-doubt, a fortune- teller reading a chart, tongue-in-cheek reassurances to the fact that "the universe is SO powerful"[39] submerged in giggles. Its intimate narrative is down to the level of its production as a communal project. In this sense, twigs' appropriation of astrology reminds us of bell hooks' reworkings of popular self-help books and new age spirituality, where hooks' Black feminist politics and thinking about love, community, and spiritual growth is informed by – yet fundamentally corrects – the way these books resituate a neoliberal version of individuality through the lens of the spiritual.[40] Writing about resurgent interest for a "new astrology" in 2019, author and cultural critic Lauren Oyler observes that astrology apps and social media deny users true agency, "not by suggesting the stars might be in control but by insinuating that taking control yourself is easy, a matter of identification."[41] Quite contrary to this assessment, twigs' *CAPRISONGS* boast less about having overcome and taking control than they narrate an ongoing struggle to allow for vulnerability despite experiences of gender-based and race-based violence, past and present, which disproportionately affect women of color.[42]

I propose *CAPRISONGS* adopts astrology as a social technology that is "spiritually oriented" to a future, a being that is not yet here. twigs' use of astrology accommo-

---

36 Theodor Adorno: The Stars Down to Earth. The Los Angeles Times Astrology Column. *Telos* 19 (1976), 13–90, here 15.

37 Adorno: The Stars Down to Earth, 17.

38 See for example: Christina Sharpe: *In the Wake. On Blackness and Being.* Durham, NC 2016; Fred Moten: *Stolen Life.* Durham, NC 2018.

39 FKA twigs: *Meta Angel,* produced by FKA twigs and El Guincho. *CAPRISONGS*, Young/Atlantic Records. 2022, TC 00:32.

40 bell hooks: *All About Love. New Visions.* New York, NY 2000.

41 Lauren Oyler: Astrology Year Zero. *The Baffler* 43 (2019), 84–89, here 89.

42 Following her lawsuit citing an abusive relationship, twigs told the *New York Times* about her difficulties in escaping her abuser and going public: "I just thought to myself, no one is ever going to believe me. [. . .] I'm unconventional. And I'm a person of color who is a female." Katie Benner / Melena Ryzik: FKA twigs Sues Shia LaBeouf, Citing "Relentless" Abusive Relationship. *The New York Times* (11 December 2020).

https://www.nytimes.com/2020/12/11/arts/music/fka-twigs-shia-labeouf-abuse.html (last accessed 26 April 2022).

dates Amiri Baraka's formulation of a new technology that essentially realizes the very humanistic ideals that – despite Adorno's assertion thereof – remain only partially implemented:

> The new technology must be spiritually oriented because it must aspire to raise man's spirituality and expand man's consciousness. It must begin by being "humanistic" [. . .]. The technology itself must represent human striving. It must represent at each point the temporary perfection of the evolutional man. And be obsolete only because nothing is ever *perfect*, the only constant is change.[43]

On a more practical level regarding the uses of technology, FKA twigs released (along with the mixtape) a series of "anti-videos" for each song; they were one to two minutes long each and mostly produced within one day. According to the artist, the prefix "anti" refers to the fact that these videos are significantly shorter than the recorded tracks, juxtaposing sound and image to the opening of a further (virtual) interval which redefines the music video on its standalone visual terms.

The anti-video for *ride the dragon*[44] features shaky black-and-white-footage of a busy street in London as somewhere in the crowd the camera spots twigs wearing a durag. Seemingly by coincidence, she assembles with a group of like-tracksuited women on the front stairs of Hackney Town Hall. As they break into dance, the video turns into color. The scene is visually interspersed with grainy stills underlining the guerilla-sensible public intervention filmed sometime during the pandemic. We hear twigs saying they are doing a TikTok, yet filming and dancing are not allowed according to the town hall official. They are asked to leave and they do, taking their equipment with them, revealing the work process of shooting a video for a brief moment– only to resume their choreography later. In the meantime, the group continues taking to the streets, stopping by a convenience store to twerk down the aisles as captured by the surveillance camera. This display of everyday joy, as it is reflected in the arrangement of images including shaky iPhone video, surveillance footage, grainy color photographs, is paired with twigs' playful yet poignant lyrics: to "ride the dragon" serves as a further formulation of toxic attachment, a high induced by substance abuse (or choking, or mouth fingering). The work of grieving and letting go of these attachments, then, is not performed by shutting herself off from the world, but rather by nourishing intimate bonds: hey, i made you a mixtape . . .

---

43 Baraka: *Ethos and Technology*, 157; for a secular formulation of this problem see Sylvia Wynter's argument for a *Second Emergence* of being human: Sylvia Wynter: The Ceremony Found. The Autopoetic Turn/Overturn. *Black Knowledges/Black Struggles. Essays in Critical Epistemology*, ed. by Jason R. Ambroise / Sabine Broeck. Liverpool 2015, 184–252.

44 FKA twigs (2022b): "ride the dragon." Directed by Aidan Zamiri and FKA twigs. 14 January 2022. Music video, 02:47. *YouTube*. Available online: https://www.youtube.com/watch?v=yDhVqgeRPJ8 (last accessed 17 April 2022).

Ride the dragon claims public space by communally obstructing its logic of surveillance, implicitly revisiting the scene of confinement in FKA twigs' earlier work *Video Girl*. twigs' audiovisuals produce generative openings in their intervals, the gaps and glitches of media time, in order to form a passage between the here and now and modes of enacting futurity/otherwise. These works actively unsettle taken-for-granted relations of power as well as the distribution of agency and vulnerability.

5 Conclusion

In her essay on the temporal politics of self-determination in radical liberation movements, US-American artist and activist Rasheedah Phillips asks:

> How does a radical movement conceive of its own future in the face of hostile visions of the future? When the future was never meant for them? How does one reconcile a temporal fatality offered by the mechanical linear timeline, with a belief in the temporal duration of one's own radical vision in change?[45]

Likewise, FKA twigs' artistic vision, as I have argued throughout this essay, does not offer grand promises of a better future to come. Instead, embracing an "Afrofuturist" sensibility in which past, present, and future collapse, she works within the gaps, intervals, and asynchronies of a violently structured present in order to manipulate, divert, and reorientate a linear temporal order bound up with taken-for-granted power relations. Thus, for twigs, and contrary to what Phillips suggests, media technology is not a mere agent of the oppression and continued subordination to the "mechanical linear timeline" of Black and other marginalized peoples. It becomes a means of a liberatory practice, however conflicted with regard to the renewed traction of algorithmically implemented social inequality in the coded biases of new media technology.[46] Despite what is arguably an interpretive investment in the emancipatory nature of art, music, time-based media, and performance put forward in this essay in relation to the histories of Black female servitude and (performance) labor, twigs' chronopolitical interventions embrace technology's ambivalences. twigs' artistic practice neither purports a notion of technological neutrality nor enacts a technological determinism. Yet precisely this refusal to construe media technology as neutral allows the artist to grapple with the power relations embedded therein and to envision futurity otherwise.

---

45 Phillips: *Organize Your Own Temporality*, 48.
46 Ruha Benjamin: *Captivating Technologies Race, Carceral Technoscience, and Liberatory Imagination in Everyday Life*. Durham, NC 2019, 3.

Bibliography

Adorno, Theodor: The Stars Down to Earth. *The Los Angeles Times Astrology Column, Telos* 19 (1976), 13–90.

Baraka, Imamu Amiri: Ethos & Technology. In: *Raise, Race, Rays, Raze. Essays since 1965*. New York, NY 1971, 155–157.

Benner, Katie / Ryzik, Melena: FKA twigs Sues Shia LaBeouf, Citing "Relentless" Abusive Relationship. *The New York Times* (11 December 2020).https://www.nytimes.com/2020/12/11/arts/music/fka-twigs-shia-labeouf-abuse.html (last accessed 26 April 2022).

Benjamin, Ruha: *Captivating Technologies Race, Carceral Technoscience, and Liberatory Imagination in Everyday Life*. Durham, NC 2019.

bell hooks: *All About Love. New Visions.* New York, NY 2000.

Browne, Simone: *Dark Matters. On the Surveillance of Blackness*. Durham, NC 2015.

Eshun, Kodwo: *More Brilliant than the Sun. Adventures in sonic fiction*. London 1998.

Eshun, Kodwo: Further Considerations on Afrofuturism. *CR: The New Centennial Review* 3/2 (2003), 287–302.

FKA twigs: *Instagram* (06 January 2022).https://www.instagram.com/p/CYZeAVotLsp/?igshid=MDJmNzVkMjY= (last accessed 19 April 2022).

Freeman, Elizabeth: Introduction. Queer Temporalities. *GLQ. A Journal of Gay and Lesbian Studies* 13/2–3 (2007).

Hamera, Judith: The Labors of Michael Jackson. Virtuosity, Deindustrialization, and Dancing Work. *PMLA* 127/4 (2012), 751–765.

Keeling, Kara: *The Witch's Flight. The Cinematic, the Black Femme, and the Image of Common Sense*. Durham, NC 2007.

Kittler, Friedrich A.: *Gramophone, Film, Typewriter*, trans. by Geoffrey Winthrop-Young / Michael Wutz. Stanford, CA 1999.

Lorde, Audre: The Master's Tools Will Never Dismantle the Master's House. In: *Sister Outsider. Essays and Speeches*, Berkeley, CA 2007, 110–113.

Muñoz, José Esteban: *Cruising Utopia. The Then and There of Queer Futurity*. Durham, NC 2009.

Oyler, Lauren: Astrology Year Zero. *The Baffler* 43 (2019), 84–89.

Phillips, Rasheedah: Organize Your Own Temporality. In: *Organize Your Own: The Politics and Poetics of Self-Determination Movements*, ed. by Romero, Anthony. Chicago, IL 2016, 48–54.

Robinson, Cedric J.: *Black Marxism. The Making of the Black Radical Tradition*. Chapel Hill, NC/London 2000.

Saxelby Ruth: Kelela Decodes Every Track from her Hallucinogen EP. In: *The Fader* (15 October 2015). http://www.thefader.com/2015/10/09/kelela-hallucinogen-track-by-track (last accessed 17 April 2022).

Sharpe, Christina: *In the Wake. On Blackness and Being*. Durham, NC 2016; Fred Moten: *Stolen Life*. Durham, NC 2018.

Minh-ha, Trinh T.: *Cinema Interval*. New York, NY 1999.

Wuthnow, Robert: Astrology and Marginality. In: *Journal for the Scientific Study of Religion* 15/2 (1976), 157–168.

Wynter, Sylvia: The Ceremony Found. The Autopoetic Turn/Overturn. In: *Black Knowledges/Black Struggles. Essays in Critical Epistemology*, ed. by Ambroise, Jason R. / Broeck, Sabine. Liverpool 2015, 184–252.

Videography

FKA Twigs (2019): *Cellophane*. Directed by Andrew Thomas Huang. 24 April 2019. Music video, 04:21. Available online: https://www.youtube.com/watch?v=YkLjqFpBh84 (last accessed 22 February 2023).

FKA Twigs: *Meta Angel*. Produced by FKA twigs and El Guincho. *CAPRISONGS*, Young/Atlantic Records. 2022, TC 00:32.

FKA Twigs (2013): *Papi Pacify*. Directed by FKA twigs and Tom Beard. 13 September 2013. Music video, 05:01. Available online: https://www.youtube.com/watch?v=OydK91JjFOw (last accessed 17 April 2022).

FKA Twigs (2022): *Ride The Dragon*. Directed by Aidan Zamiri and FKA twigs. 14 January 2022. Music video, 02:47. Available online: https://www.youtube.com/watch?v=yDhVqgeRPJ8 (last accessed 17 April 2022).

FKA Twigs (2014): *Video Girl*. Directed by Kahlil Joseph. 29 October 2014. Music video, 04:35. Available online: https://www.youtube.com/watch?v=2jhTiLuGezI (last accessed 25 April 2022).

Kelela (2015): *Rewind (Official Video)*. Directed by Eric K Yue.19 September 2015. Music video, 04:00. Available online: https://www.youtube.com/watch?v=py6PgXq0yDM (last accessed 17 April 2022).

Song Directory

Grace Jones: *Slave to the Rhythm*, produced by Trevor Horn. Manhattan Island Records 1985.

Josefine Hetterich

Queer Reproduction: AIDS Activist Pasts and Futurity in *Pose*

Abstract: This paper explores the concept of queer reproduction through an analysis of the FX series *Pose* and its revisitation of several key audiovisual documents in queer cultural history. After briefly introducing the series, the argument will be situated in discourses around queer temporality and the frame of what reproduction can come to mean in a queer context will be expanded by examining the social and cultural rather than biological processes through which queer people "birth" themselves and each other. Finally, several sequences from the series will be discussed in relation to the films and videos they reference to argue that *Pose* not only represents but also performs queer modes of reproduction through this revisitation.

Keywords: Queer Studies, Reproduction, Kinship, Temporality, Futurity, Video Activism, HIV/AIDS, Care, Trans Studies, Film

Is reproduction always already heterosexual?[1] Can it be wrested from a heteronormative frame? How do queers reproduce? And what relation to the future emerges when we turn our attention to queer reproductive labor? In this paper, I want to explore the concept of queer reproduction through an analysis of the FX series *Pose* and its revisitation of several key audiovisual documents in queer cultural history. *Pose*, which ran from 2018–2021, centers on New York City's Black and Latinx ballroom scene in the 1980s and 1990s, a queer subculture built around balls where participants compete in different categories to win trophies for their houses. The houses function as a kinship structure where house mothers and fathers take in and mentor the ballroom children, who are often estranged from their families of origin. Across its three seasons, *Pose* follows Blanca, a Black trans woman, as she starts her own house, the House of Evangelista; she adopts Damon, Angel, Lil Papi, and Ricky as her children and fights for both their survival and happiness as they navigate the AIDS crisis as well as the racism, homophobia, and transphobia that further exacerbate the epidemic. While its narrative is entirely fictional, *Pose* doesn't merely revisit this significant period of queer history, it also explicitly cites Paris Is Burning, Jennie Livingston's 1990 documentary on the New York City ballroom culture, as well as several AIDS activist videos that chronicle the actions of ACT UP, the AIDS Coalition to Unleash Power, a prominent AIDS activist group that was founded in New York City in 1987. Through these citations, *Pose* pays tribute to films and videos that have been formative for many queers across genera-

---

1 Judith Butler: Is Kinship Always Already Heterosexual? *differences. A Journal of Feminist Cultural Studies* 13/1 (2002), 14–44.

tions and differences, while foregrounding the role of Black and Latinx communities in AIDS activism. Indeed, both Paris Is Burning and AIDS activist video have been important touchstones in my relationship to my own queerness, despite the temporal and geographical distance and differences of race, class, and HIV status that separate me from many of their subjects. As a white HIV-negative cis woman who was born in Western Europe in the mid-1990s and came to queer culture in the late-2010s, my encounter with these works was not one of immediately recognizing myself in them, it was rather a process of working through my enduring fascination for them. It was the radical promise of misfitting together, of fabulously inventing new ways of being in the world and taking care of one another that kept me returning to them again and again. Beyond my personal longing for the radical queer politics and community they depict, the cultural significance of these works is attested to by the persistent resonances they produce through continual, even if hotly debated, screenings of Paris Is Burning, the re-use of video material of AIDS activist protests in countless documentaries, as well as ongoing conversations about each in academic and popular discourses.[2] In adapting these materials, *Pose* further proliferates their reach, even as it remakes them in the process by inserting its characters into them. I argue that the revisitation of these films and videos as well as the communities of care represented within *Pose's* narrative both function as modes of queer reproduction.

1 How We Make Each Other Possible: Queer Futurity and the Work of Reproduction

In his book *No Future: Queer Theory and the Death Drive*, US-American literary critic and queer theorist Lee Edelman famously asserts that "the future is nothing but kid stuff."[3] Through his frame of reproductive futurism, Edelman argues that the political is inextricably tied to the goal of creating better futures for "our children" at the expense of the present. He writes that "queerness names the side of those not 'fighting for the children,' the side outside the consensus by which all politics confirms the absolute value of reproductive futurism."[4] This perspective, which in one fell swoop dismisses the future, reproduction, and the figure of the child as antithetical to queerness

---

2 For an elaboration of the debates around Paris Is Burning, see Tavia Nyong'o: After the Ball, *Bully Bloggers* (2015). https://bullybloggers.wordpress.com/2015/07/08/after-the-ball/ (last accessed 15 August 2022); Lucas Hilderbrand: *Paris Is Burning. A Queer Film Classic*. Vancouver 2013. The revisitation of AIDS activist pasts has been charted by Alexandra Juhasz and Ted Kerr, see Alexandra Juhasz / Theodore Kerr: *We Are Having This Conversation Now. The Times of AIDS Cultural Production*. Durham, NC 2022.

3 Lee Edelman: *No Future. Queer Theory and the Death Drive*. Durham, NC 2004, 30.

4 Edelman: *No Future*, 3.

has been critiqued by several theorists who challenge the assumed whiteness and gay masculinity of Edelman's argument. Cuban American cultural studies and queer theory scholar José Esteban Muñoz cautions that "the future is only the stuff of some kids. Racialized kids, queer kids, are not the sovereign princes of futurity."[5] In offering his notion of queer futurity, Muñoz refuses to leave the future to whiteness and heteronormativity and instead calls on a "utopian political imagination that will enable us to glimpse another time and place: a 'not-yet' where queer youths of color actually get to grow up."[6] In a similar vein, US-American feminist media theorist Alexis Lothian indicates the gendering of reproduction in Edelman's argument and points to the history of feminist critiques of reproductive labor, of bearing and rearing those children – something that many queer accounts elide. She asserts that "queer worlds seem self-evidently not to include reproductive futures. Yet reproduction and heterofuturity are not always easily equated."[7] Indeed, this slippage from reproduction to heterosexual procreation, while it registers an important diagnostic queer critique of heteronormativity, nevertheless obstructs the view to what other forms of reproduction – what other futures – may be possible.

Elizabeth Freeman reminds us that "we cannot reproduce little queers with sperm and eggs, even if we do choose to give birth or parent: making other queers is a social matter."[8] Queerness does not function as a hereditary trait; rather, it is comprised of a set of sexual, social, and cultural practices and so, despite what anti-gay fear mongering may conjure up, procreation must indeed be a futile strategy for making other queers. Instead, as the Lesbian Avengers and Queer Nation have defiantly put it, *we recruit.*[9] The meanings and relational forms that amount to what we call queerness must be passed on from person to person, from generation to generation, through subcultural circuits and sometimes through something as fleeting as a covert glance. Queerness, as José Muñoz reminds us, has a "vexed relationship to evidence" because historically such evidence has been used to "penalize and discipline queer desires."[10] The resulting secrecy around deviant gender and sexual identities foreclosed many stories to be documented and preserved within official archives, but it

---

5 José Esteban Muñoz: *Cruising Utopia. The Then and There of Queer Futurity.* New York, NY 2009, 95.

6 Muñoz: *Cruising Utopia,* 96.

7 Alexis Lothian: *Old Futures. Speculative Fiction and Queer Possibility.* New York, NY 2018, 9.

8 Elizabeth Freeman: Time Binds, or, Erotohistoriography. *Social Text 84–85* 23/3–4 (2005), 60–61.

9 The Lesbian Avengers and Queer Nation, both queer direct action groups founded in New York City in the 1990s, have each used the words "we recruit" on flyers, posters, stickers, and T-shirts. The slogan can be read as a tongue-in-cheek response to the right-wing narrative that queer people were supposedly recruiting children into their lifestyle, which the Lesbian Avengers further commented on through their first action outside a primary school in New York City. There, they protested the schoolboard's rejection of teaching an LGBT-inclusive curriculum by handing out balloons to children that read "Ask About Lesbian Lives." The history of the Lesbian Avengers is chronicled on their website http://www.lesbianavengers.com/ (last accessed 15 August 2022).

10 Muñoz: *Cruising Utopia,* 65.

also produced elaborate subcultural practices that are only legible within specific publics, such as cruising and gaydar. Far from conceiving of the archive as empty, queer scholars and artists have therefore often taken an affective and at times speculative approach to the archive and its silences.[11] Moreover, queer activists have long been involved in alternative archiving projects, developing their own engaged documentary practices, and expanding the community-based preservation and circulation of queer histories.

Beyond challenging the logic of evidence, document, and archive, the lived experience of queerness also confounds a generational framework of transmission. For what makes a generation in the absence of biological parentage? The affiliation with a specific queer generation, as well as one's position as elder or youth in any given context, is not determined by descent or even age but instead may relate to how long one has been out, when one began a process of transition, or how long one has been enmeshed in queer culture or politics. It is a relational formation that can change dynamically depending on who may be able to take on the role of mentor or caregiver, yet it still borrows its designations from the language of familial structures as with the roles of house mothers and their children in ballroom, or with labels such as elder and baby gay or baby trans. In his analysis of the generational relations in ACT UP's Philadelphia chapter, Pascal Emmer suggests the term "meta-generation" to attend to the fact that seniority in the movement doesn't always map onto age and therefore complicates any straight-forward notion of intra- or intergenerational relationality.[12] While there are somewhat clearly delineated generations in *Pose* with the members of the houses taking up the roles of mothers/fathers and children respectively, there is also movement across those delineations as well as a shifting terrain of relations between them. In the pilot, we are introduced to the House of Abundance, headed by Mother Elektra and comprising the children Blanca, Angel, Lulu, Candy, Cubby, and Lemar. After some internal conflict and receiving the news about testing positive for HIV, Blanca wants to leave a mark on the world by becoming a house mother herself. When Elektra later falls on hard times, losing her source of income and housing, Blanca takes her into the House of Evangelista. The woman Elektra once mothered now mothers her, suggesting that rather than inhabiting a fixed position in this generational set up, it is possible for them to shift roles, depending on the specific context and the needs, capabilities, and resources that must be negotiated. Their meta-generational framework can be adjusted flexibly to organize and at times improvise the provision of care.

---

11 See for example Heather Love: *Feeling Backward. Loss and the Politics of Queer History*. Cambridge, MA 2007; Ann Cvetkovich: *An Archive of Feelings. Trauma, Sexuality, and Lesbian Public Cultures*. Durham, NC 2003; Christopher Nealon: *Foundlings Lesbian and Gay Historical Emotion before Stonewall*. Durham, NC 2001.

12 Pascal Emmer: Talkin' 'Bout Meta-Generation. ACT UP History and Queer Futurity. *Quarterly Journal of Speech* 98/1 (2012), 90.

For beyond simply birthing children, reproductive labor includes all those often unwaged activities that need to happen after a person is born to keep them alive – activities that have often had to be redistributed in queer communities in the face of institutional refusals. While acknowledging the longstanding work of feminist thinkers who have theorized the exploitative and unevenly distributed nature of unpaid care work along gendered and racialized lines, there has been more of an affirmative, yet critically nuanced, turn to care in queer, trans, Black, and disability studies more recently. Attending to the uneven distribution of care and therefore of life chances, many theorists such as Leah Lakshmi Piepzna-Samarasinha, Alexis Pauline Gumbs, Hil Malatino, and Marty Fink[13] see a radical potential in the ways in which underserved communities have developed alternative forms of mothering and built their own "care webs"[14] to keep each other alive. AIDS activism and ballroom, in particular its representation in Paris Is Burning, are two of the most oft-cited examples of such alternative arrangements of reproductive labor outside of the nuclear family.

By expanding the conceptual frame of reproductive labor to explore not just the ways in which queer people care for each other but also the work of passing on aspects of queer culture from person to person, across and among generations, I want to argue that *Pose* participates in the work of making other queers, of reproducing queerness. Queer reproduction, in other words, is not just how we keep each other alive but also how we make each other possible in the first place. It has less to do with procreation than with creating spaces in which queerness can gestate, flourish, and transmute, be passed on and taken up. This is not to say, of course, that making other queers has nothing to do with sex.[15] In fact, sexual encounters are probably one of the central touchstones for many queers in their own becoming – but so, I would argue, are those moments at the cinema, or the library, or in front of a TV or laptop screen, when we feel like something or someone reaches out and speaks directly to us. Arguably, both Paris Is Burning and AIDS activist video material have been formative in this way for many. Revisiting these documents, as *Pose* does, both attests to

---

13 Leah Lakshmi Piepzna-Samarasinha: *Care Work. Dreaming Disability Justice.* Vancouver 2018; Alexis Pauline Gumbs / China Martens / Mai'a Williams: *Revolutionary Mothering. Love on the Front Lines.* Oakland 2016; Hil Malatino: *Trans Care.* Minneapolis, MN 2020; Marty Fink: *Forget Burial. HIV Kinship, Disability, and Queer/Trans Narratives of Care.* New Brunswick, NJ 2021.
14 Piepzna-Samarasinha: *Care Work*, 32.
15 While queerness has always challenged the naturalized link between sex and procreation, insisting that sex cannot be reduced to a reproductive imperative while also exemplifying that in an age of assisted reproductive technology, procreation no longer necessitates sex, I do not want to entirely untether them here. Especially in relation to the AIDS crisis, our expanded notion of reproduction must encompass the ways in which queer communities taught each other safe sex practices by having sex with each other, as Douglas Crimp argues in "How to Have Promiscuity in an Epidemic." My focus in this paper, however, lies primarily with cultural rather than sexual practices of reproduction in as far as these can be separated from one another.

and nurtures, to put it in the words of Carolyn Dinshaw, a certain desire "for partial, affective connection, for community, for even a touch across time."[16] This revisitation, however, also poses ethical questions about whether this desire is welcome and what our duty of care is towards the figures we thus drag into the present.

2 Paris Is Burning, *Pose*, and the Value of Fantasy

In revisiting two very particular sets of documents that chronicle queer subcultures and are indelibly marked by death, *Pose* amplifies their already iconic subcultural status but also offers them up to new audiences and reconfigures them in the process. Whether or not this reconfiguration and re-contextualization is always done with care is, of course, up for debate. In this section, I will discuss *Pose's* citation of Paris Is Burning, outline some of the controversies that surrounded each of them and consider their relationship to fantasy.

Pose quite frequently and explicitly references the people into whose lives Paris Is Burning offered a glimpse. These references renew the questions around documentary ethics, looking relations, and power that have long surrounded Livingston's film. Paris Is Burning is arguably the theoretical object par excellence in queer studies, as it has continued to produce theoretical responses as well as popular debates in the more than thirty years since its release. Despite many seething critiques, most famously bell hooks' argument that the film constructs an ethnographic white gaze,[17] the film continues to resonate with queer audiences across time and across different localities. Tavia Nyong'o, a US-American performance and art scholar situated in Black and queer studies, challenges the "status of a representative feminist of color reaction" that hooks' piece has attained by pointing to the thrilling – if ambivalent – experience of the film that he shared with queers of color around him.[18] This is echoed by US-American media and film theorist Lucas Hilderbrand, who suggests that a focus on reception and spectatorship would allow for a more nuanced understanding of the ambivalent processes of identification and pleasure the film facilitates for queer audiences, similar to what hooks outlines in her writing on the oppositional gaze.[19] More recently, Sam Feder's documentary Disclosure: Trans Lives on Screen (2020) also attends to the nuanced ways in which spectators (who share some positionalities along the lines of race, class, gender, and sexuality with the people depicted

---

16 Carolyn Dinshaw: *Getting Medieval. Sexualities and Communities, Pre- and Postmodern.* Durham, NC 1999, 21.

17 bell hooks: *Black Looks. Race and Representation.* Boston, MA 1992, 151.

18 Nyong'o: *After the Ball.*

19 Hilderbrand: *Paris Is Burning*, 125.

in the film) related to it. While critically pointing to the ways in which ballroom has entered mainstream consciousness via the film of white lesbian filmmaker Jennie Livingston, as well as Madonna's music video for *Vogue,* thus providing (through to vastly differing degrees) recognition and monetary reward to two white women while leaving the participants of ballroom mostly empty handed, the talking head interviews in DISCLOSURE still attest to the sustenance viewers have extracted from the film.

Perhaps this shifting between a paranoid reading that seeks to expose the complicities of the film, especially in regard to who controls the means of representation, and a reparative reading that nevertheless attends to the enduring fascination that draws queer audiences to it[20] provides a model for how to attend to some of the ambivalences produced by *Pose.* The series is, after all, produced by FX, a channel that is owned by Fox Networks Group, a subsidiary of The Walt Disney Company, and therefore brings to the fore questions of co-optation and exploitation of marginal histories. The team behind *Pose* tried to attend to some of the material and structural inequalities both behind and in front of the camera by assembling the largest trans cast ever to appear in a scripted series, by including Black/ trans women like Janet Mock and Our Lady J in the writer's room, and by bringing on some of the few survivors of PARIS IS BURNING as well as members of the contemporary ballroom scene as advisors and also as the on-screen judges of the balls.[21] However, *Pose* lost some of its credit when Janet Mock called out the team of producers with her speech at the premiere of the third and last season, challenging not just her pay of only $40,000 per episode but also the tokenism and virtue-signaling that has characterized the marketing of the show.[22]

Beyond these production parameters, *Pose's* narrative and the ways in which it integrates its source materials raise further questions about its representational politics. For instance, through the storyline of Candy, *Pose* references the story of Venus

---

20 Eve Kosofsky Sedgwick: *Touching Feeling. Affect, Pedagogy, Performativity.* Durham, NC 2002.

21 Nellie Andreeva: FX's 'Pose': Ryan Murphy Sets Largest Transgender Cast Ever For Scripted Series. *Deadline* (October 2017). https://deadline.com/2017/10/pose-ryan-murphy-transgender-cast-fx-series-1202194718/ (last accessed 15 August 2022); Seth Abramovitch: 'Paris Is Burning' Emcee Junior LaBeija on 'Pose,' RuPaul and Why He Never Let Hollywood Tell His Story. *The Hollywood Reporter* (June 2021) https://www.hollywoodreporter.com/movies/movie-news/paris-is-burning-emcee-junior-labeija-pose-rupaul-1234964404/ (last accessed 15 August 2022).

22 According to Kevin Fallon at the Daily Beast, Mock's "speech ended on a note of accountability, and that meant piercing through the talking points, the ones tied up in a bow about inclusivity, opportunity, and progress that have been served to the media over the last three seasons. She mocked the standard line in a sing-song voice: 'It means so much to everyone to ensure that we enable Black and brown trans women to make it . . . That sounds good, right?' she said. 'It makes you comfortable, me talking like that. Because then I don't scare you into facing the fucking truth: You all have stomped on us.'" Kevin Fallon: Janet Mock Demands More Pay for 'Pose' in Fiery Speech at Premiere. "You Have Stomped on Us." *The Daily Beast* (April 2021) https://www.thedailybeast.com/janet-mock-demands-more-pay-for-pose-in-fiery-speech-at-premiere-you-have-stomped-on-us (last accessed 15 August 2022).

Xtravaganza, a trans woman of color who was murdered in 1988 during the shooting for PARIS IS BURNING. While the documentary only includes a brief scene of Angie Xtravaganza reacting to Venus' death, *Pose* renders that violence hypervisible. It provides the images of Candy's violated body that must be absent in PARIS IS BURNING. As contemporary debates in trans studies increasingly caution that visibility can pose as a trap for trans People of Color, putting them at an even more heightened risk for violent backlash, we have to ask what is achieved when Black trans death becomes a consumable spectacle on prime time television.[23] This also serves as a reminder that what Canadian-based race and gender theorist Jin Haritaworn and US-American literary scholar of Black transgender identities C. Riley Snorton have termed "trans necropolitics" haunts any discussion of queer reproduction.[24] As they argue, while often not cared for and even actively excluded from white (queer) spaces, "it is in their death that poor and sex working trans people of color are invited back in"[25] as the value extracted from their deaths "vitalizes projects as diverse as inner-city gentrification, anti-immigrant and anti-muslim [sic] moral panics."[26] It exceeds the scope of this essay to discuss in adequate detail the bio- and necropolitical implications of Candy's storyline in *Pose* and its resultant links to homonormative and homonationalist projects – that is to say, the ways in which LGBTQ politics are co-opted and mobilized for neoliberal and neocolonial state agendas. Yet it is nevertheless imperative to stay alert to the questions US-based philosopher and queer theorist Jasbir Puar asks in the introduction to her book *Terrorist Assemblages: Homonationalism in Queer Times*. She writes:

> How do queers reproduce life, and which queers are folded into life? How do they give life? To what do they give life? How is life weighted, disciplined into subjecthood, narrated into population, and fostered for living? Does this securitization of queers entail deferred death or dying for others, and if so, for whom?[27]

Through displaying Candy's murder, *Pose* feeds into the visual grammar of Black trans death, yet it also escapes back into fantasy in response to this violence. Throughout the course of her funeral, the character of Candy is resurrected, appearing as a lifelike ghost to find closure with the people she left behind and to triumph in a final performance at the ball. In her infamous critique of PARIS IS BURNING, bell hooks

---

23 Reina Gossett / Eric A. Stanley / Johanna Burton (eds.): *Trap Door. Trans Cultural Production and the Politics of Visibilty*. Cambridge, MA 2017.

24 C. Riley Snorton / Jin Haritaworn: Trans Necropolitics. A Transnational Reflection on Violence, Death and the Trans of Color Afterlife. In: *The Transgender Studies Reader*, ed. by Susan Stryker / Aren Aizura. 2nd ed. New York, NY 2013.

25 Snorton / Haritaworn: *Trans Necropolitics*, 74.

26 Snorton / Haritaworn: *Trans Necropolitics*, 66.

27 Jasbir Puar: *Terrorist Assemblages. Homonationalism in Queer Times*. Durham, NC 2007, 35–36.

criticizes the prominence of the ballroom scenes and reads them as reduced to mere spectacle, in arguing that

> moments of pain and sadness were quickly covered up by dramatic scenes from drag balls, as though there were two competing cinematic narratives, one displaying the pageantry of the drag ball and the other reflecting on the lives of participants and value of the fantasy.[28]

This reading, I believe, is predicated on her assumption of a white straight audience that seeks only to be entertained and for whom, in hooks' own words "it is easy to depict black rituals as spectacle."[29] Yet the experiences of queer audiences and audiences of color described above attest to the possibility of a more ambivalent reading. As a serial narrative format, *Pose* has more time than PARIS IS BURNING to build intricate narrative arcs that let the audience in on the multiple struggles the characters face as they negotiate how to make an income, find shelter, deal with sickness and violence, negotiate relations with families of origin, and fall in and out of love. Yet it similarly intersperses those narratives with scenes from the balls, providing, perhaps even more so than PARIS IS BURNING, a glossy and fabulous visual spectacle: the ballroom is beautifully lit, the participants are artfully dressed in colorful outfits with impeccable make-up, the camera moves smoothly across the floor, showing us the dancers from different perspectives, the editing picks up the rhythms of the music, building to a crescendo that matches the competition. The series' carefully choreographed, HD rendition of the balls certainly has a smoother finish than the 16mm handheld independent non-fiction look of the film, thus heightening the pageantry that hooks critiques in PARIS IS BURNING. However, I find that hooks' critique undervalues the link between those two supposedly competing narratives, for it seems to be exactly the harshness of the participants' lives that amplifies the value of fantasy and necessitates the spectacle of the balls as a moment of reprieve from the outside world, a place to come home to, a ritual celebration of their own ingenuity. What, indeed, should we make of the value of fantasy in a setting that is overdetermined by premature death? This question animates discourses around the politics of trans visibility and remains caught in an irresolvable tension since the reprieve that those spectators who share in the protagonists' hardships longingly seek may also let other audience members off the hook, providing dénouement where there is none.

---

28 hooks: *Black Looks*, 154.
29 hooks: *Black Looks*, 150.

3 AIDS Activist Video, *Pose*, and the Cost of Anachronism

This tension around the potential and pitfalls of fantasy also structures *Pose's* revisitation of AIDS video, as it adapts and re-imagines two AIDS activist protests in its second season. In this revised version, trans women of color whose contributions to AIDS activist history have often been underrepresented in both mainstream representations and subcultural archiving practices[30] are highlighted in a way that may both correct earlier misrepresentations and gloss over exclusionary tendencies in the movement.

After many of the main characters have been diagnosed with HIV in the first season, season two picks up two years later in 1990 and centers more explicitly on AIDS and AIDS activism, marking the urgency of the crisis. The first episode, titled "Acting Up," begins with Blanca and Pray Tell, the emcee at the balls and close friend of Blanca's, visiting Hart Island, the place where unclaimed bodies were buried in mass unmarked graves during the AIDS crisis. In the next scene, Blanca finds out that her T-cell count has dropped and her diagnosis has progressed from HIV to AIDS. Later in the episode, Pray Tell attends his first ACT UP meeting and subsequently urges the members of the House of Evangelista to join a protest at a church that is planned in the following days. The scene that follows is modelled on the Stop the Church action that ACT UP organized together with WHAM!, the Women's Health Action and Mobilization in New York City. In 1989, five thousand people gathered at St. Patrick's Cathedral to protest the Catholic Church's public stand against AIDS education and safer sex, and its opposition to abortion rights, exemplified by Cardinal O'Connor, the Archbishop of New York, actively discouraging the use of condoms and clean needles and claiming that "good morality is good medicine."[31] This action was documented in Robert Hilferty's *Stop the Church*[32] tape as well as in the 1991 video *Like a Prayer*[33] by DIVA TV. The video material, most of which covers the protest in front of the church, has also since been incorporated into several documentaries, such as Jim Hubbard's UNITED IN ANGER (2012) and David France's HOW TO SURVIVE A PLAGUE (2012). *Pose's* version focuses exclusively on the action inside the church. It shows the members of the House of Evangelista lead a group of people who enter the church, pass out pamphlets, and finally stage a die-in in the center aisle. Very briefly we see someone with a camcorder walk into the frame, then our view shifts to the perspective of that die-

---

30 Fink: *Forget Burial*, 6.

31 Associated Press: Vatican AIDS Meeting Hears O'Connor Assail Condom Use. *The New York Times* (November 1989). https://www.nytimes.com/1989/11/14/world/vatican-aids-meeting-hears-o-connor-assail-condom-use.html (last accessed 15 August 2022).

32 Robert Hilferty: *Stop the Church*. (Frameline Distribution, 2014). https://vimeo.com/ondemand/stopthechurch (last accessed 15 August 2022).

33 DIVA TV: *Like A Prayer*. (Deep Dish TV Vimeo Account, 2016). https://vimeo.com/178261617 (last accessed 15 August 2022).

getic camera. The diegetic video material is marked by the standard definition 3:4 aspect ratio, deviating from the rest of the episode which is shot in the 16:9 aspect ratio for high-definition television, as well as through horizontal flickering lines that make the outlines of everything appear kind of fuzzy, creating an emulated video look. In that way, *Pose* seems to gesture to its source material which was only available because AIDS video activists took it upon themselves to chronicle these actions. But while it may thus be a deferential representation of the action, it is of course not a faithful one since *Pose*'s fictional characters take center stage.

The insertion of queer and trans characters of color into a re-enacted version of this particularly notorious ACT UP action can be read as an attempt to contest the mainstream perception of AIDS activism as predominantly white, male, and cis. In this manner, *Pose's* strategy is reminiscent of the speculative modes of queer historiography and documentary practice that have been used in films such as Cheryl Dunye's THE WATERMELON WOMAN (1996) to challenge the exclusion of queer People of Color from dominant historical narratives. However, this particular revisionist take on ACT UP history has also incurred disapproval from former ACT UP members. In her book *Let the Record Show: A Political History of ACT UP New York*, Sarah Schulman laments ACT UP's lack of control over its own representation, asserts that only one white trans woman was arrested at St. Patrick's Cathedral, and claims that former ACT UP members "expressed anger that corporate representations of ACT UP inserted nonexistent people of color while ignoring the people of color who actually were there and did the work."[34] In turn, Schulman was criticized by Vicky Osterweil, who challenged the methodology of Schulman's book and expressed her disappointment at the fact that "Black trans women only appear in the book insofar as Schulman can insist upon their absence in the movement."[35] While Schulman disputed this critique in the ensuing debate, Osterweil's intervention clearly outlines the stakes of attempting to write a comprehensive history of ACT UP to serve as a model for contemporary movements. Although *Pose* certainly doesn't aim to provide a blueprint for radical organizing, its reenactment of ACT UP actions implicates it in the debates around the accuracy of this particular movement history as well as the purpose of movement histories in general. To that effect, Laura Stamm's critique of *Pose* cautions about "the cost of historicization."[36] While she applauds the gesture of reinserting trans women of color into the memory of AIDS activism, she argues that positioning one of the few representations of HIV/AIDS that focuses on trans women of color and their activism in the past obscures that both still have an urgency in the present. This echoes Alex-

---

34 Sarah Schulman: *Let the Record Show. A Political History of ACT UP New York, 1987–1993.* New York, NY 2021.

35 Vicky Osterweil: What the Record Doesn't Show. *Jewish Currents* (2021). https://jewishcurrents.org/what-the-record-doesnt-show (last accessed 15 August 2022).

36 Laura Stamm: Pose and HIV/AIDS. The Creation of a Trans-of-Color Past. *TSQ. Transgender Studies Quarterly* 7/4 (2020), 615.

andra Juhasz's and Ted Kerr's writing on "AIDS Crisis Revisitation," in which they similarly critique that much contemporary work on AIDS looks back at the early days of the crisis rather than focusing on present-day HIV/AIDS, making it "almost impossible for people to conceive of HIV in the now."[37]

While Laura Stamm justly points to the dearth of media dealing with the HIV/AIDS epidemic as an ongoing rather than historical issue, especially as it pertains to trans women, I would argue that the specific way in which *Pose* plays on its source documents has the potential to open up a relation to that history rather than necessarily relegating AIDS and AIDS activism to the past. For instance, the insertion of *Pose's* characters already partly re-signifies the action and links it to ongoing struggles by way of the shifting associations rendered by their embodied presence. When the protestors lie down in the church, they start chanting "Stop killing us!" after which there is a brief sequence where we see police rushing into the church and violently attacking protestors, dragging them away and carrying them out on stretchers. Here the accentuation of Black and brown protestors, paired with the desperate cry "Stop killing us!" which was chanted at the original Stop the Church action but, at present, is primarily known as a slogan in the movement for Black lives, prompts the viewers to consider not just the acquiescence to the suffering and death of people with AIDS but also the ongoing murder of Black people at the hands of police. A line is drawn from historical to contemporary forms of state violence in a way that highlights the centrality of racism and anti-Blackness and their entanglement with classism, homophobia, and transphobia in fueling the AIDS crisis.

The second AIDS activist action that *Pose* revisits in the seventh episode of season two, titled "Blow," is more integrated into the narrative of the season and thus even more loosely adapted. In 1991, the ACT UP affinity group Treatment Action Guerrillas wrapped a giant inflatable condom over Senator Jesse Helms' house in Arlington to protest his homophobic views and his dangerous stance on AIDS policies. The action was taped by Robert Hilferty and the video titled *TAG HELMS* is available through former ACT UP member Peter Staley's YouTube account.[38] In *Pose*, Blanca and Pray Tell, who are situated as elders, give the task to figure out how to implement this action to the children Damon, Ricky, and Lulu. The target, however, is not Jesse Helms but Frederica Norman, a real estate mogul who threatened to evict Blanca's business earlier in the season. Through this shift, the action is re-signified as a response to the racist and transphobic housing discrimination that Blanca faced, but it is also specifically used to thematize the ways in which new generations are brought into the fold

---

37 Alexandra Juhasz / Theodore Kerr: Home Video Returns. Media Ecologies of the Past of HIV/AIDS. *Cineaste Magazine* XXXIX 3 (2014). https://www.cineaste.com/summer2014/home-video-returns-media-ecologies-of-the-past-of-hiv-aids (last accessed 15 August 2022).
38 Robert Hilferty, *TAG* Helms*: When ACT UP Put a Giant Condom over Sen. Jesse Helms's House* (Peter Staley's YouTube account, 2014). https://www.youtube.com/watch?v=TS-w4Pqvkuw (last accessed 15 August 2022).

of activism – the work, in short, through which movements reproduce themselves. The narrative arc of the episode suggests that Damon, Ricky, and Lulu are feeling lost and without purpose, not in the least because this episode shortly follows the death of Candy. Through organizing this action, they come to feel empowered again, which suggests that beyond the immediate political purpose of the action, it also serves to reinvigorate the community. In both revisitation scenes, *Pose* seeks to emulate the rough and ready video look, thereby paying tribute to the documentary practices of AIDS video activists. Like the *Stop the Church* sequence, this scene establishes a diegetic camera and then switches back and forth between the regular sleek HD look of the series and the fuzzy video look, which is now emphasized even more as it is framed in a viewfinder with a red dot recording icon and battery display. This contrast makes the regular look of the series suddenly seem hyperreal but also oddly sleek, creating a sense of anachronism. Both the scenes of the balls and of the AIDS activist actions, which are familiar (at least to some viewers) in the grainy softness of 16mm film or the often blue-toned slightly slurred look of video respectively, are rendered glossy thus forfeiting the implied historicity of the traces that use and re-use would have left on the analogue materials. Perhaps it is useful to think about *Pose's* citation of these source materials – both in terms of their storylines as well as their visual registers – as a form of what Elizabeth Freeman calls "temporal drag," a "performance of anachrony" that in this case is played out not primarily on the bodies of the characters but rather on the surface of the images.[39] The future intrudes on the past, revises the past – but, we may ask, what vision for the future is offered here?

In this glossier, high production value version, the experience of fantasy that hooks critiqued in Paris Is Burning is heightened in more than one way. *Pose* constructs a vision of AIDS activism where trans People of Color are supposedly seamlessly integrated into ACT UP without having to address the internal debates around racism, classism, and misogyny – let alone transphobia – which AIDS activists were having at the time and continue to have today. This is a form of anachronism that makes the series more palatable to contemporary audiences by performing a kind of pseudo-inclusivity that goes hand in hand with "the idealization of the trans woman of color in the dominant imaginary of LGBT history" that US-American scholar of transgender history Jules Gill-Peterson identifies.[40] Gill-Peterson discusses the construction of the figure of the street queen as "a poor, transfeminine figure, often a femme of color" who is hyper visible and typically associated with certain stigmas connected to sex work and its criminalization as well as militancy, thus functioning as either "symptomatic or iconic."[41] While this figure is often taken up to perform a cer-

---

39 Elizabeth Freeman: *Time Binds. Queer Temporalities, Queer Histories.* Durham, NC 2010, 95.
40 Jules Gill-Peterson: Being Street. The Trans Woman of Color as Evidence, Imagining Trans Futures (Simpson Center for the Humanities, 12 January 2021). https://www.youtube.com/watch?v=mINM1fB8bm4 (last accessed 15 August 2022).
41 Gill-Peterson: *Being Street.*

tain kind of radicality, for example in the revised memorialization of the Stonewall Rebellion which now tends to emphasize the role of trans activists Marsha P. Johnson and Sylvia Rivera, it can also be invoked to prop up a false sense of unity in an imagined queer community. As well as reducing the complexities of the lived experiences of trans women of color to a set of characteristics that respectively makes them function as a symptomatic or iconic figure in queer discourses, this fantasy glosses over the power relations, conflicts, and complicities that continue to structure queer movements and instead constructs a de-politicized identity-based constituency that is more easily assimilable into a liberal progress narrative.

This seems to match the ways in which *Pose's* narratives sometimes lean into the same fantasies of fame and fortune but also of marriage and white picket fences that were voiced by some of the participants in Paris Is Burning. By the end of the second season, the children of the House of Evangelista have all had career breakthroughs, two are engaged to be married, and they are all moving out of their mother's house. So far, so linear. The unsettled temporality of lives marked by racist, homophobic, and transphobic violence is neatly reordered here into what Jack Halberstam describes as

> the conventional binary formulation of a life narrative divided by a clear break between youth and adulthood; this life narrative charts an obvious transition out of childish dependency through marriage and into adult responsibility through reproduction.[42]

The season concludes with a performance in which Blanca, just recently discharged from the hospital, enters the ballroom in a wheelchair from which she then dramatically rises while lip-synching to the American national anthem. At first glance, this may seem like the "fatally unsubversive appropriation" of the American dream in all its racist, misogynist, and homophobic glory that critics of Paris Is Burning have cautioned against.[43] However, this progressive onwards and upwards temporality doesn't last. After her performance, Blanca meets two homeless children named Quincy and Chilly on the street outside the ballroom. She takes them under her wings, suggesting a kind of cyclical domestic time where the work of raising children is only done to begin anew. In season three, however, these two characters are not picked up again. While there might be numerous (likely economic) reasons why they don't become part of the main cast of characters, their disappearance reminded me of the disappearance of M— from Daniel Peddle's documentary The Aggressives (2005) that Kara Keeling considers in her essay *Looking for M*— Keeling argues that at the end of the

---

42 Jack Halberstam: *In a Queer Time and Place. Transgender Bodies, Subcultural Lives.* New York, NY 2005, 153.

43 Judith Butler: *Bodies That Matter. On the Discursive Limits of "Sex."* New York, NY 1993, 128.

documentary, failing to conform to the linear time the film seeks to impose on its subjects, "M— is out of time (and unlocatable)."[44] She urges us to

> ask not the policing question attuned to the temporal and spatial logics of surveillance and control (where is M— today), but, rather, in this case, the political question of when M's visibility will enable hir survival by providing the protection the realm of the visible affords those whose existence is valued, those we want to look for so we can look out for and look after them.[45]

In the same essay, Keeling references PARIS IS BURNING, cautioning us about the "unequal calculus of visibility distribution" that becomes evident when considering that within five years of the film's release, five of the subjects of the film were dead.[46] The question that haunts *Pose*, then, is *when* Venus Xtravaganza might be. This question insists on the possibility of a future, even as the future already appears lost.

4 Queer Reproduction and Ambivalence

I don't want to close by offering a definitive verdict over *Pose's* imaginative revisitation of PARIS IS BURNING and AIDS activist video; rather, I find that the mixed feelings it left me with tellingly point to the ambivalence at the very heart of queer reproduction. Through its narrative, which centers on the alternative arrangements of care that queer and trans people have devised in the context of ballroom and AIDS activism, *Pose* represents the potency of queer reproductive labor. It situates it as a necessary survival tactic in the face of the fragmented and traumatic experiences of kinship that marked many of its characters' lives, having been exiled from their families of origin. Yet these alternative forms of kinship are also shown to be fraught with tension and uncertainty through the conflicts within the houses, as well as insufficient in the face of the fatal structural violence that costs many of the protagonists their lives. I have further argued that *Pose's* citation of iconic queer films and videos *performs* rather than just *represents* queer reproduction as it reproduces, revises, and re-circulates these materials for new audiences who may take them up in devising their own identities. Such a proliferation of queerness through cultural transmission can function as a radical gesture, insisting on caring for queer pasts and enabling queer futures. However, as the debates around visibility in queer of color critique that I referenced above teach us, visibility without protection often turns to surveillance, scrutiny, and violence for those who are most precariously positioned. In its attempt to create positive and celebratory representations of queer and trans People of Color, *Pose* constructs an occasionally

---

44 Kara Keeling: Looking For M – Queer Temporality, Black Political Possibility, and Poetry from the Future. *GLQ. A Journal of Lesbian and Gay Studies* 15/4 (2009), 577.

45 Keeling: *Looking For M*, 577.

46 Keeling: *Looking For M*, 577.

anachronistic fantasy that oscillates between a counter-narrative to a whitewashed history and a smoothed out, easy to consume story of inclusivity. It is within the queer reading practices – desirously reading both along and against the grain, drawing out what is just beneath the surface and speculatively expanding on the traces we find – that we may hold this ambivalence in suspense.

As Sophie Lewis reminds us, "the work of social reproduction brings forth new hope for revolutionary struggle, but also produces new lives for oppressors to suck and crush."[47] As such, merely reproducing other queers, whether through the cultural processes I sketched out above or through the very material work of housing, feeding, and nurturing them, does not guarantee more livable futures. But I would argue, the reproductive labor we can witness through *Pose*, both in its narrative and in the ways it revisits archival materials and engages new audiences, does mark a refusal to give up on the future, as well as a refusal to let go of the past. And for communities who have often been denied either, that is a defiant act.

Bibliography

Abramovitch, Seth: "Paris Is Burning" Emcee Junior LaBeija on 'Pose,' RuPaul and Why He Never Let Hollywood Tell His Story. *The Hollywood Reporter* (11 June 2021). https://www.hollywoodreporter.com/movies/movie-news/paris-is-burning-emcee-junior-labeija-pose-rupaul-1234964404/ (last accessed 15 August 2022).

Andreeva, Nellie: FX's 'Pose': Ryan Murphy Sets Largest Transgender Cast Ever For Scripted Series. *Deadline* (October 2017). https://deadline.com/2017/10/pose-ryan-murphy-transgender-cast-fx-series-1202194718/ (last accessed 15 August 2022).

Associated Press: Vatican AIDS Meeting Hears O'Connor Assail Condom Use. *The New York Times* (14 November 1989). https://www.nytimes.com/1989/11/14/world/vatican-aids-meeting-hears-o-connor-assail-condom-use.html (last accessed 15 August 2022).

Butler, Judith: *Bodies That Matter. On the Discursive Limits of "Sex."* New York, NY 1993.

Butler, Judith: Is Kinship Always Already Heterosexual? *differences. A Journal of Feminist Cultural Studies* 13/1 (2002), 14–44.

Cvetkovich, Ann: *An Archive of Feelings. Trauma, Sexuality, and Lesbian Public Cultures.* Durham, NC 2003.

Dinshaw, Carolyn: *Getting Medieval. Sexualities and Communities, Pre- and Postmodern.* Durham, NC 1999.

DIVA TV: *Like A Prayer.* Deep Dish TV Vimeo Account, 2016. https://vimeo.com/178261617.

Edelman, Lee: *No Future. Queer Theory and the Death Drive.* Durham, NC 2004.

Emmer, Pascal: Talkin' 'Bout Meta-Generation: ACT UP History and Queer Futurity. *Quarterly Journal of Speech* 98/1 (2012), 89–96.

Fallon, Kevin: Janet Mock Demands More Pay for 'Pose' in Fiery Speech at Premiere: "You Have Stomped on Us." *The Daily Beast* (30 April 2021) https://www.thedailybeast.com/janet-mock-demands-more-pay-for-pose-in-fiery-speech-at-premiere-you-have-stomped-on-us. (last accessed 15 August 2022).

Fink, Marty: *Forget Burial. HIV Kinship, Disability, and Queer/Trans Narratives of Care.* New Brunswick, NJ 2021.

Freeman, Elizabeth: Time Binds, or, Erotohistoriography. *Social Text 84–85* 23/3–4 (2005), 57–68.

---

47 Sophie Lewis: *Full Surrogacy Now. Feminism Against the Family.* London 2019, 165.

Freeman, Elizabeth: *Time Binds. Queer Temporalities, Queer Histories*. Durham, NC 2010.

Gill-Peterson, Jules: Being Street. The Trans Woman of Color as Evidence, Imagining Trans Futures. Simpson Center for the Humanities (12 January 2021). https://www.youtube.com/watch?v=mINM1fB8bm4 (last accessed 15 August 2022).

Gossett, Reina / Stanley, Eric A / Burton, Johanna (eds.): *Trap Door. Trans Cultural Production and the Politics of Visibility*. Cambridge, MA 2017.

Gumbs, Alexis Pauline / Martens, China Martens / Williams, Mai'a: *Revolutionary Mothering. Love on the Front Lines*. Oakland, CA 2016.

Halberstam, Jack: *In a Queer Time and Place. Transgender Bodies, Subcultural Lives*. New York, NY 2005.

Hilderbrand, Lucas: *Paris Is Burning. A Queer Film Classic*. Vancouver 2013.

Hilferty, Robert: *Stop the Church*. Frameline Distribution (2014). https://vimeo.com/ondemand/stopthechurch (last accessed 15 August 2022).

Hilferty, Robert: *TAG Helms: When ACT UP Put a Giant Condom over Sen. Jesse Helms's House*. Peter Staley's YouTube account (2014). https://www.youtube.com/watch?v=TS-w4Pqvkuw (last accessed 15 August 2022).

hooks, bell: *Black Looks. Race and Representation*. Boston, MA 1992.

Juhasz, Alexandra / Kerr, Theodore: Home Video Returns. Media Ecologies of the Past of HIV/AIDS. *Cineaste Magazine*.XXXIX 3 (2014). https://www.cineaste.com/summer2014/home-video-returns-media-ecologies-of-the-past-of-hiv-aids (last accessed 15 August 2022).

Juhasz, Alexandra / Kerr, Theodore: *We Are Having This Conversation Now. The Times of AIDS Cultural Production*. Durham, NC 2022.

Keeling, Kara: Looking For M — Queer Temporality, Black Political Possibility, and Poetry from the Future. *GLQ. A Journal of Lesbian and Gay Studies* 15/4 (2009), 565–582.

Lewis, Sophie: *Full Surrogacy Now. Feminism Against the Family*. London 2019.

Lothian, Alexis: *Old Futures. Speculative Fiction and Queer Possibility*. New York, NY 2018.

Love, Heather: *Feeling Backward. Loss and the Politics of Queer History*. Cambridge, MA 2007.

Malatino, Hil: *Trans Care*. Minneapolis, MN 2020.

Muñoz, José Esteban: *Cruising Utopia. The Then and There of Queer Futurity*. New York, NY 2009.

Nealon, Christopher: *Foundlings Lesbian and Gay Historical Emotion before Stonewall*. Durham, NC 2001.

Nyong'o, Tavia: After the Ball. *Bully Bloggers* (2015). https://bullybloggers.wordpress.com/2015/07/08/after-the-ball/ (last accessed 15 August 2022).

Osterweil, Vicky: What the Record Doesn't Show. *Jewish Currents* (2021). https://jewishcurrents.org/what-the-record-doesnt-show (last accessed 15 August 2022).

Piepzna-Samarasinha, Leah Lakshmi: *Care Work. Dreaming Disability Justice*. Vancouver 2018.

Puar, Jasbir: *Terrorist Assemblages. Homonationalism in Queer Times*. Durham, NC 2007.

Schulman, Sarah: *Let the Record Show. A Political History of ACT UP New York, 1987–1993*. New York, NY 2021.

Sedgwick, Eve Kosofsky: *Touching Feeling. Affect, Pedagogy, Performativity*. Durham, NC 2002.

Snorton, C. Riley / Haritaworn, Jin: Trans Necropolitics. A Transnational Reflection on Violence, Death and the Trans of Color Afterlife. In: *The Transgender Studies Reader*, ed. by Stryker, Susan / Aizura, Aren. 2nd ed. New York, NY 2013.

Stamm, Laura: Pose and HIV/AIDS. The Creation of a Trans-of-Color Past. *TSQ. Transgender Studies Quarterly* 7/4 (2020), 615–624.

Notes on Contributors

Daniel Baranowski is a literary scholar and works as a scientific advisor for the Federal Foundation Magnus Hirschfeld in Berlin, Germany. He completed his doctorate on the aesthetics of philosophical and cinematic representations of the Shoah. Head of the oral history projects "Sprechen trotz allem" (www. sprechentrotzallem.de) of the Foundation Memorial to the Murdered Jews of Europe (2008 to 2014) and "Archive of Other Memories" of the Federal Foundation Magnus Hirschfeld. Works primarily on topics of LGBTIQ* politics, culture, history and memory. daniel.baranowski@posteo.de

Kathrin Dreckmann is an assistant professor at the Institute for Media and Cultural Studies at Heinrich Heine University in Düsseldorf. Her recently submitted habilitation project deals with aesthetic image programs between art practice, digital image media and pop cultural production processes. Her publications focus on sound studies as well as queer theory. Kathrin.Dreckmann@uni-duesseldorf.de

Franziska Haug earned her master's degree in German studies, art education, sociology, and women's and gender studies in Frankfurt am Main. She was a research assistant at Goethe University Frankfurt/ Main and completed her PhD on literary processes of producing gender through labor as well as an associate doctoral student of the project "Epistemologies of Aesthetic Practice" at the Collegium Helveticum Zurich (Switzerland). She is currently a postdoctoral researcher in the VW-Freigeist project "Light On! Queer Literatures and Cultures under Socialism" with a PostDoc research project on queer GDR literature. She is a member of the Cornelia Goethe Centrum, the Forum of Critical Science, and the German Society for Aesthetics. Her research focuses on queer feminism, Marxism, historical materialism, pop culture, and antisemitism. franziska.haug@sprachlit.uni-regensburg.de

Josefine Hetterich received her BA in Theatre, Film and Media Studies and Sociology from the Goethe University, Frankfurt, and her MA in Gender, Media and Culture from Goldsmiths College, London. Before joining the Research Training Group "Configurations of Film," she was a staff member in Film Studies at the Goethe University, teaching classes on feminist theory, queer cinema, archive studies and AIDS video activism. Her PhD project entitled *Remembering Queer Futures* explores the modes of queer cultural production through which AIDS activism is both historicized and reanimated. Through an affective inquiry, it asks what visions of the past and future are facilitated through these projects and how they allow us to rethink temporality, historiography and kinship in the process. hetterich@tfm.uni-frankfurt.de

Sue Lèwig is a German Berlin-based artist and producer, working in the techno industry. She released with record labels Kaos, Examine Archive and Seelen. Her techno compositions bring epic downbeats, melancholic harmonies and themes of nature to the dancefloor.

Vera Mader is a research assistant at the Institute for Media Studies at Ruhr-University Bochum and, as part of the graduate research group "Documentary Practices: Excess and Privation", pursues a PhD on the theory of difference in Audre Lorde's aesthetic practice and self-writing. They studied Media and Cultural Studies and Cultural Anthropology in Freiburg, Germany and Amherst, Massachusetts. vera.mader@ruhr-uni-bochum.de

Thomas Meinecke is an author, musician, lecturer, DJ and radio host and a formative figure in German pop literature. As a member of the band *Freiwillige Selbstkontrolle*, he has participated in pop music discourse since 1980. Thomas Meinecke has written eight novels, focusing among other things on feminist theory, an approach that also shapes his writing.

Bettina Papenburg received a PhD in Social and Cultural Anthropology from Heidelberg University and a Habilitation in Media and Cultural Studies from Heinrich-Heine-University Dusseldorf. She was a Marie-Curie postdoctoral fellow and an assistant professor in Gender Studies at Utrecht University, held positions as senior lecturer in Media and Cultural Studies in Dusseldorf and Freiburg and currently acts as a guest professor in Film Studies at Freie University Berlin. In her research and teaching she focuses, among other topics, on gender, queer and postcolonial studies. She is editor of the handbook *Gender: Laughter* (Macmillan, 2017) and co-editor of the volume *Carnal Aesthetics: Transgressive Imagery and Feminist Politics* (IB Tauris, 2013). bettina.papenburg@fu-berlin.de

Peter Rehberg received his PhD from New York University in Germanic Languages and Literatures. After graduating from NYU, he worked predominantly in the fields of queer theory, popular culture, and media studies. In addition to his academic work, he also published three novels (Play, Fag Love, Boymen), worked as an editor for queer magazines, and is a regular contributor to the weekly Der Freitag, where he writes on gender and US politics. He was DAAD Associate Professor at the University of Texas at Austin from 2011 to 2016. He worked as Head of Collections and Archives at Schwules Museum, Berlin from 2018–2022. Since 2022 he is DAAD Associate Professor in German Studies, Media Studies and Queer Studies at the University of Cincinnati. peterrehberg@gmx.net

Sarah Rüß is a master's student at Heinrich Heine University in Düsseldorf. With a focus on queer theory, biopower, and affect theory, her bachelor's thesis examined the intersection of shame and queer theory. Her research explores how power structures impact queer lives and identities, including the role of emotions and affective states. sarah.ruess@uni-duesseldorf.de

Sookee, in seven solo releases so far, raised her voice criticizing capitalism and all forms of discrimination and advocating for the recognition and interests of people identifying as queer. In her studies in linguistics and gender studies, she focused on feminist theory which is very present in her work as an artist as well.

Joanna Staśkiewicz studied Social Sciences at the Carl von Ossietzky University Oldenburg and received her PhD from the Faculty of Cultural Studies at the European University Viadrina in Frankfurt an der Oder. Among other things, she was a visiting scholar (DAAD postdoctoral fellowship) at Tulane University in New Orleans and held various teaching positions. She is currently working on her DFG research project *Queering Gender, Desire, and Local Myths in (Neo-)Burlesque. A Comparative Analysis of (Neo-) Burlesque Scenes in New Orleans, Berlin and Warsaw* at the Institute for Arts and Media at the University of Potsdam. She is also an associate member of the research group *Queery/ing Popular Culture* at the University of Siegen. staskiewicz@uni-potsdam.de

Katharina Wiedlack is an Assistant Professor for Anglophone Cultural Studies at the department of English and American Studies, University of Vienna. She has taught at several universities in Europe and Russia, and the USA and published extensively in the fields of transnational American Studies, queer and feminist theory, Critical Whiteness and Disability Studies, and popular culture. Moreover, she is collaborating in artistic and activist projects in the post-soviet context. (http://katharinawiedlack.com/) katharina.wiedlack@univie.ac.at

Index